RECOLLECTIONS OF THE EVENTFUL LIFE OF A SOLDIER

including

THE WAR IN THE PENINSULA

and

SCENES AND SKETCHES IN IRELAND

RECOLLECTIONS OF THE EVENTFUL LIFE OF A SOLDIER

including

THE WAR IN THE PENINSULA

and

SCENES AND SKETCHES IN IRELAND

BY

JOSEPH DONALDSON

SERGEANT IN THE NINETY-FOURTH SCOTS BRIGADE

The Spellmount Library of Military History

SPELLMOUNT
Staplehurst

British Library Cataloguing in Publication Data:
A catalogue record for this book is available
from the British Library

Copyright © Spellmount 2000
Introduction © Ian Fletcher 2000

ISBN 1-86227-085-6

First published in 1852

This edition first published in the UK in 2000
in
The Spellmount Library of Military History
by
Spellmount Limited
The Old Rectory
Staplehurst
Kent TN12 0AZ
United Kingdom

Tel: 01580 893730
Fax: 01580 893731
E-mail: enquiries@spellmount.com
Website: www.spellmount.com

1 3 5 7 9 8 6 4 2

Printed in Great Britain by
T.J. International Ltd
Padstow, Cornwall

AN INTRODUCTION
By Ian Fletcher

There were very few occupations in the early 19th century that were regarded as being as unworthy as that of a soldier in the army of George III. After all, what were your prospects? Glory perhaps, or wealth and fame? No, when a lad joined the British army at the beginning of the 19th century his prospects were more likely to be an unmarked grave in an obscure part of Spain or Portugal as a result of death in battle or from sickness brought on by the rigours of harsh campaign life, the campaign in question being the Peninsular War, which lasted from 1808 to 1814. And, even if he survived the war, assuming he returned home with all his limbs and faculties intact, what would he return to? Certainly not a hero's welcome. For many an old soldier, discharge from the army meant a period of unemployment or a poorly paid job, with nothing but a tale to tell on a cold, dark winter's night and little to keep him warm save the memories of a distant camp fire, of comradeship and of the sounds of struggle and strife.

In spite of all this, volunteers willing to fight for king and country were never in short supply, men who joined out of patriotism, through fear of invasion from Boney's France or those simply seeking adventure. And then there were the recruits who joined the ranks of Wellington's army to seek refuge from debts, complicated private lives and other unfavourable circumstances at home, and those who were saved from prison by enlisting for service in the army. The British redcoat was, therefore, regarded as being 'the scum of the earth', to use Wellington's oft-quoted phrase. Yes, we all know that Wellington went on to say that it was wonderful that they had become such fine fellows, but that was in the 1830s, long after the war had ended. But when, following the victory at Vittoria, an angry Wellington wrote his despatch to Lord Bathurst, he did indeed refer to his men as 'the scum of the earth', and he meant it, after watching them spend the night of 21 June 1813 engaged in plundering the abandoned French baggage train instead of carrying on an effective pursuit of the beaten French. There were indeed times when British troops did become mere scum.

One can imagine, therefore, the shock and despair of the parents of Joseph Donaldson when their 16 year-old son announced to them that he had 'gone for a soldier'. It was all too much for Joseph's father to bear as can be judged from the most affecting story in Joseph's lively *Recollections*. Fortunately, Joseph Donaldson returned safe and well to his family in Scotland and, in the best traditions of story-telling, he 'lived happy ever after', if only for a few years. However, much water had passed beneath the bridge between Donaldson's departure from his native Glasgow and his return years later, and his story is told here in the pages of his most engrossing tale, *Recollections of the Eventful Life of a Soldier*.

I shall not dwell on the background to the book – this is very well covered by the Introductory Notice on page iii – suffice to say that the tale originally appeared in three volumes, *Recollections of the Eventful Life of a Soldier, The War in the Peninsula* and *Scenes and Sketches in Ireland*. Indeed, the first edition of *Recollections* appeared in 1825, which adds to its value by way of pre-dating the first volume of Napier's great *History of the War in the Peninsula* by three years and thus avoids the 'Napier factor', later diarists often resorting to drawing upon the great work to bolster their memoirs when their own memory had failed them. This edition, which combined all three works, was originally published in 1852.

Joseph Donaldson served in the Peninsula with the 94th

(Scotch Brigade) which was part of the famous 'Fighting' 3rd Division which was commanded by the fiery Welshman, Sir Thomas Picton. This meant, of course, that Donaldson witnessed many of the greatest and most terrible episodes of the war, such as the desperate and bloody street fighting at Fuentes de Oñoro and the siege and storming of the fortress of Badajoz, probably the most terrible episode of them all. But it wasn't all blood and guts and, in fact, it was a long time before Donaldson even joined Wellington's main field army, having spent seven months at Cadiz as part of the Allied garrison there. Donaldson finally caught up with Wellington's army during its sojourn within the Lines of Torres Vedras, those impassable hills and forts which so effectively thwarted Masséna and brought about an end to the third French invasion of Portugal. From here on, Donaldson served until the close of the war at Toulouse on 10 April 1814.

Joseph Donaldson was a keen observer of events in the Peninsula and his *Recollections* are strewn with vivid descriptions, of colourful vignettes and of heart-rending scenes. He strikes a nice balance between good, gripping action and the pleasantries and unpleasantries of everyday life in Wellington's army. And he was not merely looking back through rose-tinted spectacles. No, Donaldson was a level-headed soldier who realised that many improvements could have been made in Spain to better the soldiers' lot, such as tents – which did in fact appear in 1813 – and good shoes. 'Nothing renders a soldier more uncomfortable as having wet clothes about him; or, I believe, hurts his health more, when exposed to it', he wrote during one bout of bad weather. 'Much more attention ought to have been paid to the quality of the shoes served out to the army,' he went on to say, 'for they in general are of the very worse kind, and it was no uncommon thing for our shoes to be in tatters before we had worn them a week.' And, prior to the issue of tents in 1813, he wrote of campaign life in general, 'the blue canopy of heaven was our covering, the earth our bed, and a single blanket our bedclothes.'

When, in later years, he reflected on his time in the Peninsula he probably considered the agony of the storming of Badajoz as his most painful memory. His account of the assault on the night of 6 April 1812 is gripping enough but it is his description of the terrible aftermath of the storming which really brings home the harrowing nature of the events of the subsequent two days. When the 19 year-old Donaldson visited the area of the breaches, where the 4th and Light Divisions had attacked forty times without success, he was struck by the savage nature of the defences and, as he said, 'I could not wonder at our troops not succeeding in the assault.' He then returned to the scene of his own division's assault, at the castle walls. There, at the foot of those tall, forbidding walls, he saw, among scores of other dead soldiers, a man from the 45th Regiment who, as he wrote, 'when wounded, had fallen forward on his knees and hands, and the foot of the ladder had been, in the confusion, placed on his back. Whether the wound would have been mortal, I do not know, but the weight of the men ascending the ladder had facilitated his death, for the blood was forced out of his ears, mouth and nose.' Donaldson then goes on to describe a woman and her child, desperately searching the breaches for her husband, whom she eventually found, an ice-cold, bleeding corpse. It is difficult, looking back over the years, to imagine anything like the scenes at Badajoz on the day after the storming, but certainly Donaldson's description leaves one feeling numb with horror and is vivid enough to bring the terrible event closer to us.

It is also very interesting to note Donaldson's claim that, when the town had surrendered, the successful stormers 'were allowed to enter the town for the purpose of plundering it.' And he is not the only diarist to allude to this. Indeed, some claimed that the town would be given up to them for plundering should they be successful. Of course, under the convention of the day Wellington's men should have been allowed not only the privilege of sacking the town but of slaughtering the garrison as well. This is not as barbaric as it sounds and, indeed, writing after war, Wellington claimed that had he put the garrison of Ciudad Rodrigo to the sword when he stormed the town in January 1812, it would have saved him 'the flower of his army' at Badajoz. But, as we know, it was not to be. Donaldson thought the sacking of Badajoz to be a terrible event, as it truly was, adding, 'it was productive of nothing but bad consequences, and for the interests of humanity, and the army at large, I hope such licence may never recur, should we be again unfortunately plunged into war.' It was during horrific episodes such as Badajoz that his religious beliefs were sorely tested, for Donaldson was a very religious man, something which comes out forcibly towards the end of the war. Perhaps he was finding it difficult to reconcile his religion with the events happening around him, such as the deaths of many good men including his own friends.

Fortunately for Donaldson and the 94th, nothing as horrific as Badajoz ever took place again although similar events took place following the storming of San Sebastian in August 1813, an event to which he was not privy. His *Recollections* continued after Badajoz and include really wonderful descriptions; the triumph at Salamanca, the miseries of the retreat from Burgos, the 'awful grandeur' of the Pyrenees and, finally, the peace following the untidy and unsatisfactory battle of Toulouse.

Donaldson's place in the literary history of the Peninsular War is assured by this most entertaining and graphic account of the war. Furthermore, he is the only diarist from the 94th, a regiment which, given that the two regiments served side by side in Picton's 3rd Division in the Peninsula, was in 1881 rather appropriately amalgamated with the 88th (Connaught Rangers). Unfortunately, it appears that many members of the public claimed that Donaldson's *Recollections* were the work of 'some literary figure' and that they may not have been genuine. Well, perhaps this is a mark of their quality and accuracy, for it is difficult to imagine anybody writing in such detail about the war without having been a participant. No, these *Recollections* are definitely the work of Joseph Donaldson. Sadly, he did not live long after their publication, dying in Paris in October 1830 at the early age of 37. It is over 190 years since he set foot in Portugal but time has done little to diminish the value and appeal of his *Recollections,* a classic book which ranks amongst the most graphic and enjoyable of the many memoirs of the Peninsular War.

Ian Fletcher
Rochester, 2000

RECOLLECTIONS

OF THE

EVENTFUL LIFE OF A SOLDIER.

BY THE LATE

JOSEPH DONALDSON,

SERGEANT IN THE NINETY-FOURTH SCOTS BRIGADE.

> " I will a round unvarnish'd tale deliver—
> Of moving accidents by flood and field,
> Of hair-breadth ' scapes i' the imminent deadly breach,
> And with it all my travel's history."
>
> SHAKSPEARE.

" The romance of real life certainly goes beyond all other romances."

MISS EDGEWORTH.

NEW EDITION.

EDINBURGH:

ROBERT MARTIN, 3 BROWN STREET.

———

MDCCCLII.

INTRODUCTORY NOTICE.

THE ensuing narrative was originally published in three successive volumes, entitled respectively,— "Recollections of the Eventful Life of a Soldier"— "The War in the Peninsula"— and "Scenes and Sketches in Ireland." Although these volumes were eminently successful, the form in which they were brought out rendered them accessible to only a comparatively small portion of the community. They are now collected into one volume, and published at a price which brings the work within the reach of all classes of people.

The narrative, from its outset to its close in 1814, embraces a period of about twenty-one years, fifteen of which relate to the author's boyhood, and the remaining six to his career in the army. The circumstance of the work having been published anonymously will account for the scrupulous care with which he has avoided making any such allusions as might be calculated to draw aside the veil of his incognito. In this edition, however, the author's name, the number of his regiment, and the rank he held in it, are given ; the names of places, so far as they could be ascertained, and of individuals, so far

as was deemed prudent, which were left blank in the
early edition, have been supplied in this—but in other
respects the original text has been preserved. The
only part of the soldier's story which begets a feeling
of disappointment is its abrupt termination. The
vicissitudes of his subsequent career might have
formed an interesting, though melancholy, sequel to
the present volume. The few particulars we have
gathered refer chiefly to that period of his life.

While in Ireland in 1814, about a year previous
to the conclusion of the narrative, the author married
the individual of whom, under the name of Ellen
M'Carthy, he speaks in such high terms of admiration in the " Scenes and Sketches." By this union
he became the father of ten children, seven of whom
died in early life. In 1815, he returned with his
family to Glasgow, where he underwent various
changes of fortune, more particularly adverted to in
the narrative, which induced him " to resume the
uniform of a soldier." He accordingly embarked
with his family for London, and enlisted in the service of the East India Company, in which he was
soon promoted to the rank of recruiting sergeant.
This occupation, while, contrary to his wishes, it
imposed on him the duty of remaining in this
country, afforded facilities for indulging those literary
and scientific predilections which had distinguished
him in the Peninsula ; and he now endeavoured to
turn them to advantage by the study of anatomy
and medicine. Thus occupied, he remained in London, until, in 1817, he was removed to Glasgow,
where he began and completed writing from memory
the interesting " Recollections " which form the

first portion of this volume, the proceeds of which enabled him still farther to prosecute his studies at the University, where, "exchanging the tartan for the broad-cloth," he mingled unobserved among the other students. In consequence of his great dislike to the revolting practices which at that time characterized the recruiting service, he applied to Captain William Marshall, Superintendent of the East India Company in Edinburgh, who, through the influence of Colonel Hastings, got him transferred to the situation of head-clerk in the Glasgow Military District Office, where he remained for some years. During this period, he completed, in rapid succession, the consecutive portions of his " Eventful Life." In 1827, having procured his discharge, he was enabled, on the trifling proceeds of his literary labours, and by dint of severe economy and close application, to take the degree of surgeon. Shortly afterwards, he removed to the town of Oban in Argyllshire, where he continued to practise his new profession with as much success as a field so circumscribed would permit, till the year 1829, when, wearied with the proverbial drudgery of such a life, and anxious to give greater scope to his talents, he once more embarked for London, leaving his wife and children in Scotland. With "manners and dispositions not framed in the world's school," it is scarcely matter of surprise that in such a place as the metropolis he failed to procure the employment he sought. He remained there several months, occasionally solacing his dreary hours with that species of literary composition which was his chief delight. Besides contributions to periodicals, he completed a work, entitled " Life in

Various Circumstances," which, had not the MS. been unfortunately lost, with other property, on its way from France two years afterwards, might have precluded the necessity of this brief and imperfect notice. Unsuccessful in London, he proceeded to Paris, where, while attending the anatomical academies, he died in October, 1830, of pulmonary disease, at the early age of thirty-seven.

His widow, from whom the foregoing particulars have been obtained, still lives, the sole support of three surviving children. Since her husband's death, and for some years previous, Mrs Donaldson has suffered severe privation and poverty. The sole dependence to which she and her family can look forward with hope, is the recorded Reccllections of her husband's misfortunes, which are now published for her behoof.

EDINBURGH, *March.* 1838.

AUTHOR'S PREFACE.

THE present Work was first published in separate volumes, within a twelvemonth of each other, under the title of "Recollections of an Eventful Life," and "The Peninsular War." The favourable reception they met with from the Public, even in their unavoidably imperfect state, far exceeded my most sanguine expectations. Many, indeed, alleged "that they were the production of some book-maker," and others "that some person of literary ability must have assisted the soldier." Neither, however, is the fact. Such as the narrative is, it was composed and written by me without the slightest assistance. Indeed, I think it strange that scepticism on that point should have been excited. Why should not a soldier (if he has cultivated his natural abilities) express himself in a tolerable manner as well as an individual of a different class? It would be more strange if a particular grade of men were to engross all the talent existing; and it is only the presuming arrogance of rank, or the overweening conceit of literary pedantry,

which would seek to shut the door against the
exercise of talent, merely because the individual
does not enjoy any of the arbitrary distinctions
which they themselves have created.

As to my being really an actor in the scenes
I have described, I believe little doubt now exists
in the public mind. I could at once dissipate
it, by giving my name and the number of my
regiment; and I would have done so, were it
not that it might point out too minutely some
ill-favoured characters which I have given in the
work. Fear for myself would not prevent me;
but I have no personal enmity to gratify, and I
shall feel sufficiently satisfied, if the picture drawn
deter others from following their example.

My unsettled situation caused the former
edition of the work to be so hurriedly written, that
many errors escaped notice, which, in the present,
I have endeavoured to amend. The two volumes
are now thrown into one, forming a continued
narrative down to the close of the war, and
several incidents added, which were omitted in
the first edition. If in its former state it excited
an interest in the public mind, I trust it is now
rendered more worthy of its approbation. I am
aware that there are still imperfections in it that
will require indulgence—an indulgence, however,
which, I am persuaded, will be readily conceded
to the humble station of

THE AUTHOR.

THE

EVENTFUL LIFE

OF

A SOLDIER.

CHAPTER I.

I was born in Glasgow: my father held a situation in a mercantile house, that enabled him to keep his family respectable. I was the only surviving child, and no expense would have been spared on my education, had I been wise enough to appreciate the value of it; but, unfortunately for me, that was not the case. I had early learned to read; but novels, romances, and fairy tales, were my favourite books, and soon superseded all other kinds of reading. By this means, my ideas of life were warped from reality, and the world I had pictured in my imagination was very unlike the one in which I lived. The sober realities of life became tiresome and tasteless. Still panting after something unattainable, I became displeased with my situation in life, and neglected my education—not because I disliked it; on the

contrary, I was fond of learning, and used to form
very feasible plans of study, wherein I omitted
nothing that was necessary to form the accomplished
gentleman. I could pleasingly, in imagination, skim
over the whole course of literature, and contemplate
my future fame and wealth as the result; but when I
considered how many years of arduous application
would be required, I was too impatient to put it into
practice. I had acquired too great a facility in
raising castles in the air, and embellishing them with
my fancy, to submit to the drudgery of building
on a more stable foundation. Thus, straining at
shadows, I lost substantial good.

Amongst other books which fell into my hands, when
very young, was Robinson Crusoe. It was a great
favourite; and at that time, I believe I would willingly
have suffered shipwreck, to be cast on an island like
his. An island to one's self, I thought, what a happiness! and I have dreamed for hours together, on
what I would do in such a situation. I have often
played truant to wander into the fields, and read r v
favourite books; and, when I was not reading,
mind was perfectly bewildered with the romant..,
notions I had formed. Often have I travelled
eagerly to· the summit of some neighbouring hill,
where the clouds seemed to mark the limits of the
world I lived in, my mind filled with an indescribable
expectation that I would there meet with something
to realize my wild ideas, some enchanted scene or
other; and when I reached its summit, and found
those expectations disappointed, still the next similar
place had the same attraction. The sky, with the
ever-varying figures of the clouds, was an inex-
haustible field for my imagination to work in; and
the sea, particularly those views of it where the
land could not be seen from the shore, raised indescribable feelings in my breast. The vessels leaving
the coast, thought I, must contain happy souls; for

they are going far away,—all my fancied happy worlds were there. Oh, I thought, if I could once pass that blue line that separates the ocean and the sky!—then should I be content; for it seems the only barrier between me and happiness.

I was often beat for being absent from school, and urged to tell the cause. The reason I felt, but could not describe; and, the same fault recurring again and again, I was at last set down as incorrigible. What most surprised my friends was, that I never had any companions in my rambles; but a companion would have spoiled all my visions. Never did I enjoy so pure unmixed delight, as in those excursions: I feel not now, as I then did, the novelty of life and nature; but memory cherishes with fondness her first-born feelings, and I regret that those happy days are gone for ever.

> So ill exchanged for riper times,
> To feel the follies and the crimes,
> Of others or my own.

In some old romances which I had read, the life of a shepherd was described in colours so glowing, that I became quite enamoured of it, and would not give my parents rest until they procured such a situation for me. It was in vain that they assured me I would find every thing different in that life from what I imagined. I could not believe it. They made some agreement with a farmer, from whom they got their milk and butter, to take me out with him to his farm, that I might learn the truth by experience. I set off with him on his butter-milk cart, my mind filled with the most extravagant anticipations of my new employment, and arrived at the farmer's house at night. Next morning I was called up at four o'clock to my new avocation, and an old man was sent out with me to shew me my charge. I was left by him on a bleak hill, with four-score sheep, and told that

my breakfast and dinner would be brought out to me.
I sat down to contemplate the scene: there were no
sylvan groves, no purling streams, no shepherds
piping in the dale,—nothing but peat-bog was to be
seen for miles around; the few scathed hills which
reared their heads above the blackened soil were
covered with heather, which still retained its winter
suit; the shepherds had none of the appendage,
attributed to them in poetry or romance, they had
neither pipe nor crook, and shepherdesses there were
none. I tried to transform the female servant, who
was in my master's house, into a shepherdess; but it
would not do. It was a horrible caricature; she was a
strong masculine looking Highland girl, any thing
but lovely or romantic. Surely, thought I, there
must be some mistake here. I never spent a day so
lonely and tiresome. My flock seemed to think they
had got a fool to deal with, for they ran in every
direction but the right one. It is true I had a dog,
but he did not understand my language. We had
not been long enough acquainted; and, by the time
night came, I was pretty well convinced that the life
of a shepherd was not what I had imagined it. Day
after day passed, without realizing any of my expectations. My feet got sore running through the rough
heather; and I returned to my parents about a
month after, completely cured of my predilection for
a shepherd's life. One would think that this disappointment would have rendered me more cautious
in forming opinions from the same source—but no!
Indeed, it was ever my misfortune to pay dearly for
my experience, and to profit little by that of others.

CHAPTER II.

I FOUND few boys of my own age, who entered into my notions. One, indeed, I did find equally extravagant, and we were scarcely ever separate. Tired of living under the control of our parents, we determined to make a bold push at independence. We mustered as much money as bought the sixteenth of a lottery ticket. In the interval between buying and drawing—how we did dream! It never entered our minds that we would get less than the share of a prize of £ 30,000 ; and, of course, the disposal of the cash was the constant theme of our conversation. At last the wished for day arrived, on which we were to receive intelligence of the fate of our ticket. We did not go to inquire concerning it until night. With hearts fluttering with apprehension, we went to the shop where we had bought it. I would not go in, but sent in my companion. I durst scarcely look after him. To such an intense pitch of interest was my mind wrought up, that the criminal on his trial for some capital crime could not wait with more dreadful anxiety for the verdict of the jury, than I did for my companion to come out. He did come, but I was afraid to look him in the face, lest I should read disappointment in it. I waited for him to speak, but his tongue refused its office. I at last ventured to look in his face, and there I read the truth. Had he spoken and told me it was a blank, I might have doubted him, and thought he only joked me ; but I could never doubt the expression of despair which I saw there depicted. Not a word was exchanged, we walked on in stupified vexation. After wandering about for some time unconscious of where we were going, he at last burst into tears. I

could have willingly joined him, but I suspected that
something else preyed on his mind. On asking him
what distressed him so much, he said that part of the
money with which he had purchased his share of the
lottery ticket was the balance of an account, due to
his father, which he had received without his knowledge. He depended on the receipt of his prize to
pay it with interest, but now those hopes were
blasted ; he could never face home—his countenance
would betray him, and his father was very severe.

He said he was determined to go to Greenock,
and engage with some merchant vessel bound to
Surinam. He had an uncle a planter there, and, of
course, when he should arrive, there would be no
danger of him ; his uncle would procure his discharge
from the ship, and the result, that he would become
a gentleman. I listened eagerly to this. We had
often expatiated on the pleasure of seeing foreign
countries, and I resolved to accompany him, not
doubting but his uncle would provide for me also,
for his sake. Any thing like adventure was always
welcome to me, and my mind was soon decided.

We had no money, however, to carry us to
Greenock ; but I recollected a person who owed my
father money, and I proposed to go and ask it in my
father's name. This was the first time I had ventured to do any thing so glaringly dishonest, and I
hesitated long. I passed the door a dozen times
before I mustered effrontery enough to go in ; but it
was drawing near the hour of shutting up, and I was
obliged to resolve. I went in and asked the money.
The candle burned dimly, and I stood as much in the
shade as possible, but I am sure he noticed my
embarrassment. However, he gave the money, and
we hurried out of the town immediately.

We travelled all night, and next morning arrived
in Greenock. After getting some breakfast, and
brushing ourselves up a little, although we were very

tired, we resolved on looking out for a vessel. On inquiry, we learned that there was no vessel in the harbour bound for Surinam. This was a disappointment; but, we thought, if we were once in the West Indies, we would find little difficulty in getting to the desired spot.

The first vessel we came to, was a ship bound for Kingston, Jamaica. We went on board; and, inquiring for the captain, asked if he wanted any men. He looked at us with a smile of contempt, eyeing us from head to foot, " *Men*," said he, laying a particular emphasis on the word, (for neither of us exceeded thirteen years of age,) " it would be a pretty vessel that would be mann'd with such *men as you*—Whaur hae ye come frae na ? Ye 'll be some runawa weaver callans frae Glasgow, I'se warrant ye ; but ye had better gang hame again, for I 'm thinkin' ye 'll like the sea waur than the loom." We were galled by his reply ; but consoled ourselves with the idea that some one else would be glad to get us.

After trying several other vessels with nearly the same success, at last, tired and crest-fallen, we were going home to our lodging, when an old man, who had seen us going from one vessel to another, accosted us, and asked if we wanted a ship. Replying in the affirmative, " you need not want that long," said he, " for if you go with me, I will soon find one for you. Where do you wish to go ?"

" To Surinam."

" Then, you could not have come in a better time, for there is a vessel lying in the roads ready to sail for that place."

" Do you think they will take us ?" said we.

" Oh, to be sure they will, and glad to get you. I'll take you on board now if you like."

We assented, and he went to procure a boat to take us on board.

When he was gone, a sailor, who was standing by

and saw us talking to the old man, came up, and
asked us what he had been saying. Having told him,
he said the sooner we were off out of that the better;
for the fellow, who had been talking to us, was one
of a set of rascals in pay of the press-gang ; and that,
instead of putting us on board of a vessel such as he
described, he would put us on board the Tender;
and that there was actually no such vessel in the
roads as the one he had mentioned. We lost no
time in taking his advice, and hurried home to our
lodgings.

When there, my spirits began to sink; and the
thought of how I had left my parents, and the distress
they must be in about me, completely overcame me,
and I burst into tears ; and my companion feeling
as bad as myself, we resolved to return home, and
ask forgiveness of our parents ; but, being fatigued
with travelling, we put off our return until next
morning.

When we got up next day, our minds had recovered
some of their former elasticity, and we felt less disposed to return than we did the preceding evening.
The idea of the ridicule which we should have to
encounter from our acquaintance, and, on my part,
the stigma which would be thrown on my character
for drawing the money in my father's name, seemed
to be insurmountable barriers in the way, so we
walked into the town with our minds still undecided.

In crossing the main street, we met one of our old
school-fellows, who had run away from his parents
about six months before. He had just returned from
the West Indies ; and having leave for a few days to
go to Glasgow to see his friends, he had got himself
rigged out in the jolly-tar style — his jacket and
trowsers of fine blue cloth, white stockings, short-
quartered shoes, a black silk handkerchief tied loosely
round his neck, over which the collar of his checked
shirt was folded neatly down — a glazed hat on his

head, and an enormous quid of tobacco in his cheek. In fact, he was so completely metamorphosed, that we scarcely knew him; for when at school, he was remarked for being a soft, dull sort of boy.

On seeing us, he seized a hand of each, and exclaimed, " Oh, my eyes! Joe and Bill! how are ye, my hearties? what has brought you to Greenock: be ye looking out for a birth?" We were expressing our pleasure at having met him, when he said, " Don't be standing here in the street. Let's go and get a glass of grog." We remarked, that it would look very odd for boys like us to go into a tavern and call for liquor; but Tom thought that a very foolish objection, and leading the way into a tavern, we followed him. As he walked in before us, I perceived that he had altered his manner of walking quite to the rocking gait of the veteran tar. I certainly thought that Tom had been an apt scholar; he seemed to be as finished a sailor as if he had been twenty years at sea. From being a boy of few words, he had acquired a surprising volubility of tongue, along with an affected English accent. He could curse and swear, chew tobacco and drink grog; and although we perceived much affectation in what Tom said and did, still we were disposed to think him a very clever fellow. When seated over our grog, we disclosed our minds to him, and inquired if he could assist us in getting a vessel. Tom looked rather grave on this subject, and sinking his voice from the high English accent he had acquired so rapidly, said he was not sure whether he could get a vessel for us or not; " but," said he, " in the mean time drink your grog, and we will see about that after."

Warmed by the liquor, Tom began and gave us an account of his voyage, which, as he afterwards owned, he painted in very extravagant colours. We were so charmed with his description, that we gave up all idea of going home, and adjourned from the tavern to Tom's lodgings, where he displayed to our wondering eyes the treasures he had acquired by his West India voyage—conch shells, cocoa nuts, and stalks of Indian corn, which were designed to grace his mother's chimney-piece, and excite the wonder of her visiters.

Between the liquor we had drunk, and what we had heard and seen, we were in high spirits, and went out to perambulate the town ; but, going up the main street, towards the head inn, I met my father full in the face. He had just arrived from Glasgow in search of us. I thought I would have sunk into the earth. Confounded and ashamed, I stood like a felon caught in some depredation. Tom ran off, and left William and I to manage affairs as we could. My father was the first who broke silence. — " Well, Joseph," said he, " will you tell me the meaning of this jaunt you have taken ? But I am going to Mr C——'s, and you had better come with me, and we shall talk over the matter there." We followed him without saying a word, and when we were seated in Mr C——'s, he again asked my motive for leaving home. I looked in William's face, and saw he was determined. I then said we were resolved on going to sea, and that we had come to Greenock for that purpose. Mr C. and my father said every thing they could to dissuade us from our foolish resolution, but to little purpose. The idea of the ridicule we would have to bear from our acquaintance if we returned, and Tom's exaggerated description of the pleasures of a sea life, had confirmed us in our determination.

" Well," said my father (after he had reasoned the matter with me, and painted what a sailor's life was in reality, with little effect,) " I might exert the right I have over you, as a parent, in forcing you to return, but I will not. If you have so far forgot your duty to me, and to yourself, after all that I have done

for you, as to throw yourself away as a common ship-
boy, where you can have no opportunity of learning
any thing but wickedness, you may do it, but
remember my words — *you will repent it,* when you
will perhaps have no father to question the propriety
of your conduct. Indeed, after the dishonest action
you have been guilty of at home, I don't know but
your presence would be more disagreeable to me
than your absence, unless you altered much for the
better ; and if I have any very anxious wish that you
would return, it is more on your poor mother's
account than my own. Oh, how could you leave us
in the manner you did, without a cause ?— The first
night you were absent from home, your mother was
frantic. She wandered from place to place in search
of you—and was sure you were not in life—that some
accident had befallen you. When she knows the
truth, how cruel must she think you ?— O! Joseph,
after all our care and attention, I am afraid you
will bring down our gray hairs with sorrow to the
grave."

Here the tears came into my father's eyes, and his
voice became choked. I could bear it no longer,
and burst into tears. My first impulse was to throw
myself at his feet, and beg forgiveness ; but the
obstacles which were in the way of my return before,
again recurring to my mind, prevented me, and I
only wept in sullen silence.

" Say no more to him now," said Mr C. " Give
him until to-morrow to think on what you have said ;
and if he be then of the same opinion, we shall
procure a good ship for him, and see him properly
fitted out." My father took his advice, and did not
resume the subject that day. He wrote, however, to
William's father, telling where his son was.

Next morning, he arrived, and insisted on taking
him home by force, and even beat and abused him in
the house we were in ; but my father and Mr C.

interfered, and represented to him how foolish his conduct was, as he might be sure the boy would take the first opportunity of running away again. He was at last brought to reason, and agreed to be guided by my father. We were again asked what we had determined on doing, and I replied that we were fixed in our determination of going to sea.

It was then proposed to get us bound immediately, as my father could not be spared from his business, and was obliged to return next day. Mr C. took us to a friend of his, a Mr G. a respectable merchant and ship-owner, who was in want of apprentices at that time for some of his vessels. We were there bound for three years, and attached to a letter-of-marque brig, which carried 18 guns, loading at that time for New Providence.

The afternoon was spent in purchasing the necessary articles to fit me out. When that was finished, my father, feeling uneasy on my mother's account, resolved to return to Glasgow that night. Before going away, he said, " I could almost wish your mother saw you before you went away—and yet, perhaps it would be better that she would not. You will soon find yourself among very strange company ; and if I am not wrong informed, company from whom you will be able to learn little that is good ; but I trust you will remember the religious instruction you have received from your parents, when you are far from them ; and although you have grieved and disobeyed your earthly parents, I hope you will not forget your Creator. Remember his eye is on you wherever you go ; and although you may be bereft of every other stay, still he will be ever with you, to succour, and to help, if you call upon him. Farewell, my boy, God help you !"

My heart sunk within me. As the coach started, I saw him wipe the tears from his eyes. I must surely be a hardened wretch, thought I, to persist so resolutely in what I know to be wrong, and what is breaking the heart of my parents; but I was roused from my reflections by some one slapping me on the shoulder. It was Tom—" Well, my boys, so you have got bound to our owner—have you?"

" Do you belong to Mr G. also?" said I.

" To be sure, and I don't think but I shall get into your ship too, although she sails so soon; for I don't like the one I am in."

We felt well pleased that Tom was to be our shipmate; and in the contemplation of all the good fortune that I thought awaited me, I am ashamed to say, that I nearly forgot mў distressed parents.

As for William, the moment his father set off, (for my father and his went up to Glasgow together,) the poor fellow seemed quite relieved! His mother had died when he was very young, and his father being a man of a morose severe disposition, he scarcely knew what parental tenderness was.—How different from me! He had some excuse for what he had done; but I had none.

Tom went up to Glasgow next day, to see his friends; and a day or two after, William and I were sent on board, to commence our seamanship. The first day or two passed away well enough. There was little or nothing to do. The third day, the mate called us aft to the quarter deck. " Do you see that flag?" said he, pointing to the mast head. It had got entangled in the signal halliards. " Now let me see which of you will get up first and clear it."

Will and I got on the shrouds, and mounted with great alacrity, until we got to that part of the shrouds which takes a sweep outwards to meet the edge of the top. Will was up over it in a twinkling; for he had been used to mount the rigging of the vessels at the Broomielaw; but I thought it a dangerous-looking place, and seeing a hole through the top, by the side of the mast, I proceeded to squeeze myself through

it ; which being an offence against the laws of good
seamanship, (as the sailors' name for it denotes, being
called the *lubber's hole,*) the mate seized a rope's end
on deck, and running up the shrouds after me, called
out, " You young dog! is that the way you are
taking ?"

I made haste to rectify my error by taking the
same route that Will had pursued ; but, in my hurry,
from the fear of the rope's end, when I reached the
edge of the top, I let go the hold with my feet, and
being suspended by my hands, would soon have
dropped on the deck, or into the sea, had the mate
not caught hold, and assisted me up. Will had by
this time got as far as the cross-trees ; but he was
foiled in his attempts to climb up the royal mast.
The mate, however, thought we had done enough for
once, and we were ordered down ; but our exercise
at this kind of work being continued every day while
in harbour, we soon became expert at it.

CHAPTER III.

At last, the long-expected day of sailing arrived,
and among the first of the men who came on board
was Tom. He had received liberty to join our ship,
and, men and boys, we mustered about sixty hands.
The greater number, when they came on board, were
" half-seas-over," and the ship was in great confusion.

Towards evening, it began to blow fresh, and I
became miserably sick. No one took any notice of
me, unless when I went to the weather-side of the
vessel to vomit, when some one or other of my
tender-hearted shipmates would give me a kick
or a push, and, with an oath, bid me go to leeward.

In this state, I was knocked about, from one place to another, until at last I lay down in the waste of the vessel, on the lee-side, with my head opposite to one of the scuppers.* I had not been long there, when some one came running to the side. I looked up to see who it was, and saw poor Tom in nearly as bad a plight as myself. I was too sick to speak to him, or I would have asked why he had omitted this in his description of the pleasures of a sea life.

I had not seen William from the ·time I became sick ; but at that time I could feel interested for no one, or about any thing. I only wished I were on shore, and nothing should ever tempt me to put my foot on board of a vessel again.

Night came on, and the weather being cold, I began to wish that I could get below. I crawled to the first hatchway I could find, which happened to be the steerage. As this place was appropriated to the petty officers of the ship, and they being all employed on deck, I was allowed to get down unmolested. There were some of the cables coiled in the steerage ; and as I had experienced the inconvenience of being in the way, I crept in as far as I could, beyond the cables, where some old sails were lying, and there, although not relieved from sickness, I was at least free from annoyance.

I had not been long there, when the steerage mess came down to supper ; and I quaked with terror when I heard the gunner say, " I wonder where all those boys are. I can't get one of them to do either one thing or another."

" They 'll be stowed away in some hole or other, I 'll warrant ye," said the boatswain, " but if I had hold of them, I would let them feel the weight of a rope's end."

---

* Scuppers, the holes by which the water runs off the deck.

I strove to keep in my breath lest they should hear me, but at the moment my stomach heaved, and in spite of all my efforts to suppress it, I made such a noise that I was overheard.

"Who the devil's that?" cried the boatswain; "some one of the rascals stowed away in the cable tier — hold the lantern, and I'll haul him out whoever he is."

Already I thought I felt the rope's end on my shoulders, when I was unexpectedly relieved from my apprehensions, by the mate calling them on deck to arrange the watches for the night. While they were gone, I squeezed myself in behind some boxes, where I was pretty sure they could not get at me. When they came down again, they had forgotten the circumstance; and those whose watch was below got into their hammocks.

A little before day-light, I felt inclined to go on deck, as I was nearly suffocated in my hiding-place, and slipping out cautiously, got up the ladder without disturbing any of them. I had felt pretty well settled, when my head was down; but whenever I got up, the sickness returned, and my stomach being completely empty, my efforts were most distressing. An old sailor who was standing near me advised me to take a drink of salt water. I thought it was a rough cure; I tried it, however, but it was no sooner down than up again.

"Take another drink," said he; I did so—the same result followed. He advised me to take a third.

"Oh, no," said I, "I can take no more."

I then leaned over the lee bow of the vessel; and whether it was the fresh air or the salt water I know not, but I soon got better; and in the course of an hour or two I began to move about pretty briskly.

While I was stirring about, the carpenter came forward to me and inquired if I was sick. No, I said.

" Will you have any objection to attend our mess ?"

" I don't know, what have I to do ?"

" Only draw our provision, and boil our kettle morning and evening."

" Very well—I am willing."

He took me down to the steerage, and shewed me where things lay. When breakfast-time came I got their kettle boiled, and brought down their mess of bargoo, and sat down to take my breakfast with them ; but before I had taken half-a-dozen spoonfuls, it began to discompose my stomach ; and getting up to pass them for the deck, the motion of rising brought the contents of my stomach up to my mouth. I endeavoured to keep it down, but was obliged to give it vent, and it flew like water from a fire engine over the mess. The boatswain, who was a surly old fellow, and who had been the principal sufferer, rose up in a fury, and seizing the wooden dish that held the bargoo, threw it at my head. I escaped the blow of the dish, but the contents came right on my face and blinded me. I tried to grope my way up the ladder, but they did not give me time to get up, for they threw me out of the hatchway. When I got to my feet the whole of the seamen on deck gathered round, and began to jeer me on my appearance ; but I managed to flounder on through them to the head, where I got some water and washed myself. Ah! thought I, this is hard usage ; yet I could scarcely refrain from laughing at the idea of spoiling their mess.

I walked about the deck for some time, ruminating on my folly in exchanging my comfortable home for a place like this. Towards dinner-time, the carpenter came and asked me to prepare the mess-dishes for dinner, but I told him he might find some one else, for I would not do it.

" The more fool you are," said he, " you will soon find yourself worse off."

I was then obliged to shift my things into the forecastle amongst the crew. Here I found William lying in one of the births, so sick that he could not lift his head. When he saw me he beckoned me to him. " O Joseph," said he, " this is misery. I wish we were at home again ; but I will never live to return."

" No fear of that," I said, " I was as sick as you are, and I am now nearly well."

At this moment the vessel gave a heave, and down I came on the deck. William began to make cascades, and I was soon as bad as ever, and got tumbled into the birth beside him. Shortly after, the seamen's dinner was brought down, and having served themselves, one of them called out " You green-horns, in there, will you have some beef and biscuit ? "

" No, no," said I, " but if you will be kind enough to open my chest, you will find a cake of gingerbread in it—I will thank you to hand it to me."

While he was searching for the gingerbread, he cast his eyes on a large case bottle, filled with whisky, which Mr C. had given me when I parted with him. He immediately gave up his search for the gingerbread, and hauling out the bottle and holding it up, he cried, " D——n my eyes, messmates, if I ha'n't found a prize."

" Here with it," cried a dozen voices at once, and in spite of my remonstrances, they deliberately handed it round until there was not above a glass left.

" Oh shame," said one of them, " give the boy a drop of his own grog ;" but I could not look at it —the smell was sickening.

" No, no," said I, " send that after the rest."

" Right," said one of them, " boys have no use for grog."

" Will you give me the gingerbread now ? " said I.

" Oh, by the bye, I had forgot that, here it is for you, my hearty."

The most of them went on deck, and left William and I to reflect on the justice of their appropriation of my property. However, the liquor was a thing I cared little about, and it gave me the less uneasiness. We were now allowed to lie quietly enough until night, when those whose watch was below came down to go to bed — one of them came to the birth, where William and I were lying, and seizing him by the neck, cried out, " Hollo, who the devil's this in my birth ?"

" It is two of the Johnnie-raws that are sick," replied one of them.

" Johnnie-raw or Johnnie-roasted, they must get out of that, for I want to turn in."

Out we were bundled, and during the whole course of that night we were knocked about from one place to another, by each succeeding watch.

Next morning early, the word was passed for the boys to go aft to the quarter-deck. It was hard rooting them out ; but at last we were mustered—six in all. When we were assembled, the mate addressing us, said, " I think I have given you long enough time to recover from your sickness. You, Tom, have no right to be sick. You were at sea before." I looked at Tom : there was not a more miserable looking object amongst us. I could scarcely allow myself to believe that he was the same being whom we saw swaggering on the streets of Greenock a few days before. We were then appointed to different watches. William and I were luckily appointed to the same one, which being on duty at the time, we were ordered to scrub the hen coops, and feed the fowls, while the men washed the deck. The boys were always made the drudges in every thing dirty and disagreeable. But the duty of the ship was little in comparison to the way in which we were teased and ill used by the sailors. I have often been roused up after a fatiguing watch, and just when I had fallen into a profound sleep, to go and fetch a drink of water for some of the crew. A fellow, of the name of Donald M'Millan, was one of our chief tormentors. He used to invent new mortifications for us; and he was of so brutal and savage a disposition, that he would beat and abuse the boys for the most trifling fault, and often without cause. I am sure, if the conduct of the men had been reported to the captain, he would not have allowed the boys to be used in the manner they were. But we were afraid to say any thing concerning our usage, knowing that they could find numberless methods of tormenting without openly beating us.

I began, however, to get used to the sea; and taking courage, I strove to get through as well as I could. It was, nevertheless, with a great effort that I could prevent my spirits from sinking under the many hardships and contumely I had to endure. Nothing but the hope of leaving the vessel when she returned home kept me alive. Poor William lost all heart; he became melancholy and moping, and used to cry for hours together, when we were on watch at night. In this state he was ill calculated for the duty he had to perform, and was brow-beaten by almost every one in the ship. This sunk his naturally buoyant spirits; and at length he became so accustomed to ill usage, that he seemed afraid I would also turn against him. I, however, had known him in happier days; but his feelings were morbidly acute, and little calculated to struggle through the ill usage which a ship apprentice had to endure.

As we proceeded on our voyage, the weather became delightful; and getting into the trade winds, we got on so pleasantly, often for days together, without changing a sail, that had we not been tormented by the seamen, we would have been comparatively comfortable. But the only happy periods I enjoyed were, when my turn came to look out aloft —seated on the crosstrees, away from the din of the deck, with the clear blue sky above, and the sea extending far as the eye could reach beneath. It was there I almost realized some of the fairy scenes I had pictured in my imagination. I felt myself in an enchanted world of my own, and would sit watching the clouds as they passed along, comparing their shape to some romantic image in my mind, and peopling them with corresponding inhabitants. So lost was I in those reveries that I did not feel the time passing; and when the man came up to relieve me, I have often volunteered to stop his two hours also. When I came down on deck, I felt as it were cast from heaven to earth, and used to long for my turn to look out again. These were the only pleasures I enjoyed unmolested and unenvied; for few of my comrades required any pressing to allow me to remain in their place. The nights were now delightful; the moon shone in " cloudless majesty," and the air was so cool and pleasant, that it was preferred by the seamen to the day; instead of going below, they often gathered in knots on the deck, and played at various games, or told stories. Many of them were good at this. One of them, a Swede, had as large a collection as any person I ever knew : they were those of his country — mostly terrific — ghosts and men possessed of supernatural powers, were the heroes of his stories.* The flying Dutchman, and

---

* One of the stories he narrated was of a seaman with whom his father had sailed. He was a wonderful fellow : he could arrest a ship in full sail. When he wanted liquor, he had nothing to do but bore a hole in the mast, and out flowed rum, brandy, or any liquor he wished for. He once had committed some crime, for which he was sentenced to be flogged ; the crew were assembled, and the culprit stripped and tied up ; the boatswain raised his brawny arm to give the lash, but by some invisible power his arm was arrested in the air, and he stood with it stretched out, unable to bring it down. The master-at-arms raised his cane to strike the boatswain for his seeming neglect of duty, and his arm was arrested in like manner. The

many other naval apparitions, were talked of and descanted on with much gravity. Sailors, in general, are very superstitious, and these stories were listened to with the greatest attention.

One night the weather was hazy, when I was appointed to look out a-head along with an old sailor, who was remarkable for being an attentive listener when any stories were telling. The moon was up; but a dense curtain of clouds hid her almost completely from our view. The wind came in gusts, and swept the clouds along in irregular masses. Sometimes a doubtful light would be thrown around us; again a dark cloud would intervene, and we could scarcely see the end of the jib-boom. The wind whistled through the rigging of the vessel occasionally with a low murmuring sound; then it would rise gradually to such a fury, that we could scarcely hear each other talk. We were anxiously looking out, when he asked me if I did not see something like a sail a-head. I replied that I did not. He pointed to the place where he imagined he saw it. I looked again. A partial gleam of light, occasioned by a cloud of lighter texture passing over the moon, being thrown on the place, I really thought I saw something

captain, enraged to see both boatswain and master-at-arms in the strange position, drew his sword, and raised it, to let it fall on some of their heads, when he shared the same fate. Thus all three stood with their arms upraised in air; nor would our hero release them from their awkward position, until he was pardoned and taken down. Some time after, he committed another crime; but they were afraid his power was too potent on board for them to proceed against him there: therefore he was conveyed ashore, and tried. In addition to the alleged crime, they brought forward a charge of dealing with the devil. The proof was reckoned conclusive, and he was sentenced to suffer death. He gave himself no uneasiness about it. The day arrived on which he was to be executed; and the guard entered his prison for the purpose of conveying him to the place of execution. When they entered, he was busily drawing a ship upon the wall with chalk; he requested them to wait a moment until he would finish it. They did so. When he had done, he bade those about him adieu; and lifting his foot, as if it were to step into his mimic ship, he disappeared from their eyes in a moment, and was never heard of after like a sail. He did not wait for any more investigation, but gave the alarm. The mate came forward to see it; but the light was so uncertain, that he could not decide on what it was. The watch gathered about the bows of the vessel, every one having something to say on the subject. One pretended he saw a sail plainly—she was a square-rigged vessel, with all her sails set; another said she was schooner rigged. Ominous whispers now began to go round, intimating that her appearance was any thing but natural. The mate, hearing some hints that were dropped, said, " There was a cursed deal too much of that ghost story-telling of late; and he would lay his head to a marlin-spike, that this would turn out to be no sail after all." At this moment (luckily for his prediction) the moon broke through in all her splendour; and as far as the eye could reach, not a speck on the surface of the dark blue waters could be traced. The laugh was now turned against those who had pretended to see the sail; but they only shook their heads doubtfully, and wished that nothing bad might follow. I venture to say that every one on board joined in that wish.

CHAPTER IV.

A FEW days after that, we fell in with a vessel which we hailed, and found she was bound for Greenock from Jamaica. She brought to; and all those who wished to send letters to their friends were ordered to make haste and write them. I got out my writing materials; but I was at a loss what to say. Had I been inclined to tell the truth, I would have been at no loss; but I could not bear the idea of owning how grossly I had been deceived in my ideas of a sailor's life. However I believe I gave them room to think that I did not like it very well. I had lost so much time in resolving what to write, that the letters were called for before I had time to give any particulars. When I was sealing my letter, I ardently wished I could insinuate myself inside of it.

Nothing particular occurred during the rest of our voyage, until a few days before we made the land. One morning early a sail appeared to windward. The captain, looking at her through his telescope, was of opinion that she was a French privateer. All hands were called to quarters; and as she bore down upon us, the captain's opinion was confirmed, for she fired a gun, and hoisted French colours. We were well manned, and carried as many guns as she appeared to do. Every thing was prepared for action; only the guns were not run out, and the ports were down. The captain had ordered all the men, with the exception of the petty officers, to lie down on the deck, concealed behind the bulwarks, until he should give the word of command. She was bearing fast down upon us, when I was ordered to the magazine to hand up ammunition. I was frightened enough when on deck; but when below, I became much more so. It was not long before a broadside was fired. I was sure it was from the enemy, and, stunned with the noise, fell flat on my face. " God be merciful to me !" said I : for I was sure we were going to the bottom. In a minute after, I was surprised with the men cheering on deck. I mounted the ladder ; and venturing my head up the hatchway, saw the strange ship a good way to leeward, making all the sail she could. On inquiring, I found that she had borne down close on us, thinking we were an unarmed merchant ship, and ordered us to strike. The reply we gave was what had alarmed me so much ; for our men, starting to their feet on the word of command from the captain, ran out the guns, and gave her a broadside. She was so completely taken in by the reception she met with, that she sheered off without firing a shot. The captain's orders were, not to deviate from his course, else we might have captured her.

We now drew near the land, and the lead was frequently hove to ascertain what sort of a bottom we had.* Pieces of sugar-cane, melons, and fruit of various kinds, were floating about; birds, in great numbers, hovered about the ship; and every thing intimated that the land was nigh. It was my turn to look out aloft, and I felt sure of the bottle of rum which is usually given to the man who espies land first. I was not long up, when I thought I saw land off the lee bow. I watched it attentively. It became better defined every minute. I was positive it was land, and I sung out, " Land, ho!" with a joyous voice. The intelligence ran through the crew; and I saw them skipping about on deck, seemingly delighted with the news. The mate came up beside me to see where the land lay. I pointed it out to him; but it soon altered its appearance, and began slowly to move up from the verge of the horizon, and in less than ten minutes not a vestige of the appearance remained. To me it looked like enchantment; but I learned from the mate that such sights were not uncommon, and were termed by the seamen, " Cape Flyaway."

In the course of the day we made the real land, but were too late to get into the harbour that night. However, next morning early we got in, and came to anchor nearly opposite Fort Charlotte, town of Nassau, after a passage of six weeks. As we entered the harbour, we found a sloop-of-war lying there; and some of our men, afraid of being pressed, took a boat, and made towards the shore; but the officers of the man-of-war observing them, they sent a boat in pursuit. Our fellows pulled hard, and would have made the shore before them, had they not fired a musket

* There is a cavity in the bottom of the lead, which is filled with tallow, to which sand or gravel, composing the bed of the sea, adheres.

shot or two, and obliged them to lie to. They were
then all taken on board the sloop-of-war ; but in the
course of the day they were sent back, with the
exception of Donald M'Millan, who had given some
insolence to the officers ; and they sent word that they
had kept him to teach him better manners. The
boys did not mourn much at his detention, nor, I believe, did any of the crew ; for his disposition was
such, that every one hated him.

We were not long at anchor before we were surrounded by canoes from the shore, with black fellows
in them, selling fruit of various kinds, not common
in Britain. Here we got rid of some of our money,
in exchange for bananas, guavas, and pine apples ;
and I almost forgot all my sufferings in the novelty
of the scene around me. The white sandy beach, the
light ornamented wooden buildings, walks bordered
by palm and cocoa-nut trees, with the singular dresses
of the planters and their negroes, were objects which
made me think myself in a new world. In the course
of the day we got off fresh beef and plenty of vegetables, which was a treat, having had nothing but salt
provision from the time of leaving Greenock ; and to
complete our happiness, we got an extra allowance of
rum sent from the owners of the cargo.

Next day we began to deliver the cargo. There
was no quay, but wharfs here and there to the different stores. When the tide was in, we got our boats
unloaded by means of a crane ; but at low water we
were obliged to push the hogsheads from the boats
into the sea, and wading up to the middle to roll them
out before us to the shore. This was most fatiguing
and disagreeable work ; therefore we were not sorry
when it was finished. On Sundays, (the negroes'
market-day in the West Indies,) the half of the crew
alternately got leave to go ashore. William and
I happened to be of the first party, and we were
delighted with every thing around us ; but we could

not discover that the inhabitants were disposed to give their money away for nothing any more than at home. Nor could we find any thing to justify the notion, that a rapid fortune could be acquired there, without similar exertion to that we had been accustomed to see in other places. After taking a view of the town, and purchasing some shells and other curiosities, we came on board well pleased with the holyday we had had on shore. Soon after this, we began to take in our cargo, which consisted principally of rum, cotton, and coffee.

As yet it had been delightful weather, only excessively warm in the middle of the day ; but the mornings and evenings were very pleasant. The third morning, after we began to take in our cargo, came on sultry and close. The air was oppressive — the clouds hung low and heavy, and ere long the rain burst out in torrents. This had not continued ten minutes, until we were up to our knees in water on the deck. It poured down so fast that it could not escape by the scuppers. The earth seemed threatened with another deluge. The whole face of the heavens was dark as night. The crew were all employed in striking the top-gallant masts, lowering the yards, and making every thing snug. " This is shocking rain !" said I to an old sailor who stood near me.

" Yes," said he ; " but we will have worse than rain bye and bye." He had scarcely said so, when the heavens seemed to open, and a flash of lightning burst forth, so strong and vivid that it took the sight from my eyes. A clap of thunder followed so loud and long, that it must have appalled the stoutest heart. Flash after flash succeeded each other, and the peals of thunder were incessant. I thought the last day was come. Heaven and earth seemed jumbled together in one mass of fire ; and the continued noise of the thunder struck my imagination as the result of the fabric falling to ruin.

Towards the afternoon the wind blew with great fury. The vessels in the harbour began to drag their anchors, and before night many of them were on shore; but we were well moored, and did not stir. The storm continued the greater part of the night; and such a night I hope I will never see again. No one would go below. We did not know the moment the lightning might strike the vessel, and perhaps send her to the bottom. It is in vain for me to attempt to convey any adequate description of that dreadful night in words. No one can form an idea of its awfulness, unless he had seen it. The men stood huddled in groups, on the deck, in silence. Indeed it was useless to speak, for they could not be heard; nor scarcely could they see each other, unless when the lightning shot its awful glare athwart their faces, and made their horror visible for an instant; and the livid cadaverous colour it shed over their countenances, gave them an expression truly appalling.

About one o'clock in the morning, the storm began to moderate: the flashes of lightning became weaker, and less frequent; the awful roaring of the thunder changed into a hoarse growl, and at length died away. By two the storm had so much subsided, that the seamen, with the exception of the harbour watch, went below to their hammocks.

I was surprised next morning, when I got up at sunrise, to see no vestige of the night's storm remaining. All was calm and serene, save a pleasant breeze from the shore, which brought the most delicious odours along with it. The sun rose with unusual brightness, and all nature seemed renovated. We could not, indeed, have imagined that there had been a storm the preceding night, if the effects of its fury had not been visible in the roofless buildings and stranded vessels around us.

Our vessel had suffered little or no damage. We

got on with our loading, and in a short time we were ready for sea. The day before we sailed, the owners sent a present of a bottle of rum to each man, to hold a sort of " chevo," as the sailors called it. The decks were cleared, and we sat down in groups with our bottles, and commenced drinking. All went on very well for a time. The song and joke went round, and harmony and good humour prevailed. But when the drink began to operate, some of them who had differences during the voyage began to " tell their minds." The result was, that they came to high words, and from that to blows. The rest of the crew took different sides, according as they were interested ; and the deck soon became a scene of confusion and bloodshed. I had drunk little, and mounted into the foretop to be out of " harm's way ;" and from thence saw the combat, without danger of getting any of the blows which were dealing out so plentifully. The mate came forward to try to quell the disturbance ; but they knocked him over a kedge anchor that lay on the deck, and broke one of his ribs.

At length the disturbance died away, and I came down on deck. Some deep drinkers had gathered the bottles which had escaped destruction during the fight, and were emptying their contents. Others were lying insensibly drunk and vomiting. Broken bottles, with their contents promiscuously mixed on the deck with the blood of the combatants, lay scattered about in every direction. I never saw such miserable-looking wretches as they were next morning. Most of them were " horrified." Almost all of them bore marks of the late fray—black eyes, swelled lips, sprained thumbs, &c. &c. As the vessel was to sail that day, the captain, in order to bring them about a little, served them out their grog, and they quickly got to rights again.

We got up our anchors, and set sail with a fair wind. I could not describe the emotions I felt, when

I saw the vessel's head turned homewards. I was all joyous anticipation of meeting with my parents. " I shall never leave them again," thought I. " I shall obey them in every thing, and we shall be so happy. I have seen my folly, and I shall make a good use of my experience."

Nothing particular occurred on the passage home, until we got near the British coast, when the weather became extremely cold. The look-out aloft was no longer a pleasant birth. I have often been so benumbed when the man came up to relieve me, that I could scarcely move my limbs to come down upon deck. The weather had been rough for some time, but one afternoon it began to blow uncommonly hard. The wind was fair, however, and the captain seemed unwilling to take in sail, but the gale increasing, he ordered the top-gallant sails to be handed. William and I, with another boy, went up to hand the main top-gallant sail. The vessel was pitching dreadfully. William went to the weather, and I went to the lee earing, to haul in the leach of the sail. The part which bound the yard to the mast gave way, and it pitched out with such violence, that William was shook from his hold, and precipitated into the sea. I got a dreadful shock. This was an awful moment. Every pitch that the vessel gave, the yard was thrown out from the mast with such force, that it was a miracle I escaped. The other boy had got in on the mast, but it appeared impossible for me to follow him. Nothing could save me, unless the despairing hold that I retained, and I could not have kept it long, for every shock rendered me weaker ; but some of the seamen were sent up with a loose line, and succeeded in bracing the yard to the mast, and I was relieved from my perilous situation.

Poor William ! I saw him fall. " O God !" he cried, as he fell. I heard no more. The next moment he was swallowed by the waves. They told me he never rose. It was impossible to do any thing to save him in such weather with any effect. His fate made a great impression on my mind, for he was my only companion. He was a clever boy, warm-hearted, and kind in his disposition, although he had become quite broken-hearted. Nor did he seem relieved from his melancholy by the prospect of returning home; for he was sure that his father would do nothing to get him free from the ship; and even if he did, he could feel little pleasure in the anticipation of his usage there. " O Joseph!" he would often say, " if I had a father and mother like yours, how happy would I be! but I may truly say that I am an orphan! To be sure, while my mother was living, she was every thing that was good and affectionate to me; but when she died, I lost the only friend I had in the world, for my father never was kind to me, and after he married again, I never had a happy minute in the house; and if I were to go home again, even supposing that he would get me free from the ship, things would be worse than before. But I am sure I will not live to return. There is a heavy something hangs on my mind, that tells me I will not see the end of this voyage; but I do not feel grieved at it, I rather feel a pleasure in the idea. Then I will be free from ill usage and persecution; and what makes me long for my death, is the hope that I will meet my mother in heaven, never to part from her again." I could not forbear weeping when he spoke in this manner; and I tried to cheer him as much as I could, by putting him in mind of our former schemes of happiness and fortune; but he only shook his head, and said, " This is not the world we dreamed it was; but even so, I have no friends, no prospects, and death appears to me to be the only thing that can alter my situation for the better" Poor fellow! he little thought it was so near.

The gale still continued to increase, and all our

sails were taken in, with the exception of a close-
reefed fore-top-sail. The wind veered about, and
blew a hurricane. Some of the sails were torn in
ribbons before they could be handed. The sea ran
mountains high. The sky was darkened, and the
flapping of the sails and rattling of the blocks made
such a noise that we could scarcely hear our own
voices. The sea broke over us in such a way that
boats, spars, and camboose, were carried off the deck,
and the helm became almost totally unmanageable,
although four men were constantly at it. When a
sea struck the vessel, she creaked as if her very sides
were coming together. The men were obliged to
lash themselves to every place where they could find
safety, to prevent their being washed overboard; and
in this manner we stood in awful suspense, waiting
the issue of the storm. One minute she would rise
perched, as it were, on the verge of a precipice; the
next, she would descend through the yawning gulf as
if she would strike the very bottom of the sea, while
vivid flashes of lightning contributed to throw a
horrific glare over the scene.

Three days were we tossed about in this manner,
every day expecting it to be our last, for we thought
it impossible that the ship could weather the gale.
During that time we could not get below, the hatches
being battened down, and we had to subsist on dry
biscuit, or eat raw pork with it, for we could get
nothing cooked.

On the fourth day the storm abated, and the
weather cleared up, but the vessel rolled so that we
expected her masts to go overboad. After the gale
we fell in with some vessels which had suffered
severely, one in particular had lost all her masts.
We were at this time near the mouth of the Channel;
and next day, we made Cape Clear. I could not
express what I felt at again seeing the shores of
Britain. My imagination was hard at work drawing

pictures of the future. We ran up along the Irish
coast with a fair wind, and at last came in sight of
the well-known Craig of Ailsa; and passing it, the
Cumbrays, and the Clough light-house, we anchored
in Greenock roads. I was in transports of joy at the
idea of getting home again; but a doubt would often
cross my mind, whether my father might feel inclined
to get me free from the vessel, after so obstinately
persisting in going to sea; I, at least, felt sensible
that I did not deserve such indulgence. The day
after we arrived, however, my mind was set at ease,
for my mother came from Glasgow to see me, and
the first words she said, were, " Well, Joseph, are you
tired of the sea?" The tears came into my eyes, but
I could not speak. " I find you don't like it," said
she: " you have found out, I believe, that your
father's description of a sea life was a true one—well,
we must try and get you home again." A day or
two afterwards, my father came to Greenock, and
having settled matters with the owners, I went home
with him on the coach, fully resolved that I should
be more wise in future. I had a joyful meeting with
my friends, and, for a time, all went on pleasantly;
but my restless disposition still remained the same,
and I soon grew tired of home. My parents expected a miraculous change in me; and when they
found that my voyage had made me little wiser, any
indiscretion was generally checked with an allusion
to my former conduct. This irritated my feelings.
Those boys who used to associate with me now
avoided my company; most of them, I believe, by
the injunction of their parents. There were two
boys with whom I had been on the most friendly
terms—their parents and mine were very intimate—
they were constant playfellows of mine before I went
to sea, and I had occasionally seen them after my
return, without their seeming any way reserved towards me. Some months after I came home, however,

I happened to be diverting myself with them in
their court-yard, we were playing at *hide-and-seek*,
having hid myself in the straw-house, I heard their
father call them and ask who was with them ; when
they told him, he said, " Never let me see you in that
boy's company again, for he ran away from his
parents, and he may induce you to do the same."
This went like a dagger to my heart. It humbled
me severely in my own eyes. I waited until he went
into the house, and then slunk away like a felon.
From that day I thought every one who looked at
me were passing similar observations in their minds.
My temper became soured, and I grew melancholy
and restless. I brooded continually over the indignity
which I conceived I had suffered.   " Then," said I
to myself, " I have become an object of contempt to
every one. I can never endure this—I will not
remain in Glasgow."

CHAPTER V.

ONE evening, in January, 1809, returning from
dinner to school, brooding over my real or imaginary
evils—my mind in such a state of despondency that
I could almost have taken away my life,—I determined to leave Glasgow, for, I thought, if once out
of it I should be happy. In this state of mind, walking down the High Street, I met a soldier. The
thought struck me instantly that I would enlist,
although I rather felt a prejudice against the army.
Yet, by enlisting, I would get out of Glasgow, and
to me that was every thing. I followed the soldier,
and asked him where his officer lodged. He shewed
me the place, and I enlisted, with the proviso that he
would send me out of the town immediately. I was
sent to Paisley, and remained with the party there

until the recruits were ordered to march for head-
quarters. When I came into Glasgow to join them,
in passing through the Bridgegate, I met my mother.
I had never written to my parents, nor had they
heard of me from the time I enlisted. I could
scarcely define my feelings : shame—grief—a sort of
sullen despair—a sense that I had cut myself off
from the world—that I had done my worst, and a
determination to push it to the utmost—were mingled
together in my mind. My mother first broke silence.
" Poor, infatuated boy !" said she, the tears flowing
down her cheeks, " what new calamity have you
brought on yourself by your wild, inconstant disposition ?" I told her I had enlisted, and was going
that day to join my regiment,—" Alas !" said she,
" you have now finished it. Now you are lost to us
and to yourself; but will you not come home, and
see your father before you go ?" I hesitated.
" Perhaps," said she, " it will be the last time you may
ever see him. Come, you had better go with me."
I consented, and we went home together. It was
near four o'clock. My father generally came home
at that hour to dinner. My mother met him as he
came in, and explained matters to him. He strove
to assume an air of calmness ; but his countenance
shewed the emotions that were working in his mind.
We sat down at the table to dinner ; but no one
seemed inclined to eat. My father cut some meat
on his plate, but instantly pushed it from him. He
rose from his seat, and walked about the floor with a
rapid pace. He opened his waistcoat.—He seemed
suffocating. I could no longer endure to see the
convulsive agony with which his whole frame was
agitated. I sunk on my knees at his feet, and cried
out, " Forgive me, O father—forgive me !"

He looked at me for a moment ; then, bursting into
tears, he said, " God forgive you ! God forgive you !
my poor unfortunate boy. Alas !" said he " I had

none out you. I had formed schemes for your advancement in life. I saw you had some talent, and was determined to spare no expense in making you fit to fill a respectable situation. I had figured to myself you going in and out with me, happy and contented—a credit to yourself and to your parents ; but, alas! those hopes are now fled for ever : for the first news I hear of you, may be, that your corpse is bleaching on the Continent—a prey to wolves and eagles." Then, as if correcting himself for drawing such a picture—"But your life is in the hands of God. Yet even now, are you not lost to me? May I not say that I am childless?—I give you my forgiveness freely, and also my blessing; and if you should survive, oh! may you never have a son that will cause you such agony as I feel at this moment. Farewell! my poor boy; I am afraid I may say, Farewell for ever!" With these words he rushed into an adjoining room, and threw himself on his knees, I suppose to pray for that son who had repaid all his kindness with ingratitude and disobedience. My mother was wild with grief. It was the hour at which we were to march. I tore myself out of the house in a state of distraction, and joined the party, who were now on the road to Airdrie. My mind was in such a state of agitation, that I scarcely knew where I was going. I walked on before the party, as if some evil thing had been pursuing me, anxious, as it were, to run away from my own feelings.

I am scarcely conscious of what passed between that and Dunbar; it seems like a confused dream. But the parting scene with my father often recurred to my memory; and although it is now fifteen years since it took place, it remains in it as fresh as yesterday. The step I took at that time has been to me the source of constant and unavailing regret; for it not only destroyed my fair prospects in life, and fixed me in a situation that I disliked, but I believe it was

the means of breaking the heart of a parent, whose
only fault was that of being too indulgent. I felt
sensible of his tenderness, and I am sure I loved him.
But mine was a wayward fate. Hurried on by impulse, I generally acted contrary to the dictates of
my own judgment — " My argument right, but my
life in the wrong."

He has long gone to his eternal rest ; but while he
lived, he was a man—take him all in all—whose
equal will be rarely found ; for it could truly be said
of him, that " even his failings leaned to virtue's side."

When our party arrived in Dunbar, where the
regiment lay, after being finally approved, and the
balance of my bounty paid, which was about four
guineas, (after deducting necessaries,) I was conducted
by the sergeant to the room where my birth was
appointed. When he left me, I sat down on a form,
melancholy enough. An old soldier sat down beside
me ; and, remarking that I looked dull, asked me
where I came from, when I replied, " Glasgow."

I was immediately claimed as a townsman by some
of the *knowing ones*, one of whom had the Irish
brogue in perfection, and another the distinguishing
dialect and accent of a cockney.

" You don't speak like natives of Glagow," said I.

" Och ! stop until you be as long from home as
me," said Paddy, giving a wink to his comrades,
" and you will forget both your mother-tongue and
the mother that bore you."

" Ha' ye got yere boonty yet, laddie ?" said an
Aberdeen man.

" Yes," said I.

" Than you 'll no want for frien's as lang as it lasts."

So I found ; for every little attention was paid me
that they could devise. One brushed my shoes,
another my coat ; and nothing could equal the many
professions of good-will and offers of service I
received. There was a competition amongst them

who should be my comrade, each supporting his offer by what service he would render me, such as cleaning my accoutrements, teaching me my exercise, &c. It appeared to me that I was set up at auction to be knocked down to the highest bidder. But I paid little attention to them. My mind was taken up, thinking of my folly, and ruminating on its consequences.

After holding a private consultation amongst themselves, one of them took me aside, and told me it was the usual custom for each recruit, when he joined the company, to give the men of the room he belonged to a " treat."

" How much ?" said I, putting my hand in my pocket ; for, in the passive state of mind I was then in, they would have found little difficulty in persuading me to give them all I had.

" A guinea," was the reply.

" Why didn't you ask two ?" said an old fellow aside to the spokesman, when he saw me give the one so freely. He seemed vexed that he had not.

It was then proposed to go into the town, to purchase the liquor ; and I, of course, must go along with them. Four or five accompanied me to town, and we met two or three more as if by accident. As we returned home, they lingered behind me a little, and appeared to be consulting about something. When they came up to me, one of them said, as I had been so free in treating them, they could not do less than treat me ; and led the way into a public house for that purpose. One half pint of whisky was called in after another, all protesting that they would be their share ; but when the reckoning came to be paid, which amounted to seven or eight shillings, each asked his neighbour, to lend him until he went up to the barracks. It turned out, however, that none of them had any money ; and it ended in a proposal that I should pay the whole, and they would

repay me on pay-day. This opened my eyes a little.
I thought I could see a great deal of meanness and
trick in their conduct; but I seemed to take no
notice of it.

When night came, the room was cleared, and the
forms ranged around. An old Highlander in the
room had a pair of bagpipes, which with two fifes
constituted our music, and when we were all assembled, the drinking commenced, handing it round
from one to another. After a round or two, old
Donald's pipes were called for, and the men commenced dancing with the women of the company.
The stamping, hallooing, and snapping of fingers
which ensued, intermingled with the droning sound
of the bagpipes, was completely deafening. In the
confusion some of the thirsty souls took the opportunity to help themselves out of their turn, which
being observed, caused a dispute; and the liquor being
expended, a join of a shilling a man was proposed to
" carry on the glory." I was again applied to, and
aided by this fresh supply, they kept up " the spree"
until one o'clock in the morning. When some of
them who had got drunk began to fight, the lights
were knocked out, and pokers, tongs, and tin dishes
were flying about in every direction. At last the
affair ended by the officer of the guard sending some
of them to the guard-house, and ordering the others
to bed.

Next morning I was besieged, before six o'clock,
by a band of the fellows who had got drunk the night
before, begging me to treat them to a glass to " heal
their head." I felt little inclined to drink at that
hour, and expressed myself to that effect. They then
asked me to lend them money to procure it, and they
would repay me on pay-day. I gave them what they
wanted, and I soon had the most of the men in the
room at me on the same errand. In the course of the
day I got my regimentals served out, and was sent

to drill. After drill it was intimated to the recruits who had lately joined, that they ought to treat the drill sergeant, by way of propitiating his favour. While we were talking, the sergeant who had conducted us to the regiment came up to bid us farewell.

" You are not going away to-night," said a recruit.

" I believe I will," said the sergeant, " unless you have any thing to treat me to."

" You ought to give the sergeant a supper," said a man who had joined about a month before ; " we gave our conducting sergeant a supper."

It was therefore agreed that we could be no worse than the others, and he was accordingly invited along with our drill sergeant. When night came, and we were going into town, it was moved that the sergeants of our companies ought to be invited also ; of course it was insinuated that we would be no losers by so doing. When we were all met, between sergeants of companies and their friends, whom they had taken the liberty to invite, we were a goodly company.

The supper came in, and was done great justice to by the guests. Next came the drink, and when all hearts were warmed by the rum punch, numerous were the protestations of friendship and promises of favour from the sergeants to the recruits, which were very soon forgotten. I was sitting next our conducting sergeant: he seemed very restless, and spoke often to a very loquacious sergeant who sat near him, who replied several times that it was too soon yet. At last, however, when he found we were all pretty mellow, he rose and commenced his harangue with, " I say, lads, I daresay you are all very well pleased with Sergeant A——." This was assented to by all the recruits. " Well," said he, " I just wished to inform you that it is the usual custom for the recruits to give the sergeant who conducts them a present when they receive their bounty."

The acquiescence of all present, shewed how well the sergeant had chosen the time to make his proposition.

" What is the usual sum ?" said one.

This question was put to our conducting sergeant: and after some hesitation, he very modestly replied, " five shillings each."

The money was soon collected, and he pocketed it with great glee.

At a late hour we separated, and got home to our barrack rooms without disturbance, having previously had leave from tattoo. Next day I was roused for drill at day-light; and after coming in, wishing to procure some breakfast, I was surprised to find my cash dwindled to a very few shillings. During the day, I was applied to by some of my comrades for the loan of more money; but I refused, alleging that I had little left. I could soon see that this information made a great impression on them ; for the things which they had formerly been so officious in doing for me were now left to be done by myself; and amongst all those who had been so anxious to become my comrades, I could not find one now that would accept of me, and a new party of recruits joining I was soon altogether forgot.

Next day, having purchased some little things that I needed, I found my money expended ; but I gave myself little uneasiness about it, as I had lent so much, and the following day was pay-day. When the men received their pay, I spoke to those who had borrowed the money from me, and said that I would be obliged to them for it ; but how was I surprised when some of them swore I had never lent them a farthing, and threatened to beat me for presuming to say so ! Others said they could not pay me at that time ; and more of them laughed at my simplicity in expecting repayment of any money borrowed out of a bounty ! This is strange kind of justice, thought I ; and leaving

the room, I wandered down by the sea side, thinking
on the honest men I had got amongst. I heard the
step of some one behind me, and turning round to see
who it was, I perceived one of the recruits who had
joined some time before me. His name was Dennis
——— : he was an Irishman. I had remarked that he
took no part with the others, in their professions of
kindness to me, and that on the night of the spree he
had gone to bed without joining in it. When he
came up to me, he said, " I have waited until now
to speak to you, for I would not say a word while
the bounty lasted, lest you might suspect that I was
like the others; but now I have come to say that if
you choose you can be my comrade, for mine left me
before you came to the room, to go along with a recruit; and now, that his bounty is finished, he wishes
to come back again ; but I hate such meanness, and
would never associate with a fellow of his description :
however I think you and I will agree." I was glad
to accept his disinterested offer ; and during all the
time Dennis and I were comrades, I never had reason
to repent it; for he was of a warm-hearted generous
disposition, and never flinched from me in distress.
He had no education : he could neither read nor write;
but he had a judgment, which no sophistry could
blind, and his acute Hibernian remarks often puzzled
men who thought themselves better informed ; besides
this, he had a fund of honour that never would allow
him to stoop to a mean action. One fault, indeed, he
had in common with the generality of his countrymen, and that was, when he got liquor he was a
thorough madman.

Dennis and I were now left to ourselves, to act as
we pleased, and the " knowing boys" looked out for
newer hands to fleece, some of them descending to
very mean stratagems to get drink. I remember
being in town with Dennis one evening, and having
gone into a public-house to get a glass before we

went home, one of those disgraceful animals came into the room where we were sitting, and after telling some rigmarole story, without being asked to drink, he lifted the glass from before us, and having said, " Here's your health," swallowed its contents. I was confounded at his impudence, and sat staring at him ; but Dennis was up in an instant, and knocked him down, and, as he said himself, " kicked him for falling." The fellow never made any resistance, but gathered himself up, and crawled out of the room. When he was gone, — " By my faith !" said Dennis, " I think I gave the rascal the worth of his money — that is the only cure for a 'spunge.' "

" I wonder they have no shame," said I.

" Shame !" rejoined Dennis, " shame and they might be married, for any relationship between them !"

In a short time I began to recover my spirits, and when I had any spare time, I had recourse to my old favourites, which I obtained from a circulating library in the town. It is true I could not now dream so delectably of the life of a shepherd or a sailor ; but I had the field of honour before me. To fight in defence of one's country, thought I — to follow the example of a Bruce or a Wallace—must be a glorious thing. Military fame seemed the only object worth living for. I already anticipated my acts of valour, charging the enemy, driving all before me, and coming back loaded with honour and a stand of French colours ; receiving the praise of my command- ing officer, and a commission. On I went in my career of arms, and it was impossible to stop short of being a general.

In these day-dreams of promotion and honour, I did not look particularly to the situation I was then in ; or even very attentively at the intermediate ground I had to go over : but these were trifles in my estimation at that time. I must confess, how-

ever, that a damp was often thrown over these fine
speculations by some harsh words from the drill
sergeant, or some overbearing conduct of my superiors. Or when I saw a poor fellow taken out, and
receiving a flogging for being ten minutes late from
tattoo, I could not help thinking the road to preferment rather rough. Be that as it may, I believe I
had by this time caught a portion of military
enthusiasm ; and " death or glory" seemed very fine
words, and often, when walking alone, have I ranted
over the words which Goldsmith puts into the mouth
of the Vicar of Wakefield, when his son leaves him
to go into the army,—" Go, my boy, and if you fall,
though distant, exposed, and unwept by those who
love you, the most precious tears are those with
which heaven bedews the unburied head of the soldier."

The miserable retreat of our army to Corunna,
and the account given of it by some of those who
had returned, often lowered my too sanguine anticipations ; but nothing could permanently keep down my
ever active imagination. In this state of mind, I felt
a relief from the melancholy I had previously sunk
into ; but still I was far from being contented ; something was continually occurring which made me draw
comparisons between my present way of living, and
that which I had enjoyed at home. There were few
of those with whom I could associate, that had an
idea beyond the situation they were in :* those who
had were afraid to shew they possessed any more
knowledge than their comrades, for fear of being
laughed at by fellows who, in other circumstances,
they would have despised. If a man ventured to
speak in a style more refined than the herd around
him, he was told that " Every one did not read the
dictionar' like him ;" or, " Dinna be gi'en us ony o'

---

* This is not to be wondered at when we consider how the army was at
that time recruited ; it is very different now.

your grammar words na." If a man, when accused
by his superiors of something of which he was not
guilty, ventured to speak in his own defence, he was
called a *lawyer*, and desired to give no reply. If he
said that he thought it was hard that he should be
condemned without a hearing, the answer was,
" Be silent, sir! *you have no right to think ;* there
are people paid for thinking for you — do what you
are ordered, sir, right or wrong."

If he did not join with his neighbours in their
ribald obscenity and nonsense, he was a Methodist,
— if he did not curse and swear, he was a Quaker—
and if he did not drink the most of his pay, he was
called a miser, a mean scrub, and the generality of
his comrades would join in execrating him.

In such society it was a hard matter for a man of
any superior information or intellect to keep his
ground ; for he had few to converse with on those
subjects which were most congenial to his mind, and
to try to inform his comrades was a vain, and by them
considered a presumptuous attempt. Thus, many
men of ability and information were, I may say,
forced from the intellectual height which they had
attained, down to the level of those with whom they
were obliged to associate ; and every thing conspired
to sink them to that point where they became best
fitted for *tractable beasts of burden.*

Blackguardism was fashionable, and even the
youngest were led into scenes of low debauchery and
drunkenness, by men advanced in years. Many of
the officers, who, at least, *ought* to have been men of
superior talents and education, seemed to be little
better, if we were allowed to judge from the abominable oaths and scurrility which they used to those
under their command, and the vexatious and overbearing tyranny of their conduct, which was too often
imitated by those beneath them.

It redounds much to the honour of those who

superintend the discipline of the army at present, that the situation of the soldier has been much ameliorated since that period.

Let it not be thought, however, that there were not many exceptions to this general character which I have drawn, (some of whom I will have occasion to mention in this narrative,) who have shed a lustre around the military character that has often served to conceal its defects.

CHAPTER VI.

About the beginning of May, we got the route for Aberdeen. On the march I have nothing interesting to take notice of, unless the kindness which we experienced from the people where we were billeted on the road, particularly after we crossed the Frith of Forth.

We arrived in Aberdeen, after a march of ten days, where we had better barracks, and cheaper provisions than in Dunbar ; but the barracks being too small, a number of our men were billeted in the town, and not being in the mess when pay-day came, it was a common thing for many of them to spend what they had to support them in drink ; and some of them were so infatuated as to sell even their allowance of bread for the same purpose. They were then obliged (to use their own phraseology) to " Box Harry," until the next pay-day ; and some of them carried this system to such a length, that it was found necessary to bring them into barracks, to prevent them from starving themselves.

If I may be allowed to draw a conclusion from what I have seen, the men's morals are no way improved by being lodged out of barracks; for, while here, the principal employment of many of them when off duty was drinking, and associating with common women ; and I think, if any thing tends to depreciate the character of the soldier in the eyes of his countrymen, in civil life, more than another, it is this habit of associating publicly with such characters. This total disregard of even the appearance of decency, conveys an idea to the mind that he must be the *lowest of the low.* But many of them seem to be proud of such company ; and it is quite a common thing to meet them on the streets arm in arm.

This debasement of feeling and character, I imagine, arises from the system of discipline pursued by many commanding officers, which teaches the soldier to believe that he is a mere piece of machinery in the hands of his superiors, to be moved only as they please, without any accordance of his own reason or judgment, and that he has no merit in his own actions, independent of this moving power. Such a belief has naturally the effect of making a man so little in his own eyes that he feels he cannot sink lower, let him keep what company he may.

But let soldiers be taught that they have a character to uphold ; give them to understand that they are made of the same materials as those who command them, capable of feeling sentiments of generosity and honour ; let officers evince by their conduct that they believe that the men they command have feelings as well as themselves, (although it would be a hard task to make some of them think so ;) let them be encouraged to improve their minds, and there will soon be a change for the better in the army — one honourable to all concerned.

The doctrine which teaches that men are most easily governed when ignorant, is, I believe, now nearly exploded ; and I can say from my own experience, and also safely appeal to all unprejudiced individuals of the army, whether they have not found men having some intellectual cultivation the best soldiers.

We had been about three months in Aberdeen, when we received orders to hold ourselves in readiness to sail for Jersey ; and four transports having arrived for us, we prepared to embark.

This was a busy scene. We had been on good terms with the townspeople, and many of them attended us to the pier. As we marched down, the old women stood in rows, exclaiming,—" Peer things ! they are gaun awa to the slauchter." While the boys were ranked up, marching before our band, with as much importance as if they considered themselves heroes ; and no doubt, the fine music, and the sight of the soldiers marching to it, gave them high ideas of a military life ; and perhaps, was the incipient cause of their enlisting at a future period. Indeed, I must confess that when I heard the crowd cheering, and our music playing before us, I felt at least a foot higher, and strutted with as much dignity as if I had been a general. I almost felt proud at that moment that I was a soldier.

Once embarked, however, and fairly out to sea, my enthusiasm soon evaporated. Stowed like any other part of a cargo, with only eighteen inches allowed for each man to lie on, we had scarcely room to move. The most of the men became sea-sick, and it was almost impossible to be below without becoming so. The women particularly suffered much ; being crammed in indiscriminately amongst the men, and no arrangement made for their comfort.

No incident of any consequence took place on this voyage, with the exception of a severe gale of wind, which forced us to run into Dungeness ; but it soon abated, and proceeding on our voyage, we made the island of Jersey, and disembarked at St Oban's harbour ; from whence we marched through St Helier's, to the Russian barracks near Groville.

All kinds of liquor, tea, sugar, and fruit, were here uncommonly cheap ; but bread was dear, and what we had served out as rations was quite black and soft, something in consistence like clay. Brandy was only a shilling a bottle ; wine two shillings ; cyder three-halfpence a quart ; and tobacco fifteen pence a pound.

The jovial drinking fellows amongst us thought this another paradise—a heaven on earth ; and many of them laid the foundation of complaints here which they never got rid of.

It was during the time we were here that the jubilee (on his late Majesty's entering the fiftieth year of his reign) was celebrated. We were marched to the sands between St Helier's and St Oban's, where the whole of the military on the island were assembled. We were served out with eighteen rounds of blank cartridge per man, and the *feu-de-joie* was fired from right to left, and again taken up by the right, thus keeping up a constant fire until it was all expended, The artillery, with the various batteries, and shipping in the harbour, joined in the firing ; and altogether formed an imposing scene.

When we arrived at our barracks, we got a day's pay in advance, and, with great injunctions not to get drunk and riotous, we were allowed to go and make ourselves merry until tattoo-beating. Dennis and I resolved to hold the occasion like the others, although he said he did not admire this way of " treating us to our own."

We went to one of the usual drinking-houses ; but it was full, up to the door ; volumes of tobacco smoke issued from every opening ; and the noise of swearing and singing was completely deafening.

We were obliged to go farther off to get a house to sit down in. At last we found a place of that description, and went in. After a glass or two, we became quite jovial ; and Dennis insisted that our

host and his wife should sit down along with us. He
was a Frenchman and spoke little English ; but
Dennis did not mind that, and there soon commenced
a most barbarous jargon—Dennis laying off a long
story, of which, I am sure, the poor man did not
understand a syllable. Yet he went on, still saying
at the end of every sentence, " You take me now ?"
—" You persave me now, don't you ?" While our
host, whose patience seemed pretty well taxed, would
shrug up his shoulders with a smile, and looking at
his wife, who seemed to understand what was said
nearly as well as himself, he would give a nod and
say,

" Oui, monsieur—yees, sare."

Dennis having got tired of talking, asked the landlord if he could sing. This completely puzzled the
Frenchman. At last, after every method had been
tried in vain to make him comprehend, Dennis said,
" You do this," and opening his mouth, he howled
out a line of an Irish song. The Frenchman, seemingly frightened with the noise that Dennis had
made, started to his feet and exclaimed,

" Me no chanter."

" Och! the devil's in ye, for a liar, Parly-vu. But
no matter, I'll give you a song—a true Irish song,
my jewel," and he commenced with the " Sprig of
shillelah and shamrock so green." .He had got as far
as " An Irishman all in his glory was there," quivering and spinning out the last line of the verse to a
prodigious length, when a rap came to the door, and
the voice of the sergeant of the picquet, asking if
there were any soldiers in the house, put an unpleasant end to his melody. Previous to this, however,
Dennis had taken up a spade handle, to represent the
shillelah, and it was with difficulty that I prevented
him from bringing it down on the sergeant's head.

We were then escorted to the guard-house, for
being out after tattoo, which we found so full that

we could scarcely get admittance. Dennis cried and
sung by turns, until he fell fast asleep. I was so
stupified with the drink I had taken, that I scarcely
knew how I felt. Next morning, however, we were
released along with all the others who had been confined the preceding evening,

We had been about three months in Jersey when
the order came for our embarkation for Portugal ; but
only six women to every hundred men were allowed
to accompany us. As there were, however, a great
many more than that number, it was ordered that they
should draw lots, to see who should remain. The
women of the company to which I belonged were
assembled in the pay-sergeant's room for that purpose. The men of the company had gathered round
them, to see the result, with various degrees of interest depicted in their countenances. The proportionate number of tickets were made with " to go" or
" not to go" written on them. They were then placed
in a hat, and the women were called by their seniority
to draw their tickets. I looked round me before they
began. It was an interesting scene. The sergeant
stood in the middle with a hat in his hand, the women
around him, with their hearts palpitating, and anxiety
and suspense in every countenance. Here and there
you would see the head of a married man pushed
forward, from amongst the crowd, in the attitude of
intense anxiety and attention.

The first woman called, was the sergeant's wife—
she drew " not to go." It seemed to give little concern to any one, but herself and her husband. She
was not very well liked in the company. The next
was a corporal's wife—she drew " to go." This was
received by all with nearly as much apathy as the
first. She was little beloved either.

The next was an old hand, a most outrageous
virago, who thought nothing of giving her husband a
knock down when he offended her, and who used to

make great disturbance about the fire in the cooking
way.   Every one uttered their wishes audibly that
she would lose : and her husband, if we could judge
from his countenance, seemed to wish so too. • She
boldly plunged her hand into the hat, and drew out
a ticket ; and opening it, she held it up triumphantly,
and displayed " to go."   " Hurra " said she, " old
Meg will go yet, and live to scald more of you about
the fireside."   A general murmur of disappointment
ran through the whole.

" Hang the old wretch !" said some of them, " she
has the devil's luck and her own."

The next in turn was the wife of a young man,
who was much respected in the company for his
steadiness and good behaviour.   She was remarkable
for her affection for her husband, and beloved by the
whole company for her modest and obliging disposition.   She advanced with a palpitating heart and
trembling hand, to decide on (what was to her, I
believe) her future happiness or misery.   Every one
prayed for her success.   Trembling between fear
and hope she drew out one of the tickets, and
attempted to open it : but her hand shook so that she
could not do it.   She handed it to one of the men to
open.—When he opened it, his countenance fell, and
he hesitated to say what it was.   She cried out to
him, in a tone of agony, " Tell me, for God's sake,
what it is."

" Not to go," said he, in a compassionate tone of
voice.

" Oh, God, help me ! O Sandy !" she exclaimed,
and sunk lifeless in the ,arms of her husband, who had
sprung forward to her assistance, and in whose face
was now depicted every variety of wretchedness.
The drawing was interrupted, and she was carried by
her husband to his birth, where he hung over her in
frantic agony.   By the assistance of those around her,
she was soon recovered from her swoon ; but she

awoke only to a sense of her misery. The first thing
she did was to look round for her husband, when she
perceived him she seized his hand, and held it, as if
she was afraid that he was going to leave her. " O,
Sandy, you'll no leave me and your poor babie, will
you?" The poor fellow looked in her face with a
look of agony and despair.

The scene drew tears from every eye in the room,
with the exception of the termagant whom I have
already mentioned, who said, " What are ye a' makin'
sic a wark about? let the babie get her greet out. I
suppose she thinks there's naebody ever parted with
their men but her, wi' her faintin', and her airs, and
her wark."

" Oh, you're an oul hard-hearted devil," said Dennis,
" an unfeeling oul hag, and the devil 'ill never get
his due till he gets you;"—and he took her by the
shoulders and pushed her out of the room. She would
have turned on Dennis; but she had got a squeeze
from him on a former occasion, and I daresay she did
not like to run the risk of another.

The drawing was again commenced, and various
were the expressions of feeling evinced by those concerned. The Irish women, in particular, were loud
in their grief. It always appeared to me that the
Irish either feel more acutely than the Scotch or
English, or that they have less restraint on themselves
in expressing it. The barrack, through the rest of
that day, was one continued scene of lamentation.

I was particularly interested in the fate of Sandy
and his wife. I wished to administer consolation;
but what could I say? There was no comfort that I
could give, unless leading her to hope that we would
soon return. " Oh, no," said she, " when we part
here, I am sure that we'll never meet again in this
world!"

We were to march the next morning early. The
most of the single men were away drinking. I slept

in the birth above Sandy and his wife. They never
went to bed, but sat the whole night in their birth,
with their only child between them, alternately em-
bracing it and each other, and lamenting their cruel
fortune. I never witnessed in my life such a heart-
rending scene. The poor fellow tried to assume some
firmness ; but in vain : some feeling expression from
her would throw him off his guard, and at last his
grief became quite uncontrollable.

When the first bugle sounded, he got up and prepared his things. Here a new source of grief sprung
up. In laying aside the articles which he intended
to leave, and which they had used together, the idea
seemed fixed in her mind, that they would never use
them in that way again ; and as she put them aside,
she watered them with her tears. Her tea-pot, her
cups, and every thing that they had used in common
—all had their apostrophe of sorrow. He tried to
persuade her to remain in the barrack, as we had six
miles to travel to the place of embarkation ; but she
said she would take the last minute in his company
that she could.

.The regiment fell in, and marched off, amid the
wailing of those who, having two or three children,
could not accompany us to the place of embarkation.
Many of the men had got so much intoxicated that
they were scarcely able to walk, and the commanding
officer was so displeased with their conduct, that in
coming through St Helier's, he would not allow the
band to play.

When we arrived at the place where we were to
embark, a most distressing scene took place, in the
men parting with their wives. Some of them, indeed,
it did not appear to affect much ; others had got
themselves nearly tipsy ; but the most of them seemed
to feel acutely. When Sandy's wife came to take her
last farewell, she lost all government of her grief.
She clung to him with a despairing hold. " Oh,

dinna, dinna leave me!" she cried. The vessel was hauling out. One of the sergeants came to tell her that she would have to go ashore. " Oh, they 'll never be so hard-hearted as to part us !" said she ; and running aft to the quarter-deck, where the commanding officer was standing, she sunk down on her knees, with her child in her arms. " Oh ! will you no let me gang wi' my husband ? Will you tear him frae his wife and his wean ? He has nae frien's but us — nor we ony but him — and oh ! will ye mak' us a' frien'-less ? See my wee babie pleadin' for us."

The officer felt a painful struggle between his duty and his feelings : the tears came into his eyes. She eagerly caught at this as favourable to her cause, " Oh ay, I see you have a feeling heart — you 'll let me gang wi' him. You have nae wife : but if you had, I am sure you wad think it unco hard to be torn frae her this way — and this wee darlin'."

" My good woman," said the officer, " I feel for you much ; but my orders are peremptory, that no more than six women to each hundred men go with their husbands. You have had your chance as well as the other women ; and although it is hard enough on you to be separated from your husband, yet there are many more in the same predicament ; and it is totally out of my power to help it."

" Well, well," said she, rising from her knees, and straining her infant to her breast : " it 's a' owre wi' us, my puir babie ; this day leaves us friendless on the wide world."

" God will be your friend," said I, as I took the child from her until she would get into the boat. Sandy had stood like a person bewildered all this time, without saying a word.

" Farewell then, a last farewell then," said she to him, " Where 's my babie ?" I handed him to her — " Give him a last kiss, Sandy." He pressed the infant to his bosom in silent agony, " Now, a 's owre ;

farewell Sandy! we'll maybe meet in heaven:" and
she stepped into the boat with a wild despairing look.
The vessel was now turning the pier, and she was
almost out of our sight in an instant; but as we got
the last glimpse of her, she uttered a shriek, the knell
of a broken heart, which rings in my ears at this
moment. Sandy rushed down below, and threw
himself into one of the births, in a state of feeling
which defies description. Poor fellow, his wife's
forebodings were too true! What became of her
I have never been able to learn.

Nothing occurred worthy of remark on our voyage
from Jersey to Lisbon. When we made the mouth
of the Tagus, we got a Portuguese pilot on board.
He had scarcely reached the gang-way when he was
surrounded by all the men on deck; for his appearance was grotesque in the extreme. He was about
four feet and a half high, and had on a jacket and
breeches of what would have puzzled a philosopher to
tell the original; for patches of red, yellow, blue, &c.
were mingled through the whole dress, without any
regularity. A pair of red stockings, and an enormous
cocked hat, completed his costume. His complexion
was of the same hue as a well-smoked bacon ham;
and the whole contour of his face bore a striking resemblance to the ape tribe. "Blessings on your
purty face, my honey," said Dennis, as he eyed him
narrowly, "you have made your escape from some
showman. May I never sin, if I don't think I have
seen you tumbling on a rope at Donnybrook fair."
Our hero passed on, taking no notice of the compliment Dennis had paid him, to take the helm from the
seaman on duty; but the tar, giving him a contemp-
tuous look, called out to the captain, " Will I give the
helm to this here *thing?*"

" Certainly," said the captain, laughing. The
sailor, however, did not seem sure about him; and,
as he passed on to the forecastle could not help

throwing a doubtful look behind at his *substitute*. He proved to be a good pilot, however, and managed the vessel well.

We passed Fort St Julian, and sailed up the Tagus as far as Belem, where our pilot gave the order to "let go de ank." The attention of those on deck was soon drawn towards a number of people who were sitting in a row, beneath the walls of a large building, seemingly very busy at something. After watching their motions for some time, we discovered that they were picking the vermin off themselves! There was none of that *modest pressing* between the finger and thumb, for fear of being seen, which we may observe in our dirty and indigent neighbours at home. It was absolute open murder! in all its varieties ; and truly they had their hands full of work ; for although we looked at them for a length of time, the carnage still continued as fierce as ever. It appeared to me that a new breed sprung Phœnix-like, from the remains of their predecessors. This is a *biting* sample of Portugal, thought I, turning away in disgust from the scene ; but I soon got accustomed to it ; for in Spain and Portugal, the latter particularly, the *peocha* seems quite at home, not confined to the poor alone ; for I have seen the family of a rich fidalgo, male and female, assembled on the sunny side of the house, "*sharp shooting*" publicly, without seeming to feel any shame.

So far from that, it appeared to be the most interesting of their forenoon amusements.

Next morning we disembarked and marched up to St Domingo convent, part of which had been converted into barracks. In the course of the day Dennis and I got into the town. We promised ourselves much from the view we had had from the river the preceding evening ; but were miserably disappointed when we got into the streets ; for mountains of filth were collected in them, so that we could scarcely pass ; and the smell of oil and garlic issuing from the shops was quite sickening.   The most of the streets were very narrow.

The population seemed composed of monks and friars, for we met them at every step either begging, or walking in procession with the sacrament (or host) to some sick person.   On these occasions they were preceded by a bell, which warned the passengers of their approach ; whenever it was heard, they were down on their knees in a moment, in the very middle of the mud, and continued praying and beating their breasts until it passed.   Poor Dennis was sadly puzzled the first time he met one of these parties : he was a Catholic, and of course could not avoid follow- ing the example of the *Christianos* around him ; but he had a great aversion to kneeling in the dirty streets.   The procession was fast advancing, and he had been two or three times half down on his knees and up again ; at last, a lucky thought struck him —he snatched the hat out of the hand of a Por- tuguese who was kneeling before him, and deliberately placing it on the ground, kneeled down on it, and went through the ceremony with great gravity — thus saving both his conscience and his breeches.   The fellow who owned the hat durst not move until the procession had passed ; and then, without giving him time to speak, Dennis clapped the hat, dirty as it was, on the owner's head, and walked off.

The fruit market was opposite to the convent gate ; and it certainly was to us a novel and a pleasing sight.   The finest fruits, which at home were rare and high in price, we found here as plenty and as cheap as gooseberries.   Pine apples, peaches, and grapes, of the largest size and most exquisite flavour, with oranges, lemons, and pomegranates, were arranged on the standings, in the most tempting and tasteful manner.   Dennis and I walked through amongst them with a strong desire of tasting them, yet fearful that our finances would not enable us to buy any.   I ventured, however, to ask for the worth of a vintin (about three halfpence English) of oranges ; after giving the woman the money, and pointing to the fruit, I held out my hand to receive them, but she beckoned me to give her my hat, and to our surprise, she nearly filled it.

The fragrant and delicious odour which perfumed the market place, and the sight of the beautiful fruit and flowers, made it a much more attractive place of resort, than the dirty streets filled with the abominable stench which issued from their cook shops. My opinion of the interior of Lisbon was certainly very low ; and I think, if a stranger wishes to see Lisbon, and leave it with any idea of its grandeur, he ought to contemplate it from the river, but never set his foot on shore, for he will then feel nothing but disgust.

CHAPTER VII.

WE remained only seven days in Lisbon : on the evening of the seventh we were turned out, marched down to Belem, and embarked by torch light for Cadiz. I do not remember any thing worthy of notice which took place on this voyage, only that it was tedious.

When we made the bay of Cadiz, we found a large fleet of British vessels there before us. The French had possession of all the surrounding country, with the exception of the Isle of Leon and Cadiz ; and these were closely besieged. When we first arrived, we were not sure on which side of the bay we might be required to land ; but we were served out with flints and ammunition, and our commanding officer issued a circular to the men on board the different transports, ordering us to hold ourselves in readiness

for immediate action, and exhorting us to remember
the honour of our country and regiment.

That evening, our light company, with those of the
other regiments, forming a light brigade, under the
command of Major-General the Hon. Sir William
Stewart, landed and marched to the out-post at the
town of Isla. Next day, the remainder of the troops
disembarked; and entering Cadiz, we occupied part
of the bomb-proof barracks under the ramparts, where
we remained with Lieutenant-General Graham, who
was chief in command.

I could not say that our reception by the inhabitants, on landing, was very flattering. Here and
there, amongst the crowd, you could hear a " Viva
Englese ;" but the greater number received us with a
gloomy suspicious silence. Setting aside other causes,
it was really not to be wondered at, that the inhabitants should feel little attachment to the English, when
we consider that they had suffered so severely by
Nelson and the British fleet, about four years before,
and that the shattered remains of some of their vessels
were still lying in the bay.

Cadiz was, in my opinion, a much cleaner town
than Lisbon, and in point of situation, more picturesque. From the ramparts on the Atlantic side
of the town, the view was very fine : to the left, we
could see the African shore, with its mountains stretching out until their outline was lost in the distance.
Before you the prospect was unconfined, and the eye
was lost in the wide world of waters, unless when it
was arrested by a passing sail, or brought nearer the
town by the noise of the breakers lashing the dark
sides of the rocks, which ran out into the sea, and
here and there shewed their heads above water. On
the side of the town next the bay, the Rota, Bay of
Bulls, with the town of Port St Mary's, Porto Real,
Isla, Checuelina, and Cape Trafalgar, brought the eye
round to where it set out.

When we had any thing to wash, we were obliged to go outside the walls to some of the cisterns, a short distance from the town. It was here I first learned to wash my own clothes. I was awkward enough when I began, but practice soon made me expert at it.

In one of these washing excursions, I happened to pass a chapel ; and seeing people engaged at some ceremony in it, my curiosity prompted me to enter. A corpse lay on a bier, with the face uncovered, and a bunch of flowers were placed in its hands, which were joined together in a praying attitude. The priest was performing the service of the dead over it ; near him stood two little boys, with silver censers waving in their hands, filled with burning incense. The whole service seemed to me impressive enough. After it was finished, the corpse was removed to the outside of the chapel, and deposited in a hole in the wall resembling an oven ; it was then covered with quick lime ; the mouth of the hole shut up with a stone, which fitted it ; and the people retired.

As yet, none of the troops had been brought into action, with the exception of the light companies, who had some slight skirmishing at the outposts. The French had attempted nothing of any consequence. They were very busy, however, prosecuting the siege —building batteries in every direction. There was one battery, called Fort M——. It lay on the French side, at the extremity of a point of land, stretching down from Porto Real into the bay, opposite to Pun-tallis. From this, had they manned it, they might have annoyed our shipping very much ; and it was resolved that we should take possession of it.

Accordingly, one evening the three first men from each company of the regiment to which I belonged were turned out, in marching order, for that purpose. At the quay, we were joined by a detachment of artil-lery, and were conveyed across the bay in man-of-war

ooats. On our passage we were joined by a party of
seamen and marines ; who, with a captain-command-
ant, surgeon, two subalterns, one of whom acted as
adjutant, a lieutenant of artillery, and a midshipman,
made in all about one hundred and fifty men.

When we reached the fort, we used every precaution to avoid alarming the French if there had been
any there ; but it was quite unnecessary, for their
picquet had retired, without firing a shot. After
placing a picquet in front, we set to work, and got
up three guns, which we had brought with us. This
kept us busy enough until morning ; when we got a
better view of the isolated place we had taken possession of. The fort itself was about a hundred yards
square ; but it had been completely demolished on its
sea face, by the seamen of our fleet when the French
advanced to the siege, and the others were all more
or less in ruins. The bomb proofs were nearly all
destroyed. In what remained there was not shelter
for the half of our men ; and by a rule of division,
often practised in the army, that little was made less
by the officers appropriating the half of it to themselves.

Day had not long dawned when the French gave
us a salute from a small battery, in the village at
Fort Lewis ; but when we got our guns mounted, it
was soon silenced. From that time we commenced
with redoubled exertion to work at the battery
— building up the parapets, and laying platforms for
more guns. We were supplied with materials, viz.
fascions, gabions, and sand-bags, from Cadiz.

Here we were wrought like slaves, I may say,
without intermission ; for our worthy adjutant, who
aimed at being a rigid disciplinarian, and was a great
amateur in drill, was determined that no hard labour,
or want of convenience for cleaning our things, should
tempt him to deviate from a clean parade and formal
guard-mounting every morning, even although we

had been out all night under the rain on picquet, or
carrying sand-bags and digging trenches up to the
knees in mud. All the varied forms of duty known
in a militia regiment, with which he was best acquainted, were by him deemed indispensable ; and
in a place where we had no convenience for keeping
our things in order, not even shelter for them, this exactness was certainly, to say the least of it, unneces-
sarily teasing. We were also obliged to stand sentry
on different parts of the battery, full dressed, where
there was no earthly use for us, unless for show ; and
I could perceive no reason the commandant and he
had for their conduct, unless that, feeling the novelty
of their situation — in command of a fort — they
wished to ape, with their handful of men, all the importance of leaders of an army.

We were driven from guard to working — working
to picquet — picquet to working again, in a gin-horse
round of the most intolerable fatigue ; which we never
could have borne for any length of time, exposed as
we often were to sun and rain, in a climate like that
of Cadiz. But, even with all this we had the mortification to find our best endeavours repaid with the
most supercilious haughtiness, and the worst of usage.
We were allowed little time to sleep ; and that little
often interrupted.

But let it not be imagined that our officers participated in all this fatigue : they knew how to take care
of themselves ; and they could sit and drink wine in
their bomb-proof at night, as comfortably as in a mess-
room at home. And it was a common amusement of
the commandant, when he got warmed with it, to
order the drum to beat to arms in the middle of the
night — when the poor wretches who had perhaps just
lost sense of their fatigue in sweet oblivion, would be
roused up, and obliged to go to their several posts
on the ramparts ; and when permitted to go below to
our births, we would scarcely be lain down, when we

were again roused to commence working. This was the usual routine the most of the time we were here.

It may be well to remark, however, (for the benefit of those officers who may wish to follow the example,) that the commandant had a most *ingenious* method of assembling his men quickly: he used to stand, with his fist clenched, at the top of the ladder leading from the bomb-proof, ready to knock down the last man that came up; and as some one must necesarily be last, he of course was sure of the blow; and as he was a strong muscular man, it used to *tell* (as we military men term it) on the poor fellow's head.

One man, I remember, who had suffered in this way, remonstrated, and threatened to complain to his colonel; but the answer was a second " knock-down," and an order to confine him between two guns in an angle of the battery, where he was exposed to the inclemency of the weather for many days and nights without covering; and when his health was impaired by this usage, he was still kept in the fort, although it was the usual practice to send the sick to the general hospital in Cadiz. He was not allowed to leave the place until we all left it; and then it is probable, if he had ventured to complain, he might have been flogged in addition to all he had suffered, for presuming to say any thing against the Hero of M——.

We had now got up six guns and two mortars on the fort, which was all we could mount to have any effect. We were supported by a Spanish man-of-war and six or eight gun-boats; and with them, we used to bombard the small village at Fort Lewis, and annoy the working parties coming down from Porto Real to build batteries. We often made great havock amongst them, with spherical case-shot. One day in particular, I remember, we brought down an officer who was riding on a white horse at the head of his

party, and we saw them carry him off in a litter from
the place where he fell.

About this time a severe gale came on, by which
a great number of vessels were stranded on the French
side of the bay; most of them were abandoned by
their crews, who got safe over to Cadiz; but one
transport, containing the flank companies and staff of
a battalion of the fourth regiment, ran ashore near
Port St Mary's, and they were all taken prisoners.
They had their colours with them, and I heard afterwards that they had put them under the coppers and
burned them, rather than let them fall into the hands
of the enemy. Many of these vessels were richly
laden; and as they were sure ultimately to fall into
the hands of the enemy, being also considered fair
prizes when they ran ashore on an enemy's coast, we
procured a couple of boats, and succeeded in securing
part of the cargo of those nearest us, which was
principally silk, with some pipes of wine and salt
provision.

The stranded vessels, that lay along the shore, were
often visited by straggling parties of the French, who
used to carry off heavy burdens of the cargo. This
stimulated some of our men to follow their example;
but there was great risk in the adventure. They
could only go at night, and run all hazard of their
absence being discovered: that, however, might be
averted by the sergeants, who of course shared in the
booty; but the marsh which they had to cross was
very dangerous, the road uncertain, and they might
have been taken by the enemy's picquets; but notwithstanding these obstacles, there were many who,
either out of a spirit of adventure, or a love of gain,
despised them all, and were well repaid for their
trouble by the valuable articles which they found.

Our party often fell in with the French stragglers,
who were there on the same errand; but they were
quite friendly, and when any wine or spirits were got

in the vessels, they used to sit down and drink
together, as sociably as if they had been comrades
for years. What every man got was his own, and
there was seldom any dissention.

One night I happened to be of the party. We
had made our burdens, parted with our French
friends, and left the vessel on our way to the fort.
The party of the French had left it also. We had
not proceeded far, when we missed one of our comrades ; and fearing that some accident had befallen
him, we returned, and near the vessel saw him struggling with some one. We hastened up to him ; but
before we reached the spot, the person with whom
he was engaged fell to the ground with a groan. At
that moment, we saw our comrade stoop, and tear
something from him. " What is the matter ?" said
one of our party. " Come away," said he, " and I'll
tell you as we go along ;" and he passed us on his
way to the fort.

We were anxious to see who his antagonist was ;
and on raising him up, we found that he was one of
the French party, who had been with us in the vessel.
He had been stabbed in the left side with a Spanish
knife, which still remained in the wound. One of
the party withdrew it. The blood flowed out of the
wound with great force. The poor Frenchman gave
a deep groan—a convulsive quiver—and expired.

" This is a horrid cold-blooded murder," said I.
" Where is S—— ?" At this moment we heard the
noise of footsteps approaching, and thinking it might
be the comrades of the Frenchman who had been bar-
barously assassinated, we left the place precipitately,
our minds filled with horror at the savage deed.

On our way to the fort we overtook S—— ; but
none of us spoke to him. He, however, strove to
extenuate his conduct, by saying that he observed
the Frenchman find a purse in a chest that he had
broken open, and seeing him linger behind his party,

for the purpose of secreting it about his person, he
went up to him, and asked a share of it. The man
refusing this, a scuffle ensued, and he stabbed him in
his own defence, the Frenchman having attempted to
stab him. We knew this to be false ; for the Frenchman had no weapon in his hand, or near him ; and
we had no doubt, from what we knew of S——'s
character, that he had perpetrated the murder for the
sake of the money, which was gold doubloons. He
offered to share it with us ; but not one of us would
touch it ; and from that time forward, he was shunned
and detested by all who knew of the murder. He
never prospered after. I even thought that his countenance acquired a demon-like expression, that rendered it repulsive ; and we had not been long in
Portugal, when he went to the rear and died in great
misery. After that we never returned to the vessels.

The Spaniards had a number of hulks moored in
the bay which Lord Nelson made for them, on board of
which they kept their French prisoners, who, we understood, were very ill used, nearly starved, and huddled
together in such a way that disease was the consequence. Many of them died daily. They were
kept until sun-set, and then thrown over board, and
allowed to float about in the bay. Every tide threw
some of them ashore, and the beach was continually
studded here and there with them. When our men
discovered any of them, they scraped a hole in the
sand, and buried them ; but they were totally unheeded by the Spaniards, unless when they practised
some barbarity on them—such as dashing large
stones on their heads, or cutting and mutilating them
in such a way that the very soul would sicken at the
idea.

I was one night on picquet, and along with the
sergeant reconnoitering the ground in front of the fort,
as the French picquets were in the habit of coming
close down on us when it was dark. We saw some-

thing white moving amongst the weeds near the shore, to the left of the battery; and we went down in that direction to see what it was; but in an instant we lost sight of it. When we came to the place where we first saw it, we found the body of a man extended on the ground. This was not an uncommon appearance; but as we had seen something moving when we were first attracted to the spot, I was induced to feel the body, to ascertain whether it was dead, and to my surprise, I found him warm, and assisted by the sergeant raised him up. It struck us that he had only fainted, and we rubbed him for some time with our hands. He at last began to recover, and his first action, when he came to himself, was to fall down on his knees at our feet, and cry "Misericordia." * We did not understand what he said; but we asked him, in English, how he had come there. Whenever he heard us speak, he sprung to his feet, and seizing our hands, he cried "Vous etes Anglois —Grâce à bon Dieu!" †

We threw a great-coat over him, and took him into the fort, where, placing him before a fire, and giving him some bread and wine, the poor fellow soon recovered. When it was discovered that he had no clothes on, one man took off his shirt and put it on him, another gave him a pair of trousers, and he was soon comfortably clothed. He poured out his thanks in French, but he saw we did not understand the language. He tried the Spanish with like success. He attempted a mixture of both with as little effect; but when he pressed his hand on his heart, and the big drop gathered in his eye, he found by the sympathizing tear which it excited, that no words were necessary to express the universal language of gratitude.

When he was perfectly recovered, we reported the affair to the commandant, and the artillery officer

* Mercy.   † Thank God you are English.

speaking the French language, he was questioned by him. In reply, he said he was a surgeon in the French service ; that he had been taken prisoner and confined on board one of the prison ships ; that that night he determined to make his escape, or perish in the attempt ; and having lowered himself down from one of the gun ports, quite naked, he had swam a distance of two miles ; but was so exhausted wher he reached the shore, that he sank down insensible at the time we had first seen him ; when he recovered, his first idea was that he had fallen into the hands of the Spaniards, who, he well knew, would have butchered him without mercy ; but when he found by our language that we were English, he was over-joyed. He had saved nothing but a miniature of a female, which hung round his neck, and which he seemed to prize very much, for when he recovered, the first thing he did was to feel if it were still there, and raise it to his lips and kiss it.

He was kept until next day in the fort, when he was sent over to Cadiz. He seemed distracted at the idea of going there, lest he snould be delivered over to the Spaniards ; and although he was assured to the contrary, still he seemed to feel uneasy.

It was not many days, however, after that, when he was sent back, with orders that he should be escorted to our outposts at night, and left to join his countrymen. When night came, he took leave of the men in the fort with a kind of regret. I again happened to be of the party who escorted him. After leaving our picquet, the sergeant and I conducted him up the path-way leading direct from the fort, until we suspected that we were near the French picquet, and there we told him that we would be obliged to leave him. He pressed our hands in silence : his heart was too full to speak ; but we could easily guess what were his emotions. Joy at the idea of again rejoining his countrymen, with a feeling of regret at parting with those to whom he considered he owed his life, were contending in his mind.

The night was dark, and we soon lost sight of him ; but we lay down on the ground, and listened with anxious suspense, afraid that the French outpost sentry might fire upon him before he had time to explain, and he might thus lose his life on the very threshold of freedom ; but we did not hear the sentinel challenge him, nor did we hear any shot fired. We had therefore every reason to believe he reached his countrymen in safety.

During the time we were here, an attack was meditated on the French positions, and a number of troops were landed on the fort for that purpose. A strong party of seamen was also landed at fort Catalina, who succeeded in storming it, and spiking the guns ; but in consequence of some signals being thrown up by adherents of the French in Cadiz, they were alarmed, and the troops were obliged to return without effecting what had been originally intended.

CHAPTER VIII.

WE had now been in the fort about two months ; and from the time that we had silenced the small battery that had opened on us, when we first gained possession of the place, the French had not molested us, although they occasionally fired shots at the boats passing up and down the bay. We were well aware, however, that this was only a deceitful calm before a storm ; for they had been busy all this time building batteries both in front and to our right in the village I have already mentioned, although they were hidden from our view by the houses.

At last, when every thing was prepared, they commenced their operations one night by blowing up the nouses which had hitherto masked the batteries. I was out on picquet at the time ; and we perceived them moving round a large fire which they had kindled. We suspected that they designed to attack us, and our suspicions were soon verified ; for in a snort time after, they gave a salute of grape shot, which ploughed the earth on every side of us ; but this was only a prelude. A volley of red-hot shot, at the Spanish man-of-war, succeeded, which set her on fire, and obliged her to slip her cable, and drop down the bay. A volley or two more of the same kind scattered our gun-boats ; and we were then left to bear the brunt of the battle alone. Now it began in earnest. Five or six batteries, mounting in all about twenty guns, and eight or ten mortars, opened their tremendous mouths, vomiting forth death and destruction. The picquet was called in.

There was a number of spare fascions piled up on the sea face of the battery, amongst which, for want of room in the bomb-proof, we formed huts. In one of these I lodged. They had been set on fire by a shell that fell amongst them ; and when I entered the fort, the Spanish labourers were busy throwing them into the sea. I ran to try to save my knapsack, with the little treasure which I had gained ; but it was too late—hut and all had been tossed over. There was no help for it : I did not know how soon I might be thrown over also. I was called to my gun, and had no more time to think on the subject. They were now plying us so fast with shell, that I saw six or eight in the air over us at once.

Death now began to stalk about in the most dreadful form. The large shot were certain messengers where they struck. The first man killed was a sailor who belonged to the Temeraire seventy-four. The whole of his face was carried away. It was a horrid-

looking wound. He was at the same gun with me.
" Ah! what will we do with him?" said I to a seaman
next me.

"Let him lie there," was the reply. "We have no
time to look after dead men now."

At that time I thought it a hardened expression;
but this was my first engagement. Not so with the
tar. He had been well used to them.

The French soon acquired a fatal precision with
their shot, sending them in through our embrasures,
killing and wounding men every volley. I was on
the left of the gun, at the front wheel. We were
running her up after loading. I had stooped to take
a fresh purchase, a cannon ball whistled in through
the embrasure, carried the forage cap off my head, and
struck the man behind me on the breast, and he fell
to rise no more.

The commandant was now moving from place to
place, giving orders and exposing himself to every
danger. No one could doubt that he was brave:
had it been bravery, softened and blended with the
finer feelings of humanity, he would have been a true
hero; but ——. Our artillery officer behaved like
a gentleman, as he had always done; and our subaltern in a tolerable medium: the midshipman in the
style of a brave, rough and ready seaman. But, alas,
how had the mighty fallen!—our brave adjutant,
whose blustering voice, and bullying important manner, had been always so remarkable, was now as quiet
as a lamb. Seated in an angle of the battery, shel-
tered from the shot, no penitent on the *cutty stool* ever
exhibited so rueful a countenance.

The carnage now became dreadful; the ramparts
were strewed with the dead and wounded; and blood,
brains, and mangled limbs, lay scattered in every direction: but our men's spirits and enthusiasm seemed
to rise with the danger. The artillery officer stood
on the platform, and when he reported any of our shot

taking effect, a cheer followed, and " At it again, my heroes!" was the exclamation from every mouth. When any of our comrades fell, it excited no visible feeling but revenge. " Now for a retaliating shot!" was the word ; every nerve was strained to lay the gun with precision ; and if it took effect, it was considered that full justice was done to their memory.

We had a traversing gun in the angle of the battery which had done great execution. The artillery sergeant commanded her ; and they were plying her with great vigour. In the course of the day, however, as the man was returning the sponge after a shot, and the cartridge in the hand of another, ready to reload, a thirty-two pound shot from the French entered her muzzle, she rebounded, and struck the sergeant with her breech on the breast, and knocked him over insensible. The shot had entered so far that she was rendered useless, and abandoned.

The action was kept up the whole of that day, during which we lost the best and bravest of our men. Our guns had been well directed at first ; but, towards evening, the most of the artillery who had commanded them were either killed or wounded ; and the direction of them was then taken by men who knew little about it. The consequence was that much ammunition was used to little purpose. The artillery soldier at the gun next to me was killed, and two men equally ambitious for what they considered the post of honour, quarreled about it. From high words it came to blows ; but the dispute was soon settled ; for a shell, falling between them, burst, and quieted them for ever.

I could scarcely define my feelings during the action ; but so far from feeling fear, when it first commenced, and the silent gloom of the night was broken by the rapid flash, and the reverberating thunder of the cannon, I felt a sensation something

resembling delight; but it was of an awful kind —
enthusiasm and sublimity, mixed with a sense of
danger—something like what I have felt in a violent
thunder storm.

The firing, on both sides, had been kept up without intermission from two o'clock in the morning;
but as it now became dark, it was partially suspended. I then, for the first time, ventured to go below
to the bomb-proof. The scene there was dismal —
the wounded filled the whole place, and the doctor
had not got through with the dressing of them. In
this he was materially assisted from the commencement of the action by a female, (Mrs Reston,) whose
heroism I have described in a subsequent volume.
It is matter of surprise to many, that the courage
she displayed, and the services she rendered on that
occasion, should have been entirely overlooked by
those who had the power of rewarding her, or that
her claims on the country were not more warmly
seconded by the officer who commanded in the
fort.

Here let me pause in my narrative, to pay a
tribute of respect to the memory of assistant surgeon
Bennet, who was with us during that trying period.
To a fair knowledge of his profession, he added one
of the kindest dispositions I ever knew any one
possessed of; he was absolutely without one drop of
gall in his composition; so much so, indeed, that
some of the officers endeavoured to make him a butt
for their raillery, but his native wit defeated their
purpose, and turned against them their own weapons.
Those who have been under his care will remember
him with grateful feelings. But his career was
brief; shortly after our arrival in Portugal, he
caught infection from some of the sick whom he was
attending, and died.

During the day I had little time to reflect on any
thing—all was noise and bustle; but now that I had

time to look round, and saw the ramparts covered
with the pale and disfigured corses of those who,
a few hours before, were rioting in the fulness of
health and strength, and others writhing in agony,
under the severe wounds they had received, I could
not deny that I felt my heart sink within me, and
sensations of a melancholy and solemn nature took
place of those which had before excited my mind.

When day-light came in next morning, the firing
again commenced as warmly as the preceding day ;
and the precision the French had attained with their
shot was very remarkable. We had a flag-staff of
the usual size, on which was hoisted the Spanish
colours. They had cut it across with a cannon ball,
it was repaired, and again replaced ; but it was not
five minutes up, when another shot brought it down
again. This occurring four or five times successively,
gave great offence to the sailors, who attributed all
that we had suffered to fighting under the Spanish
flag, and swore that if the union jack were up in its
place, the French would not bring it down so
easily.

" There 's that bloody Spanish flag down again,"
said one of the tars.

" Look ye, Jack ! I have got our boat's ensign
here—let me go, and I 'll soon run it up."

He went, and assisted in repairing the flag staff ;
but instead of again bending the Spanish flag to the
halliards, he put the English in place of it.

A general huzza greeted its appearance. " Now,
hang it ! we 'll beat the French dogs," said the
seamen ; but the cheering attracted the notice of the
commandant, and he ordered it to be hauled down
again. Never was an order so reluctantly obeyed.
In a few minutes, a shot cut through the flag staff.
" There it goes down again—Oh, botheration !" was
the surly reply. " Let it lie there :" and there it
lay, for no one would meddle with it. " Better to

fight without a flag at all, than under such a bloody treacherous flag as that," said an old sailor. "I never could bear it, unless when I saw it flying at the mast head of an enemy."

By this time three of our guns were rendered unfit for service, and they had made great impression on our parapet, with a breach in the end of the bomb-proof. A corporal of our grenadier company had gone below to get some refreshment, and was raising a tin with some wine in it to his mouth, when a shot entered the breach, and striking some small arms that were placed against the wall, shivered them to pieces. One of the splinters entered his head, and he fell dead on the spot. The rest wounded several of the men beside him.

A shell fell about the same time at the magazine door. A blanket was the only partition between it and the powder. We were sure all was over,—that it was impossible but that the magazine would be blown up. We stood in awful suspense for the few seconds between its fall and bursting—it burst—and already we imagined ourselves in the air; but fortunately, it did not communicate with the powder. There were two artillery men in the magazine at the time, whose feelings could not be very enviable.

In the course of the morning, General Stewart came over from Cadiz to inspect the state of the fort, when it was found that it could not stand out much longer. A reinforcement of men from different regiments was sent over to assist us, in case of the enemy attempting to storm us in our disabled state, but we received little assistance from them.

One of our sergeants, who, from his complexion, was called the "Black Prince," had installed himself commissary; and on the pretence of preventing the men from getting drunk, he seated himself beside the cask, which contained our ration wine, and fulfilled his duty so faithfully that he would not even give the men their allowance, but gave it away very liberally to any of the strangers who could " *tip him the blarney ;* " and among hands " he did not forget himself." He got rather tipsy at last ; and the men getting clamorous for their just allowance, to settle the dispute, he staved the cask, and spilt the wine about the place.

Let it be observed, however, that I do not blame the action, had his motive been to prevent the men getting intoxicated, (the best proof of which, would have been keeping sober himself;) but as the contrary was obviously the case, it could only be attributed to caprice, for he withheld the ration allowed from many of the men, while he distributed to others what they chose to ask.

The affair was scarcely worth mentioning, only that it will serve to shew on what an uncertain basis a soldier's fame rests ; for he was extolled to the skies, and subsequently got a situation in the commissariat department for that action ; while others, who had distinguished themselves by their valour and intrepid exertions, were passed by unnoticed.

It being found that we could not keep the place, boats were sent to convey us to Cadiz. Mines had been previously laid, and a major of engineers came over to superintend the operations for blowing up the fort ; but he had not taken many paces on the battery, when he was struck by a cannon shot, and fell a lifeless corpse.

It is remarkable to observe the covetousness of some men, even in the midst of danger. When he fell, the epaulettes were torn off his shoulders, and the gold watch was taken out of his pocket. The watch was afterwards recovered, but not, I believe, until the chain and seals were disposed of.

The men were now busy gathering what things they had together, and moving down to the boats. Some of them had already sailed. I had now time to reflect on the almost naked situation in which I was left, for I had thrown off my great coat at the commencement of the action, and some one had taken it away. I ran down to the bomb-proof, to try if I could find any thing to put on, but I met an engineer officer at the end of the passage, with his sword drawn, who had been inspecting the train laid to the mine. He asked me if I wished to be blown up, and ordered me off instantly.

On coming up the ramparts, I found that all the men had left the fort, with the exception of three or four, and the commandant. He was watching the motions of a strong party of French who were evidently coming down to take the place. Our ammunition was expended, but he ordered all the loose powder, grape, and ball cartridge to be collected, and having stuffed three guns (all we had left fit for service) to the muzzle with them, we watched the enemy until within about two hundred yards of the battery, when they were fired into the very middle of their column, and laid the half of them prostrate on the earth; the rest wheeled to the right about and left us to embark at leisure.

A number of the men, who had been killed, were lying on the ramparts. Some of them of the same regiment to which I belonged. We resolved on giving them some sort of burial, as the last kind office we could perform. We gathered them into a temporary hut, which had been built of mud, and, throwing it down over them, " Sleep there, brave comrades !" said we: " far distant, and ignorant of your fate, is the wife or mother who would have composed your mangled limbs." Hurried and rude was their burial, and a heartfelt sigh all their requiem, but it was more valuable than the ostentatious trappings of affected wo.

We then hurried down to the boats ; they were all gone but one, and after entering, I learned from my comrades that two men of the party who had come to reinforce us had got themselves so beastly drunk that they could not stir, and had been left behind.

We were not a great distance from the fort when it blew up, but only partially. The French were still firing, and one of the shells falling into a boat, which preceded us, burst and killed three men, besides wounding others. We were taken by the boats on board of the Invincible seventy-four, where we were very kindly treated; from that we were conveyed to Cadiz.

The regiment I belonged to had removed to Isla Camp, but we were marched up to our old barracks in the bomb-proof, and a motley looking group we were. Half naked, and blackened with the smoke of the gunpowder, we looked more like chimney sweepers than soldiers. We were received very coolly by the Spaniards. They did not seem to feel any commiseration for us on account of what we had suffered. I imagined their looks expressed vexation rather at any of us escaping alive.

When we reached the barrack, exhausted with fatigue and want of sleep, I threw myself on the stone floor. My mind was a chaos. The events of the preceding thirty hours were all jumbled together in my brain. Previous to that I had a good assortment of necessaries, with a hundred and fifty dollars, and some pieces of silk. I was now left with a pair of canvass trowsers, my shirt, shoes, and forage cap; but it was the fortune of war, and I soon forgot it all in a profound sleep. I do not know how long I slept, but when I awoke all my comrades had left the bomb-proof, away drinking, with the exception of one or two, who had been left as poor as myself.

I had received a wound in the leg from a splinter of a shell during the action. At the time I paid little attention to it, but it had now become so inflamed and swelled that I could scarcely move it. My former excitement of mind, with the fatigue I had endured, had produced a proportionate debility, and my feelings were no way enviable. Nothing could be more lonely, desolate, and heartless, than the state in which I felt myself the remaining part of that day.

CHAPTER IX.

THE day following, we marched to join the regiment at Isla Camp. Our comrades turned out to receive us, and our hearts thrilled with exultation at the encomiums passed on our bravery. The poor fellows flew with alacrity to procure wine to treat us; amongst the rest, my comrade Dennis was not backward. He and I had been separated when I went to the fort, and he was now overjoyed to see me. He seized my hand in the warmth of his heart, and shook it so long, and squeezed it so heartily, that I was ready to cry out with the pain.

"Man alive, Joseph!" exclaimed he, "is it yourself that's in it? troth, I thought I'd never see you more, for, when I saw the shot and shell flying about ye like hailstones, I said to myself, 'Poor comrade! it's all over with you;' but, thank God, here you are safe and sound."

"Scarcely," said I.

"What's the matter, my dear fellow, are you wounded?"

"Slightly, but that is not the worst of it, I have all my kit on my back."

"Och, if that's all, never fear, my boy—you'll never want while Dennis has a shirt in his knapsack, or a cross in his pocket."

And his were not empty professions; my heart glows with grateful feeling to this moment at the

remembrance of his disinterested kindness. In my
chequered journey through life I met few friends of
his description.

After supplying me with things to change myself,
he procured a canteen of wine ; and being joined by
more of our comrades, who were willing to shew their
good will, and who had come equally well provided,
we sat down in the tent, and I soon forgot all that I
had suffered.

When the wine warmed my head, I entered into a
detail of our proceedings during the time we were in
the fort, and with a feeling of pride and exultation—
" fought all the battle o'er again." My comrades,
ranged around, greedily devoured the relation ; and
their exclamations and remarks served to heighten
my enthusiasm. I can smile now at the warmth of
my feeling, and the high ideas I had then of a
warrior's fame. Yet, I must say, that there is a
feeling connected with military enterprise, which
will scarcely fail to carry all before it, particularly in
men of any imagination. Military glory or fame,
calmly considered, certainly appears a mere bauble,
an *ignis fatuus :* but shew me the man, of any soul,
who could take this view of it in the midst of battle :
there the imagination soars unconfined beyond every
trammel, and gets into the region of sublimity and
enthusiasm.

Next day we were called out. The regiment
formed square, and the remains of our party was
marched into it. We were then addressed by our
commanding officer in terms of the highest eulogy,
and held out to the regiment as a pattern. The
sergeant who had distinguished himself by staving
the wine cask, was particularly addressed, and told
that he would not be. lost sight of. We were then
dismissed ; but with the exception of this sergeant, I
do not remember any of us who were thought of after
the speech. For my own part, I know that I found

difficulty enough in getting the sum of two pounds eight shillings, in lieu of all that I had lost! The commandant, however, was soon raised to the rank of major, and not long after to that of lieutenant-colonel.

The regiments of the brigade in camp were busily employed at this time working at the batteries, which were building on the island; for which they received ninepence per day, in addition to their pay. They had also extra rations, such as coffee and sugar for breakfast, and a pint of porter daily; but the labour was very hard, and the exposure to the sun brought on sickness amongst them.

Still we had little reason to complain, for we were under the command of a general who did not think it below him to look into the men's rights and interests, and anticipate their wants. It was not an uncommon thing, in a very wet morning, to find him up at our camp, ordering an extra ration of rum to be served out to the brigade. There were also double tents provided for us; as, in consequence of the heavy rains, the single ones were found insufficient; and on every occasion he paid the most indefatigable attention to our comfort. In him was found a rare combination of the rigid disciplinarian and the *soldier's friend.* He discharged his own duty faithfully and well; and he expected every one under him to do the same, and would admit of no excuse for the non-performance of it from either officer or soldier. To those who served under his command, in that place, it will be unnecessary to say that the officer to whom I allude, is Lieutenant-General the Hon. Sir William Stewart. His name will be associated in their minds with the character of a gallant and able officer, and a steady friend to the soldier.

We generally turned out for the working party at five o'clock in the morning; and our breakfast, which

was coffee with bread, was always ready at that hour.
I remember, the first time we had it, each man came
forward with his mess-tin for his allowance, which
was measured out by the cook. We had a Highlandman in the company, who had enlisted raw from his
native hills, and who, I believe, had never seen any
thing of the kind before. When he came for his
allowance of the coffee, which was now nearly done,
the cook was skimming it off the top very carefully,
to avoid stirring up the grounds. Donald, who
thought this a scheme to keep all the good part to
himself, exclaimed, " Tam your plod ! will you 'll no
gie some o' the sik as well as the sin ?"

" Oh, certainly," said the cook, (who was a bit of
a wag,) and stirring the grounds well up, he gave
him a double proportion. Donald came in, chuckling
with satisfaction at having detected the knavery of
the cook, saying, " If she'll socht to sheat a Highlandman, she 'll be far mistook ;" and seeing the rest
of his comrades breaking bread in their coffee, he
did the same : by this time the eye of every one in
the tent was on him, scarcely able to refrain from
laughing. Donald began to sup it with his spoon ;
but after taking two or three spoonfuls, grinding the
coffee grounds between his teeth, and making wry
faces, he threw the tin, contents and all, out of the
tent door, exclaiming, " Tam their coffee ! you might
as weel chow heather, and drink pog water as that
teevil's stuff. Gi'e Donal a cog o' brochan before
ony o' your tea or coffees either."

The French had once or twice made a powerful
attack on our picquets, but were repulsed with loss ;
and the skirmishing at our outposts, and firing from
the batteries, were now carried on almost without
intermission. We expected them to make an attack
on us with their whole force ; and scarcely a night
passed without being turned out, in consequence of
movements making on their side ; notice of which

was communicated to the troops by different coloured rockets, thrown up at our outposts.

At this time we had a strong force of British here. Besides artillery and engineers, we had a battalion of guards, and nine or ten regiments of the line. There was also a strong fleet of British vessels in the bay: at one time we had three first-rate men-of-war, namely, the Caledonia, Hibernia, and Ville de Paris, besides seventy-four gun ships, frigates, and a great number of smaller vessels and gun-boats. Batteries were built on every commanding situation: one of which (St Fernando) we used to call the Friars' battery, having been built in part by these gentry, and certainly among the best deeds they had done in that part of the country. It was on a very commanding situation, extending completely across the Isthmus at its narrowest part, with a wide trench, which could be filled with water from the sea on either side.

At this time the wound on my leg, to which I had paid little attention, became so ill that I was obliged to go into the hospital; and I, in a great measure, lost sight of what was going on amongst the troops. I had now nothing to relieve the monotony of an hospital life, unless a visit from Dennis now and then, when he could gain time from working or duty; and one visit from a sergeant, (a townsman,) who joined the regiment at that time, and had brought a letter from my parents. He had been long on the recruiting service, and was considered a first-rate hand at it. After some inquiries respecting my friends and native place, I happened to remark how successful he had been in getting recruits, and expressed my surprise that he should have been so much more so than others who had been on the same service. He replied, " No wonder at it — no wonder at all. I knew Glasgow well. It was my own place — knew the minds of the young fellows better than they did

themselves — for I had been a weaver myself, and a
lazy one too. I knew how I used to feel. In winter
it was too cold, and in summer too warm to work.
When it was good trade, I could not resist the
temptation of drinking and going idle two or three
days in the week ; and when it was bad, I had no
time to work for trying to find out the cause, and
setting the government to rights. The truth is, you
could scarcely ever catch a weaver contented. They
are always complaining. Therefore, you would
never have much trouble enticing them to enlist, if
you knew how to go about it ; or much in going after
them, for whenever they got lazy, they came up and
lounged about the Cross. You could not manage
them, however, the same as a bumpkin. They were
too knowing for that. The best way was to make
up to the individual you had in your eye, and after
bidding him the time of the day, ask him what sort of
web he had in. You might be sure it was a bad one ;
for when a weaver turns lazy his web is always bad :
ask him how a clever, handsome-looking fellow like
him could waste his time hanging see-saw between
heaven and earth, in a damp unwholesome shop, no
better than one of the dripping vaults in St Mungo's
church, when he could breathe the pure air of heaven,
and have little or nothing to do, if he enlisted for a
soldier,—that the weaving was going to ruin, and he
had better get into some birth, or he might soon be
starved. This was, generally, enough for a weaver ;
but the ploughboys had to be hooked in a different
way. When you got into conversation with them,
tell how many recruits had been made sergeants,
when they enlisted — how many were now officers.
If you saw an officer pass while you were speaking,
no matter whether you knew him or not, tell him
that he was only a recruit a year ago ; but now he's
so proud he won't speak to you ; but you hope he
won't be so when he gets a commission. If this won't

do, don't give up chase—keep to him—tell him
that in the place where your *gallant honourable*
regiment is lying, every thing may be had almost for
nothing,—that the pigs and fowls are lying in the
streets ready roasted, with knives and forks in them,
for the soldiers to eat, whenever they please. As
you find him have stomach, strengthen the dose, and
he must be overcome at last. But you must then
proceed quickly to work, before his high notions
evaporate. You must keep him drinking—don't let
him go to the door, without one of your party with
him, until he is passed the doctor and attested."

"But," said I, "you would not find every one so
easily duped."—"To be sure," said he, "some of
your sentimental chaps might despise all this, but
they were the easiest caught after all. You had only
to get into heroics, and spout a great deal about
glory, honour, laurels, drums, trumpets, applauding
world, deathless fame, immortality, and all that, and
you had him as safe as a mouse in a trap.

"But, if all these methods failed, and the fellow
remained obstinately determined against parting with
liberty, the next resource was to pretend you had
been joking with him—that you had no wish to enlist
any man against his will—that you had advised many
a one not to enlist. Ask him in to take a friendly
glass, ply him briskly, send one of your party out to
put on plain clothes; let another of your men bring
him in as a young man wishing to enlist, set him
down next to the man you have in your eye. After
allowing them some conversation, put the question to
them, if they were talking about enlisting. 'Yes,
I'll enlist,' would be the reply of your man, 'if this
young man will go also.' Perhaps he might; but if
not, your last resource was to get him drunk, and
then slip a shilling in his pocket, get him home to
your billet, and next morning swear he enlisted,
bring all your party to prove it, get him persuaded

to pass the doctor, as it will save the *smart* should he be rejected. Should he pass, you must try every means in your power to get him to drink, blow him up with a fine story, get him inveigled to the magistrate in some shape or other, and get him attested; but by no means let him out of your hands."

"At this rate," said I, "men are taken into the service by as unfair means as they are pressed on board a man-of-war. Were you not afraid of complaints being made to your officers; and did the magistrates not scruple to attest men who were drunk?"

"Not at all, man," was the reply. "It was war times. As for the magistrates, we knew who to go to on these occasions. You know it was all for the good of the service."

"But had you no honour or conscience of your own?" said I.

"Honour or conscience!" said he, laughing. "Pretty words in the mouth of a private soldier. You must do your duty, you know. A good soldier does what he is ordered, right or wrong."

"But I am afraid," said I, "that you did more than you were ordered."

"Perhaps we were not ordered to do all that we did; but we were blackguarded if we didn't get men, and that was the same thing; and what's the use of a man if he can't take a hint?" *

"You must have made a good deal of money in this way."

"Money!" said he, "no, no. Did you ever hear of men making money on the recruiting service? They must have come from the north if they did. No, our money didn't do much good — it all went in raking and drinking. 'It melted awa' like snaw aff

* I do not know whether the sergeant exaggerated or not; but, in justice to the service, I must remark that such stratagems are neither authorized nor resorted to at present.

a dyke,' as the old women at home would say, and
we left Glasgow with bad kitts, and worse constitutions."

" Well," said I, " you may be glad you have left
it, for more reasons than one, and I hope you will
never return to it." The conversation was dropped,
and he soon left me ; but I could not help thinking
how many poor fellows were thus inveigled into a
profession they did not like, and rendered miserable
the remainder of their lives.

While here I was near losing my life in a very
simple manner. There was a garden behind the
hospital, which had formerly been a gentleman's
house, kept by a Spanish gardener, who raised vegetables for the Isla market. In it there was a cistern,
from which the water ran when required to water the
garden ; and this was supplied by a contrivance very
unlike any thing I have seen in Britain, although
common enough on the Continent. It was raised
from a deep well, by means of pitchers attached to
the circumference of a large wheel, which, revolving
by the power of a horse and gin, were successively
filled and emptied into the cistern. To this cistern
the men who were able brought their things to wash ;
but the gardener, who either thought that the soap
used spoiled his vegetables, or from sheer crossness,
tried every means in his power to prevent them.

One day, while here dabbling my linen, he came
to the cistern in a rage, and seizing my shirts he
threw them into a dung-hill close by. This act
was far from pleasing me, and I applied my fist to
his ear, in a very unceremonious manner. This he
returned, as is the usual custom with Spaniards, by
drawing his knife, and making a thrust at me. I saw
there was no safety unless in closing with him, to
get it out of his hand ; but as I got in upon him, he
made a lounge at me, and drove it through my coat
and shirt, grazing my ribs. I seized the hand which

held it with both of mine, and tripped up his heels.
We both came to the ground. He was now foaming
at the mouth. I could not disengage his hand ; and
it would have been a doubtful thing who would have
prevailed had not some of my comrades come into
the garden at that moment. They freed his hand
from the knife, which they withdrew and threw it
into the cistern. They then left me to manage the
Spaniard as I best could, which I found no difficulty
in doing, as he could not use his fists with much
effect. He, however, managed to bite me several
times, before I had done with him.

I was obliged to be extremely cautious after this,
as long as I was in the hospital ; for I often saw him
lurking about, eyeing me like a tiger watching his
prey, and, no doubt, if he could have got an opportunity, he would have despatched me.

We had little opportunity of knowing much about
the Spaniards here ; but what we did know gave us
no great idea of them, particularly the lower class.
They seemed to be a jealous-minded, vindictive, and
cowardly race, grossly ignorant and superstitious.
Their soldiers are complete scarecrows, (I speak of
them as I found them in every part of Spain,) badly
clothed, ill paid, and worse officered. There could
not be imagined a more barbarous-looking grotesque
assemblage of men in the world than a Spanish
regular regiment. No two men are dressed alike—
one wants shoes, another a coat, another has a slip of
blanket, with a hole cut in the middle, and his head
thrust through it, a lapell hanging before and another
behind. It is a rare thing to find one of them with
his accoutrements complete ; and their arms are kept
in such order, that if brought into action, the half of
them would be useless. On the march they have no
regularity—just like a flock of sheep ; and such
chattering amongst them, that you would take it for
the confusion of tongues at Babel !

They rarely ever succeeded at any thing unless Guerilla fighting, and then only when they could take their victims by surprise, or when they were double or triple the number of their enemy.

There are certainly many brave and noble souls amongst them, whose hearts beat high in the cause of liberty, and who have evinced it by their gallant enthusiasm; but unfortunately they are but a small number, in comparison to the millions who are sunk in slavish ignorance and superstition.

CHAPTER X.

WE had been about seven months in Cadiz, when the regiment to which I belonged was again embarked; and after a passage of eleven days landed at Lisbon. We remained there two or three days, making preparation for our advance; and were then conveyed in boats up the Tagus to Villa Franca, on our way to join the grand army under the command of Lord Wellington. From Villa Franca we marched to the convent of Alcantara, situated in a bleak moor; it had been wholly deserted by the monks, and the interior of it completely destroyed. From that we moved to Rio Mayor, where we were for the first time quartered on the inhabitants; they seemed comparatively settled and happy to those of other places, where the troops had more frequently passed. The site of this village was beautiful — the river, from which it took its name, glided past it in silent majesty, skirted with rows of large trees; between which could be seen the sloping fields of maize, interspersed with vineyards, where the bunches of large purple-coloured grapes were peeping forth, half hid by the green foliage with which they were surrounded, tempting, as it were, the passenger to try how deliciously they tasted; and some of our men could not resist the temptation, although they were forbidden fruit. There was something about this village so calm and serene, combined with the simple scenery around, which forcibly brought back to my imagination the Sabbath in a country village on the banks of the Clyde. I almost considered myself at home; and when I left it a day after, I felt grieved, as if leaving a place with which I had been long acquainted.

After halting one day here, we proceeded on the main road as far as Cavallos. Here we received information, from men going to the rear sick, that our army was retreating, after having fought an action at Busaco. This intelligence was soon confirmed by cars coming in with the wounded — those who had suffered slightly were walking, while others, whose wounds were more severe, were either sitting or lying on the cars, which from their construction were ill calculated for conveying sick and wounded men. They were about five feet long, and two and a half broad; but instead of being boarded at the sides, there were stakes placed in holes about eighteen inches apart; the wheels were about two feet in diameter, rather octagonal than round; and as they were not girt with iron, it was quite a common thing to have a piece broken out of the circumference, and of course every time the wheel turned, the whole car was violently shaken. This was drawn by a pair of oxen, yoked by the head. A peasant, with a long stick and a sharp nail in the end of it, walked before them, and every now and then run his goad into their shoulders to hasten their pace. This generally produced an awkward zig-zag trot for a few yards, when the jolting occasioned by the inequality of the wheels, caused the most excruciating torture to the poor fellows who were in them, and forced them to groan with agony. In this manner, exposed to the inclemency of the weather, and going at the rate of two

miles an hour, they had to travel to Lisbon, a distance
of forty or fifty miles, before they reached an hospital.
The wounded continued to pass during the remaining
part of the day, and throughout the whole night.

The continual creaking of their wheels was intolerable. I know of nothing in this country I can
liken it to, unless the grating of an iron door on rusty
hinges, but it was still worse than that. The Portuguese never put any grease on their wheels ; for they
think the noise of them frightens away the devil.
The consequence is, that the axletree often takes fire
with the friction, and burns completely through. I
never after could bear the noise of those cars. The
hideous grating sound was always associated in my
mind with the pallid faces and piercing groans of the
wounded whom we that day saw passing.

Next morning we got orders to march across the
country to Alcobaço, where we were to join the third
division of the army, commanded by General Picton.
This was a beautiful little village, with a very large
convent in it, occupied by Bernardine monks, — one
of the richest orders in Portugal. It was built by
Alphonso the First, to fulfil a vow made by him after
the taking of Santarem from the Moors, and for its
support he endowed it with all the land within view
of its walls, which was not a little, for the prospect
was extensive.

When we entered the village, we found it empty of
inhabitants; for they had fled with precipitation when
they heard that our army was retreating, leaving
every thing behind them, but what money or jewels
they could carry about their persons. We were
quartered in one of the passages of the convent. The
monks had all left it, with the exception of a few
who remained to superintend the removal of some of
their precious articles.

I forget how many hundred monks there were cells
for in the convent; but an idea of its size may be

formed, when it is known that a whole division of
the army, consisting of not less than five thousand
men were lodged in the galleries alone, without filling
them. Attached to it was a spacious chapel, the
whole inside of which was decorated in the most
superb style ; the walls covered with valuable paint-
ings, and in it a magnificent organ.

In the convent was the library, which contained a
selection of many thousand volumes, with philoso-
phical apparatus.

Contiguous to the church belonging to the convent
there was a Gothic mausoleum of hewn stone, in the
midst of which were two magnificent sepulchres of
white marble, containing the remains of Don Pedro
the First of Portugal, and of Dona Ignes de Castro,—
a description of whose tragical death forms a beautiful episode in the third book of the Luciad.

The kitchen of the holy fathers, which was on the
sunk floor, presented a scene of plenty, which was
not very favourable to the opinion of their severe
abstinence. It was about a hundred feet long ; the
fire-place, which was raised on cast-iron pillars in the
centre of the apartment, was thirty feet long, by
twelve wide ; a stream of water ran through the
kitchen, which was occasionally overflown to cleanse
the floor, and also supplied the tanks in which they
kept live fish. Certainly, if they lived as well every
day as they seemed to do while we were there, they
could not boast much of fasting ; for, in their larders
and kitchen, there was a profusion of every delicacy
which could be thought of. Their cellar contained
upwards of seven hundred pipes of the choicest wines,
and in the gardens belonging to the convent were
the rarest and finest fruits, besides vegetables and
plants of every description.

To judge from what we saw, they ought to have
been the happiest fellows imaginable. Good eating
and drinking, fine grounds to walk in, and plenty of

books! What could they wish for more? It is likely, however, that their usual mode of living was not so luxurious as we were inclined to think, from what we saw of their kitchen; but I suppose they considered it better to use what they could of their dainties, than leave them to the French; and, to tell the truth, the poor monks did not seem to have any great appetite while we were there: for any of our men who entered the kitchen were liberally supplied with any thing that was cooked.

Previous to the regiment being dismissed, the colonel cautioned us against taking any thing which had been left by the inhabitants. Before the division came in, I believe this order was punctually obeyed, and our men walked peaceably up and down the streets, the same as they would have done in a village at home; but when the other regiments, composing the division, arrived, the scene was soon changed; for they scarcely took time to take off their knapsacks, before they commenced breaking up the doors, and plundering every thing they could lay their hands on.

Some of our men, considering, I suppose, that they might as well have a share of the spoil as the others, joined in the throng; but they had a lesson to learn which some of them paid for rather dearly. They were not aware that there was a provost marshall* attached to each division.

And while they were busy he came upon them with his guard: the old campaigners made good their retreat, but our *innocent boys,* (as the Irish regiments in the division called them,) not being acquainted with his person or power, kept their ground, and were so warmly received, that they did not forget either him or his kindness while in the division.

An inspection was made next day of the division,

---

* The provost marshall is invested with power to inflict summary punishment on all soldiers whom he may find plundering, or straggling from their regiment.

to ascertain whether they had any plunder in their
knapsacks, and any thing found more than the regulated compliment of necessaries was taken from them.
The town fell into the hands of the French the following day, and it may be thought that it would have
been better to allow us to take the things left than
that they should fall into the hands of the enemy ;
but nothing is more subversive of discipline in an
army than the habit of plundering, exclusive of the
men, through covetousness, burdening themselves in
such a way that they cannot march. Whether the
means used to prevent it were the best and most
efficient, I do not pretend to say ; but there can be
no doubt as to the necessity of preventing it as much
as possible.

In the course of this day, the monks who had been
left departed in chaises, and took not a few boxes of
doubloons, with them. The greater part of the pipes
of wine in the cellars were staved, to prevent them
falling into the hands of the enemy. We left the
convent that afternoon, and having marched as far as
Torres Vedras, encamped outside of the town.

When I say encamped, I do not mean that we
pitched tents, for the army were not supplied with
tents, until the last campaign in 1813-14. At this
time, the blue canopy of heaven was all our covering,
the earth our bed, and a single blanket our bed-
clothes.

A newly ploughed field, on the face of a hill, was
our portion. We got out our blankets, and lay down,
expecting to get a comfortable nap, although the
weather was rather cold ; but towards morning, it
began to rain so heavily that we were soon wet to
the skin. Some, who had a little wisdom in their
heads, got up, and packed up their blankets ; but
others lay still, until they were literally floated with
water and mud, which came rolling in streams down
the ridges, in such a way that they could scarcely be

distinguished from the soil around. They were then obliged to get up, and squeeze their blankets in that wet and dirty state into their knapsacks. The rain got heavier, the longer it continued, and we stood huddled together, shivering with cold and wet. At last, an order came for us to march into Torres Vedras; but such a march I never saw, even in the worst of times afterwards. We were novices in the business, and not yet weather-proof. Had it not been that the town was so near, we would have occupied three or four miles of a line of road, we were so straggled. The ground was of a clayey nature, and with the rain that fell it had become like bird-lime. Our feet stuck fast at every step, and our shoes were actually torn off, and many of them were left lying in the clay. Some were walking barefoot; others in their stockings, without shoes; and more had one shoe on, and another carrying in their hand. We were a set of drenched and miserable looking creatures, and the officers were in as bad a plight as ourselves.

At last we reached the town and got into houses; but the village was too small, and we were crowded in such a way that we had scarcely room to sit down. In the course of the day, however, arrangements were made; and some of the regiments sent to other villages, so that we were better accommodated.

During the time we were in the Peninsula, the troops suffered much from exposure to rain; and nothing renders a soldier so uncomfortable as having wet clothes about him; or, I believe, hurts his health more, when first exposed to it. I have often wondered that no means were taken to prevent this. Many of the officers had oil-cloth cloaks that completely covered them. Some such thing for the men would have been neither expensive nor heavy to carry, and would have been the means of saving many lives. Much more attention ought also to be paid to the

quality of the shoes served out to the army, for they
in general are of the very worst kind, and it was no
uncommon thing for our store shoes to be in tatters
before we had worn them a week.

After a stay of a few days here, we removed to
Cadaciera in the same line of position, which extended
from the Tagus to the sea. We had not long taken
up our quarters in the village, where our whole
brigade was, when a peasant entered it, driving a
flock of sheep before him. In a moment, a race was
made amongst them by some of the soldiers. Others,
stimulated by their example, followed ; and in a few
minutes, officers and men were seen promiscuously
scrambling for the mutton. Dennis joined in the
throng, and had seized one of them, at the same
moment that an officer of the Irish regiment in the
brigade made a grasp at it. " Give me that sheep,
sir," said the officer in an authoritative tone.
" Arrah, be aisy, honey !" said Dennis. " Kill a
Hessian for yourself, if you plase." * The officer
relinquished his claim, and pursued another. The
poor Portuguese shepherd stood like a statue, not
knowing well what to do. At last, when he found
himself relieved from all his charge, he went away,
lamenting and muttering curses on the " *ladrones
Englese*," † to make his complaint to the general.

Soon after, a wine store was found out, and as
plundering was the order of the day, the contents of it
were soon lessened. This depredation was discovered
by the men becoming intoxicated. The most severe
investigation and search took place, and those with
whom any of the stolen property was found were

---

* I asked Dennis what the expression meant. He said that during the
rebellion, a number of Hessian soldiers had been in Ireland, and an " United
Man," having shot one of them, was busy plundering him, when one of his
comrades aked share of the booty. " Kill a Hessian for yourself, my gay
fellow," was the reply.

† English Robbers.

confined, tried by a court martial, and flogged ; but they were not the most guilty who suffered.

While we remained in this position, we were obliged to be under arms two hours before day-light, and remain until clear day ; and for a few days after, these two hours were pretty well occupied by flogging.

Terror seems to be the only engine of rule in the army ; but I am fully persuaded in my own mind that if a more rational method were taken, the character of the soldier in quarters would be as exemplary as in the field.

I cannot adduce any reasonable excuse for this wanton breach of honesty ; for we were regularly supplied with rations at the time ; but I imagine that most of the men were led into it by the example set by others, without taking time to think about the impropriety of the action. The soldier could scarcely think that there was any harm in the deed which an officer joined in. This was rather rare, however : but many of them had no objection to participate in what was stolen, which to me appeared equally blameable.

When settled in a place for any time, the brigade assembled on Sundays for divine service. We were always in full marching order on these occasions : and not uncommonly had a field day after it. If a person were to judge from the hitching of knapsacks, and wry faces that were making, during this ceremony, he would have thought the soldiers would rather have dispensed with it ; but I dare say, the anticipation of the drill that was to follow, prevented them from feeling much benefit from their devotions.

The first Sunday after the outrage already related, when the chaplain left his station, General Picton took his place.

This was the first time he had addressed us. I felt anxious to examine the features of a man who had

been so much the public talk on account of his reputed
cruelty at Trinidad. I could not deny that I felt a
prejudice against him, and his countenance did not
do it away : for it had a stern and gloomy expression,
which, added to a very dark complexion, made it no
way prepossessing ; but when he opened his mouth,
and began to pour forth a torrent of abuse on us for
our conduct, and his dark eye flashed with indignation, as he recapitulated our errors, " hope withering fled, and mercy sighed farewell." He wound
up the particular part of his speech addressed to
us with, " *You are a disgrace to your moral country,
Scotland !*" That had more weight than all his
speech. It sunk deep in our hearts. To separate a
Scotsman from his country—to tell him he is unworthy of it—is next to taking away his life.

But General Picton was not the character which
we, by prejudice, were led to think him. Convinced
of the baneful effects of allowing his men to plunder,
he set his face sternly against it, but in other respects
he was indulgent ; and although no man could blame
with more severity when occasion required, he was
no niggard of his praise when it was deserved.
Nothing could surpass his calm intrepidity and
bravery in danger, ; and his presence in battle had
the effect of a talisman, so much had his skill and
valour gained the confidence of the men under his
command.

CHAPTER XI.

FROM Torres Vedras, we removed to Alcoentre, a
small village some miles in rear of Rio Mayor ; and we
were kept pretty busy while in it, strengthening our
position, making batteries, breast-works, abattis, &c.

The general of the brigade was quartered in the same village; and as he had, or seemed to have, a great antipathy to every thing Scottish, our regiment of course was included, and he found means to annoy us a good deal. Perhaps, he believed, with many people in England, that the Scots run wild about their native hills, eating raw oats like horses, with nothing but a kilt to cover their nakedness, and that they had no right to receive any other treatment, when they entered the army, than what is usually given to any wild animal when caged. " Rousing up with a long pole" seemed to be his hobby. When exercising in the field, our regiment could do nothing right. When our guard turned out to salute him, they were either too late, or they did not present arms properly; and he would order the sergeant to drill them for an hour; while he stood by and gave vent to the harsh epithets which he was in the habit of using on those occasions. " Scottish savages— stupid—barbarous," &c.

I have often been led to think that he studied expletives on purpose. He pretended that he could not understand a word that any of us said—that we spoke Gælic; and his aid-de-camp was called to interpret, although he had no right to understand what was said better than himself, for I believe he was also an Englishman.

As a sample—he once took a fancy to the wooden cases which the Portuguese use instead of stirrup irons, and ordered his Scottish servant to get a pair for him; for although he disliked the Scots, he employed them as his servants. The man procured them; but they were not fellows.

" Well, sir," said the general, " have you got those things ?"

" Yes, sir, but they are no marrows."

" Marrows ! marrows ! what's that ? what's that ?

and calling his aid-de-camp, he asked him what " the Scottish savage" said.

" He means, sir, that they are not fellows."

" Poh! poh! you surely do not pretend to understand what is no language."

" That is his meaning in his own language, sir."

" Nonsense, sir, you are as bad as he ; go and read your dictionary."

He was very strict in duty affairs, particularly in details, which perhaps another general would not have troubled his head about. He was very fond of surprising the sentinels at the outposts, by taking circuitous routes, and keeping under cover of the bushes. On one occasion, however, he met his match, if the story reported was true : but as I only had it from report, I will not pledge myself for its truth.

One of the men on picquet was planted as outpost sentry on the road leading to Rio Mayor.

" Now, George," said the corporal to him, as he was leaving him, " mind that the general is out in front, keep a good look out, or he may surprise you, and you know the consequence. Be sure you challenge in time."

" Leave that to me," said Geordie.

A short time after (it was dusk when he was posted) he heard some one coming up the road very cautiously, as if wishing to avoid observation. At last, when about to turn the road, the individual, who was on horseback, clapped spurs to his horse, apparently for the purpose of passing him before he could challenge. There was no time to lose, and many a poor fellow might have been so confused at being taken unawares, that he would have neglected to challenge before the person was on him. Not so with Geordie. The moment he saw him quicken his pace, he challenged. The challenge was either not heard or purposely unheeded. Another challenge was given ; the general continued his gallop without answering. "You'll no tak me in that way, my gentleman," said Geordie; and as he gave the third and last challenge, he came to the present, and made a bullet whiz past the general's ear. The horse was drawn in immediately.

"What! do you mean to shoot your general, you rascal?"

"I dinna ken wha folk are in the dark; but whether you're a general or no, my orders are to fire at ony body that attempts to pass me without answering when I challenge. It's the general's orders; and I ken what I would get if I didna obey them."

"Well, sir, I am your general; and I wish to pass into the town."

"I'm no sure about ye — ye may be some French spy for ony thing I ken; and ye maun just stay whar ye are till the sergeant o' the picquet comes; he'll no be lang now, for the report o' my piece would alarm them."

At that moment the picquet arrived, and the general was allowed to proceed; but from that time, he did not trouble the outpost sentries so much.

Some time before we left these quarters to advance, an attack was made by the French, under General Junot, on our advanced posts; and we were ordered under arms to defend our position, in the event of them pushing forward. During that day, and the succeeding night, the baggage of the troops in front, along with the inhabitants of the surrounding country, filled the road leading through our village. It was a melancholy sight to see the poor natives, carrying their children, and any little thing which they were able to bring with them, moving along the road, after having left their homes and property — travelling they knew not whither, desolate and friendless. In a few days they might be reduced to beg, or perhaps (what was not uncommon in Portugal) die of hunger.

Alas! thought I, what misery war causes! I hope I will never see my own country in such a state.

The French were beaten back, and our troops resumed their former station; but few of the inhabitants returned. Not long after this, we were reviewed, along with part of the first division, by Lord Wellington. From the place where we were assembled, we could see Santarem, General Massena's head-quarters. Next day (the sixth of March) the whole army was ordered to advance, as the French had retreated in three divisions, by separate routes during the night.

This opened the campaign of 1811. From Alcoentre we marched to Rio Mayor (our former quarters when we were on our way to join the army;) but it was sadly altered,—the inhabitants had mostly all left it; the houses were in ruins; and it wore a desolate appearance. Next day we crossed to Alcaneyde. From thence we proceeded to Porto de Mos.

When we entered the latter place there was a large convent fronting us, which, as well as many of the houses, had been set on fire by the French. I never before witnessed such destruction. The finest furniture had been broken up for firewood; the very floors torn up, beds cut in pieces, with their contents thrown about, intermixed with kitchen utensils, broken mirrors, china, &c. &c. all in one heterogeneous mass of ruin, and not an inhabitant to be seen.

We had scarcely taken up our quarters, until I was called out for duty, and placed on the commissary guard. The mules with the stores had arrived, and the store-keeper looking for a place to put them in, when we joined him. At last he pitched on a chapel for the purpose. There was a large fire in the middle of the floor, on which was heaped broken pieces of the altar, wooden images, frames of pictures; even the ornamented wood-work of the organ was broken up for the purpose.

In searching for the cleanest place to set down the bags of biscuit, we found a door leading to some place apart from the chapel. As it was quite dark, I caught up a burning piece of wood to inspect the place—but what was my horror, when I entered and found the half-consumed skeletons of human beings on every side ; some lying, others kneeling, and more of them standing upright against the walls. The floor was covered with ashes, in many places still red. I stood fixed to the spot—the burning stick dropped from my hand. I informed some of my comrades of what we had seen, and we re-entered. Such an appalling sight was never witnessed. Of those who had sunk on the floor, nothing remained but the bones ; while the others, who were in a kneeling or standing posture, were only partially consumed ; and the agonized expression of their scorched and blackened features was awful beyond description.

On going to the upper end of the apartment, I perceived a bag lying on the floor with something in it. I was almost afraid to open it, lest some new object of horror should present itself. I was not mistaken in my apprehension ; for when the bag was examined, it was found to contain the dead body of an infant, which had been strangled ; the cord used for that purpose still remained about its little neck.

Next morning we continued our march to Leria, and on entering it found it burned. We were quartered in a convent outside the town, which was partially consumed, where we remained the succeeding day.

On the top of a hill, to the left of the town, was a sort of redoubt. I went with Dennis to take a view of the place, and going up to where some of our soldiers were standing, we found three children lying, two already dead, but the other was still breathing. There were pieces of biscuit lying beside them, which our soldiers had brought—but it was too late.

They had evidently perished from hunger; one of them had expired with the bit in his mouth. This was part of the horrors of war; but only a part. The wanton cruelty of the French soldiers, on this retreat, defies description.

From Leria we advanced towards Pombal, in front of which the French army had concentrated their force and made a stand; but they retired during the night, and took up a strong position at the end of a defile between Pombal and Redinha, with their right on a wood, and their left occupying the high ground above the river of Redinha, the town being in their rear. In this position our division attacked their left, the light division their right, and the fourth their centre; the rest of our army being in reserve. Their right was soon dislodged from their position in the wood, and retreated across a narrow bridge over the Redinha, followed by our light troops; but as the fords and bridge were commanded by their cannon, some time was lost before a sufficient number of troops could be passed over, to make a new disposi-*tion* to attack the heights on which they had taken post. A portion of the division crossed the river by swimming, headed by Major Lloyd; but the columns moved on towards the bridge. As we were advancing, a cannon shot from the enemy struck our column, killed a sergeant, and wounded two or three men; besides tearing our armourer's knapsack open, and scattering its contents about in every direction —the poor fellow was so frightened that he grew sick, went to the rear, and soon after died.

Our troops having passed the river, we soon drove them from their position back upon the main body, and next day their whole army was strongly posted at Condeixa. Our division was ordered to march through the mountains on their left towards the only road open for their retreat, which had the effect of dislodging them from their strong position; here our

part of the duty was very fatiguing, for the hills were
so steep that we had to scramble up the one side on
our hands and feet, and slide down in the same
manner on the other.

The French had retreated in such haste from their
position at Condeixa that they left the communication
with Coimbra unguarded, and our army communicated with Colonel Trant and the Portuguese militia,
who were in possession of it.

They were now obliged to abandon all the positions
which they had successively taken in the mountains,
and their rear guard was thrown back on the main
body at Miranda de Corvo, from which they immediately retreated, destroying part of their ammunition and baggage. At this place we passed many
dead bodies of French and Portuguese, lying on the
road; and one part of it was covered with asses,
which the French had hamstrung before they left
them. It was pitiable enough to see the poor creatures in this state; yet there was something ludicrous
in the position that the animals had taken, when thus
cruelly lamed; they were sitting in a groupe upon
their hinder end, staring in each other's faces, seemingly in deep consultation on some important subject,
and looking as grave and dull as many an assembly
of their *biped brethren* at home.

The enemy now took up a new position on the
river Ceira, leaving a division at a small village as an
advanced guard, which was attacked by the third and
light divisions, and after some hard fighting their
army retired across the Ceira during the night, destroying the bridge. The enemy suffered severely
here, for besides their killed and wounded, numbers
were drowned in crossing the river.

Having taken up another position, from which they
were driven by our division, with the first, and light,
they concentrated their whole army on the Seirra
Moito, from which they retired on the eighteenth,

and our army occupied the ground they had left.
They now continued their retreat so rapidly that our
army, with the exception of our division, the sixth,
and light, were halted for the necessary supplies of
provision to come up. From this until the twenty-
seventh we followed them through the mountains,
harassing their rear, and suffered much fatigue, for
during that time we were very ill supplied with rations,
at times wanting bread and rum for two days together,
and when we did get it, perhaps only half allowance ;
we were almost always supplied with beef, but it was
of that description that there was little nourishment
in it. The cattle were brought from Barbary, and
often had to travel many hundred miles before they
were used, with very little to eat during their journey;
the consequence was. that when killed they were
nothing more than a mass of emaciated muscle, with
a semi-transparent covering of, what would be a per-
version of language to call fat—it was more like a
coating of train oil. It was never bled properly ; and
when boiled, it was as tough and stringy as a piece
of junk. The water it was boiled in was dignified
with the name of soup : and if the blood which boiled
out of the beef, along with the wood ashes that fell
into it, constituted soup, we had it in perfection.

One day we had halted rather early ; at this time
we had been without rations for two days. Many a
curse was poured on the head of the commissary, who
was considered the responsible person.

" There comes the stores, at last," cried one of the
men.

" Where ? where ?" said those around. Every eye
was now directed to a hill at some distance, where a
long train of mules were perceived successively rising
over its summit, and bending their way towards the
division. The men were in transports of joy ; a
general cheer greeted their appearance.

" We will have full rations to-day," cried one

" and rum too," said another, " for I can see casks on
the mules."

Another cheer succeeded this discovery; and we
were dancing about overjoyed. " Who goes for the
rations?   Get out blankets for the biscuit, and camp
kettles for the rum." There were soon enough of
volunteers for this duty. The mules had by this
time got into a sort of defile.   Every eye was on
the stretch, waiting for their re-appearance.   As the
first mule emerged from the place where they were
hid, every face was dressed in smiles; but the next
second produced an effect, similar to that which a
criminal might feel, who had been informed of his
reprieve on the scaffold, and the next moment told it
was a mistake; for it turned out to be mules with
ammunition for the division.   Never did I witness
such a withering effect on men, as this disappointment produced.   We stood looking at each other for
a minute, in all the agony of hope deferred : the next
was opened by a torrent of execration on all concerned.   Those who have never experienced extreme
hunger can form no idea of our feelings.

A day or two after this, we crossed a river and
ascended a hill, where we encamped.   Dennis and I
were for duty, and both placed on the out picquet,
which was posted on the face of a hill in front of the
division.   The French were on the opposite rise, and
a small river ran at the foot of it.   We had only got
one day's rations from the time the incident mentioned
above occurred ; and as Dennis expressed it, " our
bellies were thinking our throats were cut."

I procured leave from the officer to go to the river
for water ; intending to proceed a little farther down,
to try if I could find any thing that I could eat.
Turning round the hill, I came to a mill ; and entering it, found a number of soldiers belonging to different regiments of the division busy grinding Indian
corn ; others were employed drawing a baking of

bread, which the French had left in their hurry, when
we took up our position. I attempted to help myself
to some corn, which was lying in a basket.

"Drop that like a hot potatoe," said one of the
Connaught Rangers.

I tried another basket, but it was also appropriated;
and as there were none of my regiment there, I could
not expect to succeed by force; so I left the place,
sorrowful enough, on my way back to the picquet,
with a cargo of cold water — poor cheer, certainly.
But just as I turned round the hill, I met my friend
Dennis, who had got leave from the officer on some
pretence to go down to the river. I told him my
melancholy story; he paused for a moment; then
clapping his hand to his forehead, he exclaimed, " Now
I have it! Give me the canteens."

When I gave them to him, he poured out the water,
and slung them over his shoulder.

" Now, just stand there a minute," said he, "and I'll
show you a scatter."

He then commenced running, with the canteens
clattering at his back. Those who were in the mill,
being startled by the noise, looked out to see what was
the matter. When Dennis saw them, he cried out,
" Och, ye rogues o' the world, run for your lives; for
the division has fell in, and the provost is coming
down with his guard; and every one of yees will be
taken."

They were all out in a moment.

" Which way is he coming ?"

" This way," said Dennis, pointing to the way he
had come himself. " I am on picquet, and I just run
down to give you warning."

They all took to their heels in the opposite direction, leaving the field clear to Dennis and me; and
we lost no time in filling our haversacks.

The right of the French army had retreated by the
high road upon Celerico, but the left (which we were

pursuing) had fallen back upon Govea and the moun
tains of Guarda ; and having augmented their force,
held the position in great strength.   Our army having
collected in the neighbourhood of Celerico, on the
morning of the 29th our division moved for the purpose of flanking the enemy, and the light and sixth
divisions having moved also, by different routes, in
the direction of Guarda, the attack was combined in
such a manner that the enemy were nearly surprised,
and abandoned many of their effects in their flight,
without attempting to fire a shot, notwithstanding the
strong position they occupied,* and retired on Sabugal on the Coa, leaving an advanced guard on our
side.

The position which the enemy had now taken was
very strong, the river behind which they were posted
being difficult of access, and could only be approached
by its left.

Our troops were set in motion on the morning of
the third April, to turn the enemy's left above Sabugal, and to force the passage of the bridge of that town.
A strong corps of the enemy were posted on a height
immediately above the bridge.

The light division and cavalry were ordered to
cross the river at two separate fords, upon the enemy's
left.   The fifth division and artillery were destined to
attack the bridge, and our division to cross at a ford
about a mile above the town.   The light division
crossed first, and commenced the attack, but they
were warmly received, and the action was for some
time doubtful.   Our division now crossed and

---

* Guarda lies on the top of a high hill ; we were much fatigued in ascending
it, and entered the town with empty stomachs, but we were agreeably surprised to find that the French had left their dinners for us ready cooked, as
in their haste they had left them on the fire in the different houses where they
had been lodged.   In one house where some of their officers were quartered,
and had been obliged to retreat from table, after it was laid for dinner, some
wag placed a mule's head in the centre, with a label in its mouth on which
was written 'Pour Mons. Jean Bull."

attacked their centre; while at the same time the fifth division crossing the bridge, ascended the heights on the right flank of the enemy, and the cavalry appeared in rear of their left; they made a precipitate retreat, leaving a howitzer in possession of the light division, and about two hundred killed on the ground, six officers, and three hundred prisoners.

As we descended the hill towards the river, we passed a convent or chapel, half way down; at the door lay an old man, who had been killed with a musket shot, and a genteelly dressed Portuguese was standing beside him; he spoke to us as we passed, but we had no time then to pay any attention to what he said. We learned after, from the men who were following us with the baggage, that he had been hung up by some of the French soldiers, because he would not, or could not, show them where he had hid his money. His old father who was lying at the door, had been shot, and his mother's throat cut. His sisters had been first violated by the monsters, and then cruelly used: one of them had her eyes blackened, and the other her arm broken. His life was saved by the French General, who came up just as he had been suspended, and ordered him to be cut down. Such were the tender mercies of the French soldiery!

When we had gained the edge of the river, the French columns were posted on the height above us. We passed the river under a heavy fire, and proceeded to ascend the hill. We could now see that more of our army had crossed, both to our right and left. As we advanced up the hill, we formed line. General Picton rode up in front of us, with his stick over his shoulder, exposed to the heavy fire of the enemy, as composedly as if he had been in perfect safety. "Steady, my lads, steady!" said he; "don't throw away your fire until I give you the word of command." We were now close on them; the balls

were whizzing about our ears like hailstones. The
man before me received a shot in the head, and fell.
" Why don't they let us give the rascals a volley," said
some of the men.   The left of our brigade, which was
nearest them, now opened a heavy fire ; and by the
time the line was all formed, the French had taken to
their heels.   At this moment a severe rain storm
commenced, and darkened the air so much that we
lost sight of them completely ; when the sky cleared
up, they were discovered, about a mile forward,
scrambling their way over hedge and ditch without
any regularity.   The ground which they had occupied now lay before us, strewed with the dead and
wounded ; and the Portuguese regiment belonging to
our division were busy stripping them naked.   In
this barbarous action, however, they were joined by
very few of the British.   The division to our right
and left had by this time succeeded in turning the
flanks of the French army ; and they were now
retreating in great confusion.

After waiting under arms for some time, we were
ordered to encamp on the ground we then occupied,
where we remained during that night.

THE

WAR IN THE PENINSULA

———

A CONTINUATION

OF

RECOLLECTIONS OF THE EVENTFUL LIFE
OF A SOLDIER.

EVENTFUL LIFE

OF

A SOLDIER.

***

CHAPTER I.

THE night we passed in the encampment at Sabugal was uncommonly dark, and at intervals the rain fell in torrents ; fires had been kindled in the hollow trunks of some large chestnut trees, which, burning up as high as the branches, illuminated them to the very top. The flickering lurid glare which these fiery columns threw on the naked bodies of the slain, the indistinct objects in the back ground, and the groups of soldiers which flitted around them, presented a scene at once sublime and picturesque ; it looked like the midnight orgies of some supernatural beings.

Next morning we fell in at daylight, and, in a short time after, pursued our march by the same route the French had taken the preceding day. The ground was covered with gum cistus, which had been previously burned, either through accident, or to serve some purpose, among which they had left visible marks of their confused flight, in the torn pieces of clothing and broken arms which strewed their line of march. They continued their retreat without halting until they reached Ciudade Roderigo, a fortified town on the Spanish frontier, at which place, having crossed the Agueda, they made a stand and concentrated their force. In consequence of this our army also halted, and, in a few days after, our regiment was quartered in a Portuguese village within some miles of them.

On the advance to this place, I became acquainted with a lad of the name of Henry G——. While on guard with him one day, I perceived him reading a book, which, on inquiry, I found to be Cromek's Remains of Nithsdale and Galloway Song, which he had borrowed from an officer's servant. Books of any kind were rare amongst us at that time, but one of this description had too much nationality in it, not to be considered a valuable prize in a foreign land. We read the book together, and a similarity of feeling and sentiment subsequently led to a friend ship which continued unimpaired while we remained in the Peninsula. In his romantic turn of mind and acute sensibility, he bore a strong resemblance to my former friend and shipmate, William. He had read a great deal, but, like myself, he had read with little discrimination. The effects were nearly the same in both, a propensity to day-dreaming and castle-building. Many a weary mile have we travelled together, almost unconscious of progression, charming the sense of hunger away by anticipating our future honour and preferment, and in forming romantic schemes of rural retirement, when our campaigns were ended. This peculiarity of disposition, although it might sometimes occasion us uneasiness, where others, less sensitive, felt but little, yet, on the whole, in a life like ours, where the scene was continually shifting, it rendered our minds more elastic; and the continual play of fancy which was thus excited, diversified the lights and shadows so much, that even now, I am at a loss to say, whether at that time I felt more pain or pleasure. We had only been a few days in quarters, when my friend Henry was near being involved in an affair, the consequence of which would have ruined a mind like his for ever. The captain of his company was a man of a strange disposition, which rendered him an object of dislike to both officers and men. A fellow of infinite jest, he rarely spoke but in a humorous strain ; but there was " a laughing devil in his sneer," and, like the cat, when she has secured her prey, he always felt most inclined to sport with the individual on whose destruction he was bent. It would be endless to enter into a detail of the methods by which he tormented his company, —those who served under him will remember them well ; suffice it to say, that I have known many officers who possessed bad qualities, but none who possessed fewer good ones than Captain S——.

On the march, he was in the habit of riding his mule among the ranks, very much to the annoyance of his company, and one day during the previous advance, the column was marching through fields which were fenced in by broad thin stones. The other officers finding they could not get through conveniently with the regiment, had taken a lane to the right of the column, but he continued to move on ; finding, however, that his mule could not get through the openings made, he desired Henry to overturn one of the stones. Henry made the attempt, but finding his strength inadequate to the task, and seeing himself getting behind the regiment, he passed through and rejoined his company. The captain had now to take the same road with the other officers. When he overtook the column, foaming with rage, he commenced in a measured affected style, to abuse Henry, ending with his usual phrase of encouragement, " *I'll get you a sweet five hundred.*" From that day forward, poor Henry was marked out as a butt for his caprice and tyranny. Not long after, two men of the company were ordered to be confined on a charge of selling their necessaries, one of whom happened to be Henry's comrade, and Captain S—— thinking this a favourable opportunity for carrying his promise into effect, ordered him to be confined also. A court-martial was ordered, and the prisoners warned for trial. Whether by some sinister manœuvering, or that it fell his regular turn, Captain S—— was president.

The witnesses were examined; the evidence was sufficiently clear against the other two, but none was adduced against Henry.

The president, trusting, I suppose, to his influence with the other members, proceeded (without taking any notice of the total want of evidence against Henry) to recommend the prisoners to acknowledge the crime laid to their charge, and throw themselves on the mercy of the court. Poor Henry was so struck with the flagrant injustice of this proceeding, that he could scarcely muster courage sufficient to say that he had heard no evidence against him. The president did not allow him to finish what he had to say, before he opened on him with a string of the most abusive epithets; and then, addressing himself to the members of the court—" Gentlemen," said he, " this is one of the most insolent dogs in my company. You may take my word for it, he is guilty—he confessed to me that he was, before I confined him, which I can prove." The members sat mute, as is generally the case while under the influence of a superior officer's rhetoric; and Henry had bade farewell to hope, when one of the officers, who was but a young subaltern, bursting through the blind deference too often cringingly paid to power, even in matters where discipline is not concerned, and giving way to the words which a natural love of justice prompted,— " We have no right, Captain S——," said he, " sitting

here as we do, to try the case according to the
evidence laid before us, to presume that the prisoner
is guilty, in the absence of all evidence. Nor are
we entitled to pay attention to any representation
which you may feel inclined to make, prejudicial to
his character. Sitting where you do as president of
this court—either sufficient evidence must be produced against the prisoner, or we are bound to acquit
him."

Captain S—— turned the scowl of his dark grey
eyes upon him, wherein the disappointment of baffled
revenge and rage were distinctly visible: but the
subaltern bore the look intended for his annihilation
with the utmost indifference—there even seemed to
be a smile of contempt playing on his countenance.
Captain S—— then proceeded to bring forward evidence to prove Henry's connection with the crime
for which the prisoners were tried—principally for
the purpose of proving that he had confessed his
guilt ; and, according to the president's opinion, this
evidence was perfectly conclusive. The officer
already mentioned, seeing that Henry was nearly
sinking under the influence of his feelings, said,
" Don't be afraid, my man, justice will be done you
—I believe you to be innocent—at least, I have heard
nothing yet to induce me to think otherwise ; take
time, collect yourself, and if you have any questions
to ask the evidence, or any witnesses to call in your
defence, to disprove what has been stated, speak out
fearlessly." Encouraged by the officer's kind and
manly conduct, and with his assistance, Henry cross-
questioned the evidence, and brought forward witnesses that not only disproved all that had been
stated against him, but fixed a suspicion on the minds
of those present, that the president had not only
confined him without cause, but had suborned witnesses for the purpose of bringing him to punishment.

Captain S—— seeing that his designs were frustrated, sullenly gave up the point, and poor Henry was acquitted : but had it not been for the independent character of the officer above-mentioned, he might not have escaped punishment. Courts-martial were at that time much too frequent to expect that justice would be always administered impartially by them ; and I am sorry to say it was too often evident, that individual pique influenced the decisions. In some regiments, indeed, courts-martial were resorted to, merely to give a colour to the proceedings of the officer commanding, whose wishes were oftener consulted than the ends of justice. This was not remedied by what are called company courts-martial, where the individual was tried by his peers; for I remember in one case, where I was president, the point in agitation among the members was not, " what punishment was adequate to the crime ?" but " what punishment would please the commanding officer ?" and I had some difficulty in convincing them that the former was the point they had to determine. The *surveillance*, established by the commander-in-chief over courts-martial, was a wise measure, and has altered matters very much. Indeed, too much praise cannot be bestowed on His Royal Highness, for the humane and effective policy which has been gradually introduced into the army : the situation of the soldier at present is very different from what it was twenty years ago. From the specimen Henry had got of Captain S——'s disposition, he thought it the wisest plan to get transferred from his company, which he effected shortly after.

A few days after this occurrence, our regiment was moved to the village of Fuentes de Honore, a few miles nearer Almeida : great part of the way, we moved through a wood of oak trees, in which the inhabitants of the surrounding villages had herds of swine feeding: here the voice of the cuckoo never was mute; night and day its simple notes were heard in every quarter of the wood.

The village we now occupied was in Spain, and formed a striking contrast to those of Portugal; the inhabitants and their houses wore an air of neatness, cleanliness, and comfort about them, unlike any thing we had as yet seen in the country; their dress and language were also different.

The site of the village itself was beautiful and romantic; it lay in a sort of ravine, down which a small river brawled over an irregular rocky bed, in some places forming precipitous falls of many feet; the acclivity on each side was occasionally abrupt, covered with trees and thick brushwood. Three leagues to the left of our front lay the villages of Gallegos and Espeja, in and about which our light division and cavalry were quartered. Between this and Fuentes lay a large wood, which, receding on the right, formed a plain, flanked by a deep ravine, being a continuation of that in which the village lay; in our rear was another plain, (on which our army subsequently formed,) and behind that, in a valley, Villa Fermosa, the river Coa running past it.

We had not been many days here, when we received intelligence that the light troops were falling back upon our village, the enemy having recrossed the Agueda in great force, for the purpose of relieving Almeida, which we had blockaded. On the morning we received this intelligence, (the 3d of May, 1811,) our regiment turned out of the town, and took up their position with the rest of the division on a plain, some distance behind it. The morning was uncommonly beautiful, the sun shone bright and warm, the various odoriferous shrubs, which were scattered profusely around, perfumed the air, and the woods rang with the songs of birds. The light division and cavalry falling back, followed by the columns of the

French, the various divisions of the army assembling
on the plain from different quarters, their arms glit-
tering in the sun, bugles blowing, drums beating,
the various staff-officers galloping about to different
parts of the line giving orders, formed a scene which
realized to my mind all that I had ever read of feats
of arms, or the pomp of war; a scene which no one
could behold unmoved, or without feeling a portion
of that enthusiasm which always accompanies "deeds
of high daring;" a scene justly conceived and well
described by Moore, in the beautiful song —

> Oh the sight entrancing,
> When morning's beam is glancing
> O'er files array'd,
> With helm and blade,
> And plumes in the gay wind dancing.

Our position was now taken up in such a way,
that our line ran along the frontiers of Portugal,
maintaining the blockade of Almeida by our left,
while our right kept open the communication with
Sabugal, the place where the last action was fought.

The French advanced on our position in three
columns, about three o'clock in the afternoon, and
detached a strong body of troops against Fuentes,
which was at this time occupied as an advanced post
by the 60th regiment, and the light company of our
division. The skirmishers were covered in their
advance by cavalry, in consequence of which ours
were obliged to fall back, for greater safety, to some
stone fences on the outskirts of the village, while a
party of our German hussars covered their retreat.
The cavalry now commenced skirmishing, the infantry keeping up an occasional fire. It was rather
remarkable that the cavalry on both sides happened
to be Germans. When this was understood, volleys
of insulting language, as well as shot, were exchanged
between them. One of our hussars got so enraged
at something one of his opponents said, that raising
his sword, he dashed forward upon him into the very

centre of their line. The French hussar, seeing that
he had no mercy to expect from his enraged foe,
wheeled about his horse, and rode to the rear ; the
other, determined on revenge, still continued to follow
him. The whole attention of both sides was drawn
for a moment to these two, and a temporary cessation
of firing took place ; the French staring in astonishment at our hussar's temerity, while our men were
cheering him on. The chase continued for some way
to the rear of their cavalry. At last our hussar coming
up with him, and fetching a furious blow, brought him
to the ground. Awakening now to a sense of the
danger he had thrown himself into, he set his horse
at full speed to get back to his comrades ; but the
French, who were confounded when he passed, had
recovered their surprise, and determined on rvenging
the death of their comrade ; they joined in pursuit,
firing their pistols at him. The poor fellow was now
in a hazardous plight, they were every moment gaining upon him, and he had still a long way to ride.
A band of the enemy took a circuit, for the purpose
of intercepting him ; and before he could reach the
line he was surrounded, and would have been cut in
pieces, had not a party of his comrades, stimulated by
the wish to save so brave a fellow, rushed forward,
and just arrived in time, by making the attack general,
to save his life, and brought him off in triumph.

The overwhelming force which the French now
pushed forward on the village, could not be withstood
by the small number of troops which defended it ;
they were obliged to give way, and were fairly forced
to a rising ground on the other side, where stood a
small chapel. The French now thought they had
gained their point, but they were soon undeceived ;
for being reinforced at this place by the Portuguese
caçadores, our lads came to the right about, and
attacked them with such vigour, that in a short time
they were driven back to their old ground. While

retreating through the town, one of our sergeants who
had run up the wrong street, being pushed hard by
the enemy, ran into one of the houses : they were
close at his heels ; and he had just time to tumble
himself into a large chest, and let the lid down, when
they entered and commenced plundering the house,
expressing their wonder at the same time concerning
the sudden disappearance of the " Anglois," whom
they had seen run into the house. During the time,
the poor sergeant lay sweating, and half smothered ;
they were busy breaking up every thing that came in
their way, looking for plunder ; and they were in the
act of opening the lid of his hiding place, when the
noise of our men cheering, as they charged the enemy
through the town, forced them to take to flight. He
now got out, and having joined his company, assisted
in driving the French back. No other part of the
line had as yet been attacked by the French ; they
seemed bent on taking the village of Fuentes in the
first place, as a " stepping stone," and the main body
of each army lay looking at each other. Finding that
the force they had sent down, great as it was, could
not keep possession of the place, they sent forward two
strong bodies of fresh troops to retake it, one of which,
composed of the Irish legion, dressed in red uniform,
was at first taken for a British regiment, and they had
time to form up, and give us a volley before the mistake was discovered. The village was now vigorously
attacked by the enemy at two points, and with such
a superior force, that in spite of the unparalleled
bravery of our troops, they were driven back contest-
ing every inch of the ground.

On our retreat through the village, we were met
by the 71st regiment, cheering, led on by Colonel
Cadogan ; which had been detached from the line to
our support. The chase was now turned, and although
the French were obstinately intent on keeping their
ground, and so eager, that many of their cavalry had

entered the town, and rushed furiously down the streets, all their efforts were in vain: nothing could withstand the charge of the gallant 71st; and in a short time, in spite of all resistance, they cleared the village. This regiment during the Peninsular war, was always remarkable for its gallantry. The brave Cadogan well knew the art of rendering his men invincible; he knew that the courage of the British soldier is best called forth by associating it with his country, and he also knew how to time the few words which produced such magical effects. We were now once more in possession of the place, but our loss, as well as that of the French, had been very great.

In particular places of the village, where a stand had been made, or the shot brought to bear, the slaughter had been immense, which was the case near the river, and at the small chapel on our side of the town; among the rest lay one poor fellow of the 88th light company, who had been severely wounded, and seemed to suffer excruciating agony, for he begged of those who passed him to put him out of torture. Although from the nature of his wound there was no possibility of his surviving, yet none felt inclined to comply with his request, until a German of the 60th rifle battalion, after hesitating a few moments, raised his rifle, and putting the muzzle of it to his head fired the contents of it through it. Whether this deed deserved praise or blame, I leave others to determine. The French, enraged at being thus baffled in all their attempts to take the town, sent forward a force composed of the very flower of their army; but they gained only a temporary advantage, for being reinforced by the 79th regiment, although the contest remained doubtful until night, we remained in possession of it, with the exception of a few houses on the rise of the hill at the French side.

The light brigade of our division was now withdrawn, and the 71st and 79th regiments remained as a picquet in it during the night ; next morning it was again occupied as before.   On the fourth, both sides were busily employed burying the dead and bringing in the wounded ; French and English promiscuously mixed, and assisted each other in that melancholy duty as if they had been intimate friends.   So far did this friendship extend, that two of our lads who spoke French, went up that night after dark to the enemy's picquet, and having conversed and drank wine with them, returned unmolested to their company. During this day the French Generals reconnoitered our position, and next morning, (the fifth,) they made a movement to their left with two strong columns ; this caused a corresponding movement in our line, and it was scarcely made, when they attacked our right, composed of the seventh division, with all their cavalry, and succeeded in turning it ; but they were gallantly met by some squadrons of our dragoons, and repulsed.   Their columns of infantry still continued to advance on the same point, and were much galled by the heavy fire kept up on them by the seventh division ; but in consequence of this movement, our communication with Sabugal was abandoned for a stronger position, and our army was now formed in two lines, the light division and cavalry in reserve , this manœuvre paralyzed their attack on our line, and their efforts were now chiefly confined to partial cannonading, and some charges with their cavalry, which were received and repulsed by the picquets of the first division in one instance ; but as they were falling back, they did not perceive the charge of a different body in time to form, and many of them were killed, wounded, and taken prisoners.   Colonel Hill, who commanded the picquets, was among the latter ; the 42d regiment also, under Lord Blantyre, gallantly repulsed another charge made by the enemy's cavalry. The French then attempted to push a strong body of light infantry down the ravine to the right of the first division, but they were driven back by some companies of the guards and 95th rifles.

While on the right this was going on, the village of Fuentes was again attacked by a body of the imperial guard, and, as on the third, the village was taken and retaken several times. At one time they had brought down such an overwhelming force, that our troops were fairly beat out of the town, and the French formed close column between it and us ; some guns which were posted on the rise in front of our line, having opened upon them, made them change their ground ; and the 88th regiment (Connaught Rangers) being detached from our division, led on by the heroic General M'Kinnon, (who commanded our right brigade,) charged them furiously, and drove them back through the village with great slaughter. Some time previous to this, General Picton had had occasion to check this regiment for some plundering affair they had been guilty of, and he was so offended at their conduct, that in addressing them, he had told them they were the greatest blackguards in the army ; — but as he was always as ready to give praise as censure, where it was due, when they were returning from this gallant and effective charge, he exclaimed, " Well done the brave 88th !" Some of them, who had been stung at his former reproaches, cried out, " Are we the greatest blackguards in the army now ?" The valiant Picton smiled, and replied, " No, no, you are brave and gallant soldiers ; this day has redeemed your character."

At one time during the contest, when the enemy had gained a partial possession of the village, our light troops had retired into a small wood above it, where they were huddled together without any regularity ; a French officer, while leading on his men, having been killed in our front, a bugler of the 83d regiment starting out between the fire of both parties, seized his gold watch ; but he had scarcely returned, when a cannon shot from the enemy came whistling past him, and he fell lifeless on the spot. The blood started out of his nose and ears, but with the exception of this, there was neither wound nor bruise on his body; the shot had not touched him. The phenomenon here described has been the subject of much discussion among medical men, some attributing it to the shot becoming electrical and parting with its electricity in passing the body; while others maintain, that the ball does strike the individual obliquely, and although there is no appearance of injury on the surface, there always exists serious derangement of the system internally.

We had regained possession of the village a short time after, and got a little breathing time ; a few of our lads and some of the 79th were standing together, where a poor fellow lay a few paces from them weltering in his blood. As he belonged to the 79th, they went over to see who he was ; the ball had entered the centre of his forehead, and passed through his brain, and to all appearance he was completely dead ; but when any of the flies which were buzzing about the wound, entered it, a convulsive tremor shook his whole body, and the muscles of his face became frightfully distorted; there could scarcely be imagined any thing more distressing, or more appalling to the spectator.

Within the walls of the old chapel, where our men and the French had got under cover alternately, as they were pursuing or pursued, there lay a mixture of various nations, wounded, dying, and dead, and presented a sight which no language could describe, raving, groaning, calling for assistance and drink. He must have had a hardened heart who could have beheld it without feeling deeply. One noble looking fellow of the imperial guard lay wounded through both legs, and one of his arms shattered ; he had been plundered and stripped half naked. One of our light company, of the name of James Cochran, as much distinguished for bravery in the field as for a mild and humane temper, (for they are not incompatible,) seeing the poor fellow lying in this plight, unable to help himself, and the flies irritating his wounds — threw his own blanket over him — brought some water, and left it and some bread with him ; but what was his mortification on returning that way, to find that he was again plundered of all, and left as before. The poor fellow, however, seemed to feel the most lively gratitude for what Cochran had done, and wished to force some money on him, which had escaped the search of his plunderers.

After the various taking and retaking of the village, night again found us in possession of it. On the 6th no attempt was made to renew the attack, and, as on the 4th, the army on each side were employed in burying the dead, and looking after the wounded. On the 7th we still remained quiet ; but on this day the whole French army were reviewed on the plain by Massena. On the night of the 7th, some companies of our regiment were detached on picquet to the ravine on the left of the town, and during the night I was placed one of the outpost sentries. The French picquets occupied the opposite side, and the distance between us was but trifling. The night was very dark, and the place where I was posted was amongst bushes and trees, near the river's edge. All was still, save the river gurgling over its rocky bed, or when a slight breeze set the leaves in motion, and the *qui vive* of the French sentinels could be distinctly heard.

I had been some time posted, ruminating on the awful responsibility attached to my post, as it was probable the enemy might make an attack during the night. I was straining my eyes through the thick darkness towards the spot where I imagined the French sentry was placed, at the same time eagerly listening. In the midst of this anxiety I was alarmed by the noise of something rustling among the bushes near the river. The thought struck me instantly that it must be the French picquet advancing on my post; my first impulse was to fire in the direction of the noise, but I recollected that there was a possibility of giving a false alarm, and I felt myself in a strange dilemma — I could not fire until I ascertained that it was an enemy, and before that could be done I might be surprised and killed. The noise ceased, but still I was all attention, for this did not give me confidence; sticking my ramrod in the ground, I put my ear to it, but could hear nothing. I now assumed more courage, and almost persuaded myself I had been deceived. At that moment, a burst through the bushes in my front, accompanied by a horrid yell, robbed me of all presence of mind. In the desperation which fear sometimes inspires, I dashed forward against the object of my alarm with my charged bayonet, and plunged it in the foe; he fell, and for a few seconds I had not power to move. Silence was now only broken by the smothered groan of my dying victim; and recovering myself a little, I stooped to ascertain whether it was really a French grenadier I had slain, but found it was only a poor ass's colt which had strayed from its dam, and browsing about had thus been the unconscious cause of my alarm.

On the 8th the French sentries were withdrawn at day light, the main body of the enemy having retired during the night, to the woods between Fuentes and Gallejos. On the 9th they broke up, and retired from their position; and on the 10th they had recrossed the Agueda without having accomplished the relief of Almeida. On the morning of the 11th, however, about one o'clock, A. M. the garrison having blown up part of the fortifications, made their escape past the troops who had blockaded them, in consequence of the darkness of the night—some said the carelessness of the regiments on that duty. One

regiment in particular was blamed, but the excuse
might be more properly sought for in the masterly
dispositions which the governor (General Brenier)
had made, both for the escape of the garrison, and
the subsequent retreat.

CHAPTER II.

WE were again quartered in Fuentes, but the place
was sadly altered ; the inhabitants had fled, many of
the houses were destroyed, and all of them plundered ;
although the dead had been in general buried, there
still remained some bodies lying about swelled and
blackened by the heat of the sun ; the ground was
strewed with uniform caps and clothing, and the streets
were dyed with the blood of the combatants ; the whole
place wore an air of desolation and wretchedness.
We were only a few days there when we received
orders to march along with the 7th division, for the
purpose of laying siege to Badajos, a fortified town
on the Spanish frontier, in the province of Estrema-
dura. The distance between Fuentes and Badajos
might be about 40 leagues, Portuguese, (150 miles ;)
we proceeded by Alfeyates, Penamacore, and Castello
Branco, where we were quartered in a Franciscan
convent for two days. From thence we marched to
Villa Valhe, where boats were ready for us to cross
the Tagus. This was a romantic spot : the side on
which we lay previous to passing was a plain, the
opposite one a mountain, which rose abrupt and precipitous, clothed with trees and bushes to the top,
throwing its dark shade on the bosom of the river,
which rolled along at its base, deep, dark, and rapid.
Here it was reported Lord Wellington had lost his
two orderly dragoons some days before. He had

received information that the French army under
Marshal Soult was coming down in great force on
Beresford's army, and he was so anxious to get forward, that when he came to the river, and found the
bridge of boats not thrown across, he plunged in
followed by his orderly dragoons, (certainly a most
hazardous attempt;) the current was so strong that
the dragoons with their horses were carried away and
drowned, his lordship only escaping by the superior
strength of his horse.

Having crossed the river, we proceeded by a
winding road cut in the face of the hill to Niza; this
was a most distressing march, being up hill the whole
way. Passing Alpalhao, we reached Porto Legre
two days after. From this we marched to Arronches,
and from thence to Campo Mayor, situated about ten
miles from Badajos, where we remained for some
days, while preparations were making for the siege.
This was a very handsome town, walled, but very
slightly fortified; one building in particular, a small
chapel, called Capella des Ossos, is worth noticing.
It had been erected to commemorate some massacre.
The whole interior was built up with skulls and
thigh bones, laid across, and two skeletons, one on
each side, were built into the wall.

On the 25th of May we marched towards Badajos,
which the French had gained possession of in the
beginning of the campaign, through the treachery of
the Spanish governor, at the very time Lord Wellington had promised relief, and given orders to hold
out. When we first came in sight of the town, its
spires appeared above the hill which rises on the
Campo Mayor side of it, as if the town lay immediately beneath, but we found it was still a great way
off; we then took a circuitous route to the left of the
town, and having crossed the Guidiana, we encamped
about three miles from it, on the slope of a small hill
which skirted the Elvas road; here we constructed

huts in the best manner we could, with bushes and branches of trees.

On the night of the 29th, the stores and ordnance having arrived, we marched down towards the town, for the purpose of breaking ground : it was fortunately very dark, and as we kept the greatest silence, the French were not aware of our approach. When we reached the place where it was intended we should open the trenches, we formed a line across the front of the town, where two thousand intrenching tools had been laid. We were then told our safety depended on expedition, for if the French discovered our presence before we had worked ourselves under cover, a warm salute might be expected. The officers were dependent on our exertions for safety ; and it was remarked in what kind and familiar tones some of those spoke, who, in greater security, would have acted the blustering tyrant. I cannot understand what makes many officers so supercilious, haughty, and morose to their men, when, by a little good humour, or friendly feeling displayed, I have no doubt they might not only make themselves beloved, but have their orders much better obeyed.

We now commenced work vigorously, and in six hours were under cover, without the French having discovered our presence. The operations of the siege were now carried on with great vigour on both sides of the river Guidiana ; the opposite one was conducted by the seventh division against fort St Christoval, an outwork that protected the advance to the bridge. By the second of June we had two batteries playing on the walls, and four were opened by the seventh division on fort St Christoval. The guns were partly served by Portuguese artillery, who behaved extremely well. The troops were told off in two parties, relieving each other every twenty-four hours.

A communication was kept up between the several trenches, and a covered way formed, which prevented the men from being so much exposed in going to, and returning from the camp; but still we suffered severely from the enemy's shot and shell, with which they now plied us hotly, having their guns constantly ready to fire at even a single individual if he put his head above the trench; and the shells fired from the garrison were thrown so as to make them fall in it. At night we could see them by the fuse, and were often enabled to get out of their way; in the day, we ran more risk, although we could still distinguish them from shot, by the whistling sound they made coming through the air.

The second or third night after the trenches were opened, Dennis and I were down on the working party. Captain S——, already mentioned, was one of the officers. They were telling off a covering party, who were to go out in front, to prevent any sudden surprise by the enemy making a sortie, when the word "shell!" was given. All eyes were instantly turned on it, watching its direction, that they might run in the opposite one. Captain S——, although so valiant on parade, seemed to have no predilection for a " glorious death" more than his neighbours; and he, in company with a brother captain, headed the retreat. They had not gone many paces, when notice was given of another shell falling in the direction they were running. By this time the first had fallen short of the trench, and a retrograde movement took place; but the captains were now in a bad plight, for the crowd was so condensed in the direction they had to go, that there was no getting through. The shell was giving intelligence by its quickened revolutions, that it was falling, but there was no means of escape, the whole were fairly wedged in and had fallen on each other; and had the shell burst among them, it would have made dreadful havock. As I threw myself down by the side of the trench, I perceived Captain S—— running about like a chicken

in a coop, seeking an opening by which he might
escape, but finding none he wormed his head into
the crowd, which had fallen in his front, and thus
remained. The shell fell in a direction that placed
me in imminent danger; but I could not refrain from
laughing at his ludicrous position; it burst, however,
without doing any injury.

On one occasion, when Dennis and I were on
duty in the trench, and at one of the batteries
with some others, at the formation of an embrasure,
we had nearly completed it, but it still required
opening and facing off towards the enemy; this
was a very hazardous business, as we were sure of
a volley of cannon shot, the moment we mounted
the parapet. "Come, my brave fellows," said the
superintending engineer officer, "which of you will
volunteer to go outside, and form the embrasure?"
Dennis and I were standing close by him, and jumped
upon the top of the breastwork. We were followed
by two more, but had scarcely appeared, when a
cannon shot striking the parapet close where I stood,
covered me with earth. "Never mind," said Dennis,
"to miss is as good as a mile." He scarcely had
finished, when he was served in the same manner—
no way dispirited, he exclaimed, "Time about is fair
play." One of the lads who worked with us began
to show symptoms of fear, "Don't be afraid," said
Dennis, "you'll never die till your time come." His
eloquence did not seem to take effect. "Go into
the trench," said Dennis, "we will do without you."
The lad was in the act of doing so, when a shot
struck him, and he fell mortally wounded. Soon
after, our dinners having come down, we were relieved
by others, and called in. The mess I belonged to
had sat down round the camp kettle, and were
beginning to help themselves, when the cry "shell!"
was given; all were to their feet in an instant, for we
found by the noise that it was coming in our direc-

tion. The others endeavoured to make their escape;
whether from a belief in Dennis's doctrine of pre-
destination, I cannot at present recollect, but instead
of running from it, I threw myself down flat in the
embrasure. I had scarcely done so, when the shell
fell within two yards of me. " Now," thought I,
" there is no chance of escape," and during the few
seconds of suspense, while the last part of the fuse
was whizzing in my ear, reflections which would have
occupied an hour at another time, on home, parents,
death, and my future fate, whirled through my mind,
like a wild and giddy dream. The shell burst, and
for a few moments I was bereaved of recollection.
Coming to myself, I scrambled out from amongst the
stuff with which I was covered. " Are you kilt ? "
asked Dennis, running up to me with an expression
of real concern : looking to myself to see whether I
was wounded, I replied, " No ;" but I had been well
frightened. " That's right, my boy," said he, " I
don't believe the shot's made that will kill any of us.
Many's the long yarn about this business I'll be after
telling to the ould women of Ireland yet."

On the sixth, the breach in fort St Christoval being
considered practicable, a detachment of the different
regiments composing the seventh division was
selected to storm it : being at night we could not see
the attack farther than the flash of their fire-arms,
which, from our encampment, looked like an exhibition of fire works ; but we understood that from the
nature of the impediments thrown in the way, although
they had advanced under a heavy discharge of shot
and shell from the town, and musketry and hand
grenades from the garrison, they were unable to
succeed, and were ordered to retire. The firing was
continued upon the breach for three days longer, and
a second attempt was made to carry it on the evening
of the ninth, with another detachment of the seventh
division. The attack was made with the utmost

gallantry, and they advanced intrepidly to the foot of the breach ; but the same obstacles presented themselves as on the first attempt, and after having suffered most severely, without being able to effect a lodgment, they were again ordered to retire. The loss in officers and men was considerable.

The men of our division, unaccustomed to failure in any enterprise, and perhaps rather conceited, were inclined to attribute the failure of these attempts to the troops composing the seventh division being mostly foreigners ; but in this opinion it is likely they were wrong, as in the subsequent storming of the town, in the ensuing year, the obstacles thrown in the way were sufficient to resist even the bravest British troops. A day or two after this affair, intelligence having been received that Soult was advancing with a large army, for the purpose of relieving Badajos, Wellington deemed it prudent to raise the siege, converting it into a blockade. From this until the seventeenth we were busy withdrawing the guns and stores, which were sent to the garrison of Elvas, as a place of security, and on the seventeenth quitted our investment of the place, and withdrew to Campo Mayor. On the morning we left it, the French cavalry were out skirmishing with a party of the eleventh hussars, who were covering our retreat, and followed us the greater part of the way.

While in Campo Mayor, where we remained for some time, a German of the sixtieth regiment, a Frenchman, and two Italians, belonging to the Chasseurs Britannique, were shot for desertion, — the former belonging to our division, the latter three to the seventh. On the morning that the sentence of the first was carried into execution, the division was assembled outside of the town, where they formed three sides of a square. The prisoner was marched past the various regiments, accompanied by the chaplain of the division, and the guard appointed to

shoot him. When his devotions were finished, he
was blindfolded by the provost marshal, and placed
kneeling on the brink of his grave already open to
receive him. He gave the signal, and the next moment
he fell pierced by half a dozen musket balls. The
different regiments then marched past the body,
receiving the word " eyes left" as they past him.

I was on the general provost guard, the evening
previous to those of the seventh division being shot.
The sergeants came with the company's books to
settle their accounts ; the two Italians were in
paroxysms of agony, crying and wringing their
hands. The behaviour of the Frenchman, who had
been taken prisoner, had volunteered into the Chasseurs Britannique, and afterwards deserted from them
to his countrymen, formed a strong contrast to that
of the others. Calm and dignified, he seemed to feel
no fear of death, nor did any complaint pass his lips,
save an occasional exclamation against the injustice
of trying him as a deserter, being a Frenchman. In
his circumstances, he argued it was natural that he
should endeavour to join his friends the first opportunity that offered. When the sergeant was settling
their accounts, the Italians paid no attention to any
thing said to them ; but he discussed every item
with the greatest exactness, and the sergeant wanting
a small coin about the value of a farthing to balance,
he desired him to procure it before he would sign
the ledger ; but though thus exact with the sergeant,
the moment he received his balance, which amounted
to some dollars, he divided every penny of it amongst
his fellow-prisoners. When the Italians received
their money, they sent for brandy, and began to
drink intemperately, endeavouring to drown their
sorrows and sear their minds ; but it had quite a
different effect, for they then broke from all restraint
in the expression of their feelings, and cried and
groaned with agony in such a manner, that they

could be heard at a considerable distance from the
guard-room. In this state they continued until
morning, when they ceased their lamentations, only
because nature was exhausted by their former violence. Quite different was the conduct of the
Frenchman : when the brandy was procured, the
Italians pressed him to take some, but he thanked
them, and refused, " No," said he, throwing a look
of mingled pity and contempt on them, " I need no
brandy to enable me to face death." He continued
to walk about with his arms folded during the whole
evening, without seeming in the least disturbed ;
occasionally, indeed, his countenance softened, and a
tear-drop gathered in his eye, but it was not permitted to linger there ; and as if ashamed of showing
the least want of firmness, he assumed redoubled
inflexibility of countenance.

I could not help admiring his manly fortitude and
courage. I had no opportunity of speaking to him,
without being intrusive ; but in silence I watched the
expression of his face, with a feeling I could hardly
describe. It was reported that he was a brother of
Marshal Soult : the truth of this I cannot pretend to
affirm. He was, however, certainly a man of a noble
mind and independent spirit. About midnight he
lay down and slept soundly until near the hour of
execution ; his courage seemed to be now even more
exalted. He cleaned himself with the greatest nicety,
conversed with his fellow prisoners cheerfully, and
endeavoured, although without success, to infuse
some courage into the poor Italians. The guard
having arrived, he took leave of those prisoners who
were confined with him ; and to one, with whom he
was more familiar than the others, he gave some private injunction, and on parting with him he said
emphatically, " Remember, I die a Frenchman." He
marched off to the place of execution with the same
collected intrepidity he had before evinced, and I

understood afterwards, that his demeanour on the ground where he was shot, was similar to that displayed while a prisoner. All admired his courage, and were sorry for his fate.

CHAPTER III.

LEAVING Campo Mayor we returned by the same route that we had come, re-crossing the Tagus at Ville Valhe, and halting at Albergeria, a village near the place from whence we had first set out to go to Badajos, and not far distant from Ciudade Roderigo, in which the French had a garrison. We remained here in camp for some time, very busy making fascions and gabions to fortify the position which our army had taken. While we lay in this encampment the weather was uncommonly warm, and the bushes and long grass, among which we had raised temporary huts, were rendered inflammable as tinder; the grass on our left had been by accident set fire to, and the flames soon spread in every direction. The whole of the soldiers were turned out to stop its progress; but in spite of their endeavours, it communicated to a wood which lay on the face of a steep hill in our rear, burning with the greatest fury. The night happened to be very dark, and there could scarcely be any thing more grand or awful: the whole mountain was in a blaze of fire, and the noise and crackling of the trees burning was like the noise of a hurricane; it was a scene which a person could stand and gaze at it in mute astonishment, without being able to define the sensations which were raised in his mind. The wind fortunately carried the fire to the rear of our encampment, or it might have been productive of great injury, by blowing up the ammunition, &c.

From this place we removed more in advance to

Robleda, a Spanish village. The people seemed to be comfortable, the houses were extremely clean, and here we had a fair specimen of the manners of the Spanish peasantry. All their domestic concerns were conducted with the greatest regularity: they were very punctual in the observance of all the rites of their church, and in catechising their children. They seemed to me to be really pious, and from their prudent industrious habits, happy and contented. The people I was quartered on were uncommonly friendly; being able to speak the language a little, and Dennis being of the same religious persuasion, we were almost considered as members of the family. The inhabitants were mostly all employed in agriculture, and were very lively and fond of amusement, particularly of singing and dancing; here they had their fandangos and boleras every Sunday evening after mass, dressed in the gay and becoming fashion of their country, and many a ditty was chaunted in praise of General Mina and Don Julian. The village, however, proved very unhealthy: during the short time we were in it, eighty or ninety of our men left us to go to the rear sick, most of them with fever and ague, and among the number my poor friend Dennis.

On the 24th September, in consequence of the advance of the French, we were ordered to march from this to El-Bodon; and it was with unfeigned regret on both sides, I believe, that we parted with our friendly hosts.

On the 25th, at two o'clock in the morning, we were turned out to the heights above the town, which our brigade, along with one of cavalry, occupied. Our position was on a range of heights, over which passed the road leading from Roderigo to Fuente Guinaldo. Here we lay under arms until about eight o'clock in the morning, when we perceived, issuing out of Roderigo, one column of cavalry after another advancing along the road towards our post, to the amount of about forty squadrons; these were succeeded by twelve or fourteen battalions of infantry, with twelve piece of cannon. Our situation now began to get precarious, being completely separated from the rest of the army, by at least six miles. Still we had no orders to retreat — and to retreat without orders is not the custom of the British army.

One of the regiments was posted on the hill over which the road passed, and when it was seen that the French were bent upon advancing in that direction, two more regiments, the 77th British, 21st Portuguese, and the brigade of cavalry, were sent to reinforce them.

This was scarcely done, when the advanced squadrons of the enemy's cavalry and artillery made a furious attack on this post, and succeeded in taking two piece of Portuguese cannon. The Portuguese artillery behaved bravely, having stood until actually cut down at their guns, which were posted on a rising ground to the right. The 5th regiment was now ordered to charge, and they succeeded in retaking the guns. While this was going on on the right, we were attacked by another body of cavalry in front, which was met and repulsed with determined bravery by the 77th regiment. Our cavalry also were warmly engaged, and charged different bodies of the enemy which ascended on the left. Here we kept our post gallantly, surrounded by about two thousand cavalry —until at last the French infantry being brought up, we were ordered to retreat in squares on Fuente Guinaldo, supported only by the small body of cavalry already mentioned. The French cavalry seeing us preparing for retreat, rushed furiously on, and the various squares were now successively charged by powerful masses of their cavalry, one in particular on three faces of the square, but they halted, and repulsed them with the utmost steadiness

and gallantry. The French in those charges suffered
severely, having a tremendous fire poured in on them
each time. As they rushed on with impetuosity,
when they were brought to a dead stop by the points
of our bayonets, they were thrown into the greatest
confusion, and were brought down by our shot in
numbers. The whole now proceeded to retreat in
excellent order, at an ordinary pace, keeping exact
distances, ready to form up in the event of a charge
being made.

We were much annoyed by shot and shell from
the heights where the French artillery were posted,
some of which falling in the squares did great mischief,
killing and wounding several of our men, and blowing
up our ammunition. We had about six miles to
retreat in this manner before we reached the body of
the army, with the French cavalry hanging on our
flanks and rear, some of whom had even the audacity
to ride to our front, and having taken part of our
baggage, brought it back close past our columns : we
could render no assistance, as our own safety wholly
depended on keeping ourselves ready to form square.
Here General Picton showed that coolness and intrepidity for which he was so much distinguished ; for
some time he rode at the head of our square, while a
strong body of French hung on our right, waiting a
favourable opportunity to charge. The captain who
commanded us (both field officers being sick) was
throwing many a fearful glance at them, and was
rather in a state of perturbation— " Never mind the
French," said Picton, " mind your regiment ; if the
fellows come here, we will give them a warm reception."

At length we came in sight of the rest of our army,
and the main body of the French hung back, but we
were escorted into the very lines by their advanced
guard. Here, however, they met with a warm reception from some squadrons of our cavalry, which made

them retreat. We halted in rear of Fuente Guinaldo, where an intrenched camp had been formed, and remained here that night and next day, during which the French, having brought forward their infantry, took post on a hill opposite, and we expected an engagement ; but Lord Wellington, for good reasons, no doubt, deemed it more prudent to retire. When night came, we were ordered to kindle a great number of fires, for the purpose of making the French believe we still remained in our encampment. Two hours after, we commenced our retreat, leaving the fires burning brightly, and marched all night ; the road we travelled was uncommonly narrow, and various impediments in the way often caused the rear to halt. The fatigue we had undergone the preceding two or three days, and the almost total want of sleep during that time, completely overcame us ; the moment a halt was made, we dropped down on the ground fast asleep, and it was by the greatest exertion that we were able to rouse ourselves to proceed. So overpowering was its effects, that I would have been content to be taken prisoner, or even to suffer death, I dare say, had it been the alternative, had I been allowed to sleep. Indeed, some of the men could not resist its effects, and stepping aside off the road, threw themselves down, and yielded to its influence, although certain of being taken by the enemy, which they accordingly were. Next day we halted in a meadow, where, having our rations served out, we proceeded on to a village, near which our light division and cavalry had a severe skirmish with the French, whom they repulsed. The enemy then retreated to their old position, and we were quartered in a Portuguese village, on the frontiers, within a few leagues of Roderigo, where we remained until January, 1812. This was a miserable dirty place, with a few poor wretched inhabitants in it. It was designated by the soldiers, the " Hungry Village ;" as, to answer some purpose which we were then unacquainted with, we had only half rations during the greater part of the time we were in it ; to add to the rest, the officer in temporary command of the regiment at that time, was ignorant of his duty, which, in conjunction with a naturally cruel and vindictive disposition, bade fair to ruin the regiment in the few months he had the command of it. I shall not trace his pedigree to the low origin from whence he sprung, because, had he been a good man, it would only have enhanced his merit ; nor shall I particularize the deformity of his person, which he could not help ; but there will be no harm in giving a specimen of his mode of discipline while in command of the regiment, particularly as it forms a strong contrast to that of an officer whom I shall have occasion to mention in the course of this narrative.

Having neither the education nor the breeding of a gentleman, he felt jealous in the company of the officers, and lived in a retired and sullen manner He generally passed his time in gossiping with his barber or his cook, or indeed any of the men, with an affectation of entering into all their concerns. By this and eaves-dropping he became acquainted with little circumstances which another commanding officer would have disdained to listen to, and which he always made a bad use of. The full extent of his malevolent disposition was not known, however, until he got command of the regiment, when he introduced flogging for every trivial offence — in fact, the triangles were generally the accompaniment of every evening parade. In addition to this, he invented more disgraceful and torturing modes of inflicting the punishment; but all this was not enough, — he ordered that defaulters should have a patch of yellow and black cloth sewed on the sleeve of the regimental jacket, and a hole cut in it for every time they were flogged. The effects of this soon became visible : as good men were liable to be punished for the slightest fault, the barrier between them and hardened ill-doers was broken down, and as they had lost respect in their own eyes, they either became broken-hearted and inefficient soldiers, or grew reckless of every thing, and lanched into crime; those who were hardened and unprincipled before, being brought by the prevalence of punishment nearer a level with better men, seemed to glory in misconduct. In fact, all ideas of honour and character were lost, and listless apathy and bad conduct were the prevailing features of the corps at this time.

That flogging is notoriously useless in reclaiming men where they are bad, must be evident to every one who knows any thing of the service, and surely it is not politic to disgrace an individual, and break his heart for a casual error. There ought always to be an opening left for a man to retrieve a false step; but once bare his back at the halberts, and you shut it for ever.

In the regiment I. belonged to, I had a good opportunity of marking its effects, and in every instance, I have observed that it changed the individual's character for the worse; he either became broken-hearted and useless to the corps, or shameless and hardened. In two individual cases, its inefficiency to prevent the recurrence of the fault was particularly marked, — the first was desertion, and the second drunkenness. These men had received at various times upwards of two thousand lashes, but the first continued to absent himself, and the other to get drunk, periodically, although they were perfectly sure that flogging would be the result. There were men in the service to whom the excitement produced by ardent spirits seemed as necessary as food; in them this unnatural craving for liquor appeared to me to be a disease, calling for medical treatment more than punishment.

I have no doubt that many commanding officers resorted to corporal punishment from the conviction that it could not be done without; they had tried to dispense with it and could not—but I doubt much whether the experiment was fairly made. They found difficulties at the outset, and that it was more easy to exert their authority than their patience; the consequence was, that flogging was again resorted to, and they satisfied their conscience, by saying that it could not be dispensed with. The real method of accomplishing the desired end was neglected, namely, making themselves acquainted with the character and disposition of the men under their command: this, I believe, many would think incompatible with their dignity; but has not a commanding officer as good a right to make himself acquainted with the dispositions of his men, as the medical officer with their constitutions? If they did so, they would soon find other means than flogging, to make those under their command what they would wish them to be. I am aware that its frequency at one time had the effect of blinding the judgment of officers who possessed both feeling and discrimination; and I have occasionally witnessed a ludicrous waste of sympathy on some inferior animal, where nothing of the kind was felt for their fellow-creature suffering under the lash. For instance, I have known an officer shed tears when his favourite horse broke its leg, and next day exult in seeing a poor wretch severely flogged for being late of delivering an order; but I am happy to say, that the severe discipline of the old school is fast falling into disrepute, and I hope the time is not far distant when it will altogether be abolished.

The lieutenant-colonel joined when Captain L—— had been some time exercising his power in this despotic manner, and being a man of a different stamp, he was not well pleased to find the men of his regiment, whom he had always been proud of, treated

in this manner. His first order was to cut off all the
badges which Captain L—— had ordered on the
men. The frequent punishment was next done
away, and the regiment was again placed on a fair
footing; but the effect of their previous ill usage did
not so soon disappear.

This village was situated at the foot of a high hill,
which was covered with wood, and from which the
wolves were in the habit of coming down at night,
and prowling about the village in quest of prey. On
one post beside the field where the cattle were killed,
the sentries were very much annoyed by them; but I
believe they did no farther injury than devouring
some pigs and an ass, which had been left out all
night. Towards the end of December we were once
or twice marched from our village, to within a short
distance of Roderigo, for the purpose of intercepting
supplies which the French attempted to throw into
it, and the weather being extremely cold, we suffered
much on the journey. The governor of that garrison (General Renaud) while out on a reconnoitering party about this time, was taken prisoner by the
Spanish Guerilla chief, Don Julian.

In the beginning of January, 1812, we were removed for the purpose of besieging Ciudade Roderigo, and we left this miserable village in the midst
of a snow storm, and marched to Morti Agua. Next
day we forded the Agueda, and took up our quarters
in Ceridillo del Arroyo. The siege now commenced;
the light division having succeeded, on the night of
the 8th January, in storming one of the principal
outworks, (the redoubt of St Francisco,) we opened
the trenches the same night, within 600 yards of the
town, the outwark which they had carried forming
part of the first parallel. The weather was so severe,
and the cold so intense, that the army could not
encamp, but the divisions employed at the siege
marched from their different quarters and relieved

each other, alternately, every four-and-twenty hours. Our division took its turn of the duty on the 11th, and the frost was so excessive that we were almost completely benumbed, and nothing but hard working, I believe, kept us from perishing with the cold; indeed, it was said that some Portuguese soldiers actually died from its effects. Still, however, the work went on rapidly, aud on the night of the 13th, another outwork (the fortified convent of Santa Cruz) was stormed by the 1st division, under General Graham. On the 14th, the batteries in the first parallel were formed, and commenced firing from twenty-two pieces of cannon; that same night the fourth division carried all the remaining outworks, and we were established in the second parallel, one hundred and fifty yards from the town, on the 15th, on which day it fell our turn a second time for the duty.

The French kept up a very destructive fire on us during the whole of our operations, and while forming the second parallel they threw out some fire balls to enable them to see where we were working, that they might send their shot in that direction; one of them fell very near where a party were working, and by its light completely exposed them to the view of the enemy; a sergeant belonging to our regiment, of the name of Fraser, seeing the danger to which they were exposed, seized a spade, and jumping out of the trench, regardless of the enemy's fire, ran forward to where it was burning, and having dug a hole, tumbled it in and covered it with earth.

On the morning of the 18th, a battery of seven guns was opened in the second parallel, while those in the first still continued their fire upon the walls. On the 19th our division again took their turn of the duty; but as the breaches were now considered practicable, the other troops destined for the attack

were also assembled, it being Lord Wellington's
intention to storm it that night.

The attack was directed to be made in five different columns : the two right composed of part of
our division, under the command of Major Ridge of
the 5th regiment, and Colonel O'Toole of the 2d
Caçadores, were to protect the attack of the third
column, (composed of our right brigade commanded
by General M'Kinnon,) upon the principal breach ;
the left of this assault, was to be covered by part of
the .light division, who were, at the same time, to
ascend the breaches on the left ; while General Pack's
brigade made a false attack on the south of the fort.
On the right of the whole, the regiment I belonged
to were to descend into the ditch, for the purpose of
protecting the descent of General M'Kinnon's
brigade against any obstacles which might be thrown
in the way by the enemy.

Thus arranged, some time after it was dark, we
moved down from our encampment towards the
town, and our regiment having formed behind the
walls of an old convent, each section being provided
with a pick-axe and rope, we advanced rank entire
under a heavy fire from the garrison, to the brink of
the trench, where planting the one end of the pick-
axe firmly in the ground, we threw the noose of the
rope over the other, and then descended by it into
the ditch.   After descending, we moved along towards the breach.   Our orders were to remain there,
and protect the right brigade ; but our colonel finding
no obstacles in the way, pushed up the breach, leading on his regiment to the attack ; the 5th regiment,
which also belonged to the covering party, joined us
as we ascended, and together we succeeded in
establishing ourselves on the ramparts, in spite of the
obstinate resistance made by the French.   The other
troops advancing at the same time, we were masters

of the town in half an hour from the commencement
of the attack ; but the gallant General M'Kinnon was
killed by the springing of a mine, just as we gained
the ramparts. The last time he was seen alive was
when addressing a young officer who had displayed
much courage,—" Come," said he, " you are a fine lad,
you and I will go together." The next moment the
mine sprung. In the morning his body was got a
short distance from the place, wounded and blackened
by the explosion. He was much regretted, for he
was an intelligent, brave, and enterprising officer.
General Crawford, a brave and much beloved officer,
who commanded the light division, was also mortally
wounded in the assault.

The French had behaved well during the siege,
and made a tolerable resistance at the breaches the
night of the storm ; but they appeared either to be
panic struck, not expecting us to storm the town so
soon, or the individual who commanded wanted
ability, for the dispositions made for the defence
were a mere nothing, in comparison to those at
Badajos, when that town was taken some time after.
In mounting the breach, we found great difficulty in
ascending, from the loose earth slipping from under
our feet at every step, and throwing us down ; the
enemy at the same time pouring their shot amongst
us from above. After having gained possession of
the ramparts, the enemy retreated into a square in
the centre of the town, where they were pursued, and
gave up their arms.

Among the prisoners taken, were eighteen deserters
from our army, who were subsequently tried and
shot. The town was partially plundered by those
who had straggled from their regiments, but the
different columns remained formed on the ramparts
until day-night, when a party from each regiment
were sent to bury the dead, and collect the wounded,
and I was one of the number. The first we found

was Captain W. a brave and good officer. He fell
mortally wounded near the head of the breach, while
cheering on his men to the assault.

Among the wounded lay Lieutenant T. whom we
used to call Robinson Crusoe, from his wearing very
large whiskers, and always carrying a goat skin
haversack, in which he kept the greater part of his
necessaries, including his pipe and tobacco, of which
he was very fond. The other officers rather shunned
his company, from his not being very exact in his
dress, and eccentric in his habits; but he was well
liked by the soldiers, being an excellent officer, and
brave as a lion.

In this respect he was worth a hundred dandies.
A few moments before he received the wound, he
dragged a minikin officer from a hiding-place, and
brandishing his sword over him, threatened to cut
him down if he did not advance. But the poor fellow
did not go many paces farther himself, when he was
brought down by a grape shot; yet still he continued
to cheer on, and encourage the men who were
ascending.

On the ascent of the breach, lay many dead, and
among the rest my ill-fated friend Sandy, whom I
have had already occasion to mention, as parting
from his wife at Jersey. When I saw him stretched
lifeless on the breach, that scene flashed full upon my
memory, and I could not but remark how true his
wife's forebodings had turned out.

By taking the town, we became masters of one
hundred and fifty-three piece of cannon, including
the heavy train of the French army, and a great
number of stores. The Governor, (General Banier,)
seventy-eight officers, and one thousand seven hundred men, were taken prisoners.

Our division was marched out of the town in the
morning, and returned to the village where we were
quartered. On the way home we lost one of our

men, and we never heard of him after. It was suspected that he either perished among the snow, which lay thick on the ground, or that he was murdered by some of the peasantry.

CHAPTER IV.

AFTER remaining a few days in Ceridillo del Arroyo, we removed to Villa Mayor, where we remained until we received orders to march back our old route to Badajos, which we invested on the 17th of March. Our division again taking the left of the Guidiana, along with the 4th and light, while the right was occupied by a brigade of General Hamilton's division, we broke ground rather to the left of our old trenches, within about two hundred yards of Fort Picurini, a strong out-work.

On the 19th the enemy made a sortie from one of the gates, a little to the right of our trenches, with two thousand men ; but they were almost immediately driven in, without effecting any thing, having suffered severely.

On the 25th we opened six batteries with twenty-eight piece of cannon ; and having kept up a heavy fire on Fort Picurini during the day, for the purpose of destroying the defences, when it was dark, a detachment of five hundred men of our division, under the command of Major General Kempt, were ordered to storm it. They were formed in three parties, who attacked at different places at the same time ; and they succeeded, after an obstinate resistance, in gaining possession of it. Two hundred men garrisoned the place, out of which one hundred and sixty were killed, or drowned in the overflow of the river.   The colonel commanding, three other officers, and eighty-six men, were taken prisoners.

Seven cannon were found in the place, besides some stores. During the assault, the enemy made a sortie from the town, with a view either to recover the place, or cover the retreat of the soldiers who manned it; but they were driven in by a party of the detachment stationed to protect the attack.

In this affair we lost a great number of officers and men, some of them after the place was taken, the enemy having bombarded the fort from the town, when they found we were in possession of it.

The second parallel was now opened within three hundred yards of the town, in which two batteries commenced firing on the 28th. During this time the weather was so bad, and the rains so heavy, that we were working in the trenches up to the knees in mud, and the river swelled to such a height, that the pontoon bridge, over which we crossed the Guidiana, was carried away. On the 29th another sortie was made by the enemy on the right; but they were repulsed by General Hamilton's division. On the 31st twenty-seven piece of cannon were opened in the second parallel, on the walls of the town; and the firing was continued with great effect until the 4th, when another battery of six guns was opened. Practicable breaches were effected on the 5th, and we were turned out that night to storm the town; but the enemy having made formidable preparations for the defence, the attack was deferred until next night, during which time all the guns in the second parallel were brought to bear upon the breaches. This delay was productive of very serious feeling throughout the succeeding day, as we were warned at the time to be ready to storm the town the next night.

Various were the effects produced on different individuals. There was an unusual talking of relations, a recalling to mind of scenes forgotten; a flow of kindly feeling which softened down the rough soldier into something milder and more pleasing

Many letters were written during that day to absent friends, in a more affectionate style than usual ; and many injunctions given and taken, about writing, in the event of the fall of either party, to their relations.

The nearer the time drew for the intended attack, the more each individual seemed to shrink within himself; yet still nothing of fear or doubt of our success was expressed, — every feeling displayed was natural and manly. At length night came, and the appointed hour for turning out.

It was dark and gloomy ; not a single star shewed its head; the air was still, not a sound could be heard but the noise of the field cricket, and the croaking of frogs ; every word of command was given in a whisper, and the strictest silence enjoined, which I believe was unnecessary ; few felt inclined to speak. At last the order was given to advance, and with palpitating hearts we commenced our march — slow and silent, a dead-weight hanging on every mind ; had we been brought hurriedly into action, it would have been different, but it is inconsistent with the nature of man not to feel as I have described, in such a situation. The previous warning—the dark and silent night—the known strength of the place—the imminent danger of the attack,—all conspired to produce it. Yet this feeling was not the result of want of courage ; for I never witnessed any thing like the calm intrepidity displayed in the advance, after we came within range of the enemy's cannon. Being apprized of our intentions, they threw out fire-balls in every direction, and from total darkness, they changed the approaches to the garrison into a state light as day ; by this means they were enabled to see the direction of our columns, and they opened a fire of round and grape shot which raked through them, killing and wounding whole sections. A circumstance occurred at this

time, which may be worthy of notice :—A man who
had been very remarkable for his testy disposition,
and inveterate habit of swearing on all occasions,
happened to hit his foot against a stone, and
stumbled; this vexed him, and uttering an oath, he
wished a shot would come and knock his brains
out; he had scarcely finished these words, when a
grape shot struck him in the forehead, and literally
fulfilled the rash wish.   We still advanced, silent as
before, save the groaning of our wounded comrades,
until we reached a sort of moat about fifty feet wide,
formed by the inundation of the river; here we had
to pass, rank entire, the passage being only capable
of admitting one at a time.   On this place the enemy
had brought their guns to bear, and they kept up
such a fire of grape and musketry on it, that it was
a miracle any of us escaped.   When we reached the
other side we formed again, and advanced up the
glacis, forcing our way through the pallisades, and
got down into the ditch.   The ladders by which we
had to escalade the castle were not yet brought up,
and the men were huddled on one another in such
a manner that we could not move; we were now
ordered to fix our bayonets.   When we first entered
the trench, we considered ourselves comparatively
safe, thinking we were out of range of their shot, but
we were soon convinced of our mistake, for they
opened several guns from angles which commanded
the trench, and poured in grape shot upon us from
each side, every shot of which took effect, and every
volley of which was succeeded by the dying groans
of those who fell.   Our situation at this time was
truly appalling.   The attack had commenced at the
breaches towards our left, and the cannon and musketry which played upon our troops from every
quarter of the town attacked, kept up a continual roll
of thunder, and their incessant flash one quivering
sheet of lightning; to add to the awfulness of the

scene, a mine was sprung at the breach, which carried up in its dreadful blaze the mangled limbs and bodies of many of our comrades.

When the ladders were placed, each eager to mount, crowded them in such a way that many of them broke, and the poor fellows who had nearly reached the top, were precipitated a height of thirty or forty feet, and impaled on the bayonets of their comrades below; other ladders were pushed aside by the enemy on the walls, and fell with a crash on those in the ditch; while more who got to the top without accident were shot on reaching the parapet, and tumbling headlong, brought down those beneath them. This continued for some time, until at length a few having made a landing good on the ramparts, at the expense of their lives, enabled a greater number to follow. When about a company had thus got collected together, we formed and charged round the ramparts, bayoneting the French artillery at their guns. In the direction that the party I was with took, they had drawn out a howitzer loaded to the very muzzle, pointed it towards us, and a gunner had the match ready to fire, when he was brought down by one of our party; in this direction we charged until we reached the sally-port communicating with the town. In a short time the whole division were established in possession of the castle, but the contest at the breaches was still severe.

The light and 4th divisions had advanced from the trenches a short time after us, until they reached the covered way; their advanced guards descended without difficulty into the ditch, and advanced to the assault with the most determined bravery, but such was the nature of the obstacles prepared by the enemy at the head of the breach, and behind it, that they could not establish themselves within the place. Repeated attempts were made until after twelve at night, when Lord Wellington finding that success was not to be obtained, and that our division had succeeded in taking the castle, they were ordered back to the ground where they had assembled, leaving the breach covered with dead and wounded. When the governor (Philipon) found the castle was taken, he retreated into fort St Christoval, and at day light in the morning he surrendered with all the garrison ; it had consisted of five thousand men, of which number twelve hundred were killed during the siege.

When the town surrendered, and the prisoners were secured, the gate leading into the town from the castle was opened, and we were allowed to enter the town for the purpose of plundering it. We were scarcely through the gate when every regiment of the division were promiscuously mixed, and a scene of confusion took place which baffles description : each ran in the direction that pleased himself, bursting up the doors and rummaging through the houses, wantonly breaking up the most valuable articles of furniture found in them. Small bands formed, and when they came to a door which offered resistance, half-a-dozen muskets were levelled at the lock, and it flew up ; by this means many men were wounded, for having entered at another door, there was often a number in the house, when the door was thus blown open. The greater number first sought the spirit stores, where having drank an inordinate quantity, they were prepared for every sort of mischief. At one large vault in the centre of the town, to which a flight of steps led, they had staved in the head of the casks, and were running with their hat-caps full of it, and so much was spilt here, that some, it was said, were actually drowned in it. Farther on, a number of those who had visited the spirit store were firing away their ammunition, striving to hit some bells in front of a convent.

The effects of the liquor now began to shew itself,

and some of the scenes which ensued are too dreadful and disgusting to relate ; where two or three thousand armed men, many of them mad drunk, others depraved and unprincipled, were freed from all restraint, running up and down the town, the atrocities which took place may be readily imagined, —but in justice to the army, I must say they were not general, and in most cases perpetrated by cold blooded villains, who were backward enough in the attack. Many risked their lives in defending helpless females, and although it was rather a dangerous place for an officer to appear, I saw many of them running as much risk to prevent inhumanity, as they did the preceding night in storming the town. I very soon sickened of the noise, folly, and wickedness around me, and made out of the town towards the breach. When I arrived at where the attack had been made by the light and 4th divisions, what a contrast to the scene I had just left ! Here all was comparatively silent, unless here and there a groan from the poor fellows who lay wounded, and who were unable to move. As I looked round, several voices assailed my ear begging for a drink of water : I went, and having filled a large pitcher which I found, relieved their wants as far as I could.

When I observed the defences that had been here made, I could not wonder at our troops not succeeding in the assault. The ascent of the breach near the top was covered with thick planks of wood firmly connected together, staked down, and stuck full of sword and bayonet blades, which were firmly fastened into the wood with the points up ; round the breach a deep trench was cut in the ramparts, which was planted full of muskets with the bayonets fixed, standing up perpendicularly, and firmly fixed in the earth up to the locks. Exclusive of this they had shell and hand grenades ready loaded piled on the ramparts, which they lighted and threw down among the assailants. Round this place death appeared in every form, the whole ascent was completely covered with the killed, and for many yards around the approach to the walls, every variety of expression in their countenance, from calm placidity to the greatest agony. Anxious to see the place where we had so severe a struggle the preceding night, I bent my steps to the ditch where we had placed the ladders to escalade the castle. The sight here was enough to harrow up the soul, and which no description of mine could convey an idea of. Beneath one of the ladders, among others lay a corporal of the 45th regiment, who, when wounded, had fallen forward on his knees and hands, and the foot of the ladder had been, in the confusion, placed on his back. Whether the wound would have been mortal, I do not know, but the weight of the men ascending the ladder had facilitated his death, for the blood was forced out of his ears, mouth, and nose.

Returning to the camp, I passed the narrow path across the moat, where many lay dead with their bodies half in the water. When I reached the opposite side, I perceived a woman with a child at her breast, and leading another by the hand, hurrying about with a distracted air, from one dead body to another, eagerly examining each. She came to one whose appearance seemed to strike her, (he was a grenadier of the 83d regiment,) she hesitated some moments, as if afraid to realize the suspicion which crossed her mind. At length, seemingly determined to ascertain the extent of her misery, releasing the child from her hand, she raised the dead soldier, (who had fallen on his face,) and looking on his pallid features, she gave a wild scream, and the lifeless body fell from her arms. Sinking on her knees, she cast her eyes to heaven, while she strained her infant to her bosom with a convulsive gasp ; the blood had fled her face, nor did a muscle of it move ; she seemed inanimate, and all her faculties were absorbed in grief.

The elder child looked up in her face for some time with anxiety ; at last he said, " Mother, why don't you speak to me ? — what ails you ? — what makes you so pale ? — O speak to me, mother, do speak to me ! " A doubt seemed to cross her mind — without noticing the child, she again raised the mangled corpse, looked narrowly at his face, and carefully inspected the mark of his accoutrements — but it was too true — it was her husband. Neither sigh, nor groan, nor tear escaped her ; but sitting down, she raised the lifeless body, and placing his head on her knee, gazed on his face with feelings too deep for utterance. The child now drew himself close to her side, and looking at the bleeding corpse which she sustained, in a piteous tone, inquired, " Is that my father ? is he asleep ? why doesn't he speak to you ? I'll waken him for you" — and seizing his hand, he drew it towards him, but suddenly relapsing his hold, he cried, " O mother ! his hand is cold — cold as ice."

Her attention had been drawn for some moments to the child : at length bursting out, she exclaimed, " Poor orphan ! he sleeps, never to wake again — never, O never, will he speak to you or me !" The child did not seem to understand her, but he began to cry. She continued, " O my God ! my heart will burst, my very brain burns — but I can't cry — Surely my heart is hard — I used to cry when he was displeased with me — and now I can't cry when he is dead ! O my husband ! my murdered husband ! — Ay, murdered," said she, wiping the blood that flowed from a wound in his breast. " O my poor children !" drawing them to her bosom, " what will become of you ?" Here she began to talk incoherently — " Will you not speak to me, William ? — will you not speak to your dear Ellen ? Last night you

told me you were going on guard, and you would
return in the morning, but you did not come — I
thought you were deceiving me, and I came to look
for you."

She now ceased to speak, and rocked backwards
and forwards over the bleeding corpse; but her
parched quivering lip, and wild fixed look, showed
the agonized workings of her mind. I stood not an
unmoved spectator of this scene, but I did not interrupt it. I considered her sorrow too deep and sacred
for commonplace consolation. A woman and two
men of the same regiment who had been in search of
her, now came up and spoke to her, but she took no
notice of them. A party also who were burying the
dead joined them, and they crowded round striving
to console her. I then withdrew, and hastened on
to the camp, my mind filled with melancholy reflections; for many days after I felt a weight on my
mind, and even now I retain a vivid recollection of
that affecting scene. But she was not a solitary
sufferer: many a widow and orphan was made by the
siege and storming of Badajos; our loss amounting
in killed and wounded to about three thousand men.

The camp during that day and for some days after
was like a masquerade, the men going about intoxicated, dressed in the various dresses they had found
in the town; French and Spanish officers, priests,
friars, and nuns, were promiscuously mixed, cutting
as many antics as a mountebank. It was some days
before the army could be brought round to its former
state of discipline. Indeed the giving leave to plunder the town, was productive of nothing but bad consequences, and for the interests of humanity, and the
army at large, I hope such licence may never recur,
should we be again unfortunately plunged in war.

CHAPTER V.

A few days after the town was taken, I took the fever and ague, with which I was so extremely ill, that when we marched, which we did immediately after, I was unable to keep up with my regiment, and was left, with four others, about five leagues from Castello Branco, in charge of a sergeant, who was to endeavour to bring us on ; but being unable to proceed, he was obliged to put us into a house in the small village in which we were left. It was occupied by a poor widow, who had two children ; there was only one apartment in the house, in which there was a loom ; and having crept under it, I lay there for four days without bed or covering, with the exception of an old great coat, my necessaries, which I was unable to carry, having gone forward with the regiment. The poor Portuguese widow had little to give except commiseration, and seemed to feel much for me in particular, as the others could move about a little. I have often heard her, when she thought I was asleep, soliloquizing on the grief it would give my parents, were they to know my situation ; and in her orisons, which she was in the habit of repeating aloud, she did not neglect a petition for the " povre rapaz Englese." * She often brought me warm milk, and pressed me to take a little of it ; I felt very grateful for her sympathy and kindness, but I was too sick to taste it. As we were here without any means of support, the sergeant managed to press five asses to carry us to Castello Branco, where there was a general hospital forming ; on one of these I was mounted, and supported by the man who drove it. I

* Poor English Boy.

took leave of the tender-hearted widow, while the tears stood in her eyes. Such disinterested feeling I was at that time little accustomed to, and it was precious. We proceeded on our journey, but never did I endure such torture as I did on that day, and I often begged of them to allow me to lie down and die.

On the second day we reached our destination, and remained waiting in the street for two hours before the general doctor would look at us. When he did come, his countenance foreboded no good. "What's the matter with you, sir?" said he to me in a scowling tone of voice; "You ought to have been with your regiment; a parcel of lazy skulking fellows—there's nothing the matter with any of you!"

I said nothing, but I looked in his face, with a look which asked him if he really believed what he said, or if he did not read a different story in my pale face and sunken cheek. He seemed to feel the appeal, and softening his countenance he passed on to another. We were then placed along with others, in the passage of a convent, which was converted into an hospital; here I lay that day on the floor, without mattress or covering. Night came, and a burning fever raged through my veins; I called for drink, but there was no one to give it me. In the course of the night I became delirious; the last thing I remember was strange fantastic shapes flitting around me, which now and then catched me up, and flew with me like lightning through every obstacle—then they would hold me over a precipice, and letting me fall, I would continue sinking, with a horrid consciousness of my situation, until my mind was lost in some wild vagary of a different nature. For some days I was unconscious of what was passing, and when I recovered my senses, I found myself in a small apartment with others who had bad fevers, but I was now provided with a mattress and bed-clothes.

A poor fellow, a musician of the 43d regiment, was next birth to me, sitting up in his bed in a fit of delirium, addressing himself to some young females, whom he supposed to be spinning under the superintendence of an old woman, in a corner of the ceiling ; he kept a constant conversation with his supposed neighbours, whom he seemed to think were much in awe of the old dame, and he frequently rose out of his bed to throw up his handkerchief as a signal. When he recovered, the impression was so strong, that he remembered every particular.

There was a great want of proper attendants in the hospital, and many a time I have heard the sick crying for drink and assistance during the whole night, without receiving it. There seemed also to be a scarcity of medical officers during the Peninsular war. I have known wounded men often to be three days after an engagement before it came to their turn to be dressed, and it may be safely calculated that one-half of those men were thus lost to the service. Those medical men we had were not always ornaments of the profession. They were chiefly, I believe, composed of apothecaries' boys, who, having studied a session or two, were thrust into the army as a huge dissecting room, where they might mangle with impunity, until they were drilled into an ordinary knowledge of their business ; and as they began at the wrong end, they generally did much mischief before that was attained. The extent of their medical practice in most disorders was to "blister, bleed, and purge,"——what then ? why "blister, bleed, and purge again." This method of cure with poor wretches who were any thing but over-fed, and whose greatest complaint often was fatigue and want of proper sustenance, was quite à-la-Hornbook, and the sufferers were quickly laid to rest. In the field they did more mischief, being but partially acquainted with anatomy; there was enough of what medical men call *bold practice*. In cutting down upon a ball for the purpose of extracting it, ten chances to one but they severed an artery they knew not how to stem; but this gave no concern to these enterprising fellows, for clapping a piece of lint and a bandage, or a piece of adhesive plaster on the wound, they would walk off very composedly to mangle some other poor wretch, leaving the former to his fate.

Here I may be accused of speaking at random, on a subject I do not understand; but there is no man who served in the Peninsular war, but can bear witness to the truth of what I have stated. I, however, do not pretend to say there were not many exceptions to this character; and in justice to the whole, it must be admitted, that the duties of a surgeon on the Peninsula, were fatiguing and arduous in the extreme. The medical department of the French army was much superior to ours at that time in every respect; this can only be accounted for by the superior opportunity they had of studying anatomy, which in Britain is now almost prohibited — more the pity! Those who have witnessed the evils resulting to the army in particular, from imperfectly educated surgeons, must regret that government does not afford greater facilities to the study.

The ague fits having returned when the severe fever left me, I recovered very slowly; the medicine I received, which was given very irregularly, having done me no good. While in this state, General Sir John Hope, who lately commanded the forces in Scotland, happened to pay a visit to the hospital, and going round the sick with the staff-surgeon, he inquired " What was the prevailing disease?" the reply was,

    " Fever and ague."

Sir John, whose kind and humane disposition is well known, mentioned that he had heard of a cure for that disease among the old women in Scotland, which was considered infallible. The staff-surgeon smiled, and begged to hear what it was. "It is," said the good old general, "simply a large pill formed of spider's web, to be swallowed when the fit is coming on. I cannot pledge myself for its efficacy, but I have heard it much talked of." The staff-doctor gave a shrug, as much to say it was all nonsense, looked very wise, as all doctors endeavour to do, and the conversation dropped. I had been listening eagerly to the conversation, and no sooner was the general gone, than I set out in quest of the specific. I did not need to travel far, and returned to my room prepared for the next fit; when I felt it coming on, I swallowed the dose with the greatest confidence in its virtues, and however strange it may appear, or hard to be accounted for, I never had a fit of the ague after, but got well rapidly, and was soon fit to march for the purpose of joining my regiment, which I overtook at Pollos. They had been quartered for some weeks in a village on the frontiers, from whence they advanced, and having passed Salamanca, were now in this place, which was situated on a rising ground on the bank of the river Douro, our army occupying the one side, and the French the other.

In this place we were in the habit of turning out of the town during the night, and lying under arms in the field; in the day we occupied the village, still wearing our accoutrements. Fuel was uncommonly scarce; the inhabitants in the best of times, having only the pruinings of their vines for that purpose, and we were obliged to cook our victuals with stubble. While here there was an understanding, I believe, between both armies, that each should have the use of the river without molestation, and

our men and the French used to swim in it promiscuously, mixing together, and at times bringing
brandy and wine with them, for the purpose of
treating each other ; but though thus friendly to our
men, the French soldiers studiously avoided coming
near the Portuguese, whom they knew by the dark
colour of their skin. This friendly feeling between our
soldiers and the French was remarkably displayed
during the whole war, whenever we were brought
in position close to each other, or either party were
taken prisoners, and it could only be accounted for
by the respect excited by the bravery of each nation,
and a similar generosity of sentiment, for in this the
French were not deficient. How different were our
feelings in this respect from many of our countrymen at home, whose ideas of the French character
were drawn from servile newspapers and pamphlets,
or even from so low a source as the caricatures in
print shops ; but I myself must confess, in common
with many others, that I was astonished when i came
in contact with French soldiers, to find them, instead
of pigmy spider-shanked wretches, who fed on nothing but frogs and beef tea, stout, handsome looking
fellows, who understood the principles of good living,
as well as any Englishman amongst us ; and whatever
may be said to the contrary, remarkably brave soldiers.

During the time we lay in this position, a German
belonging to our band deserted to the enemy, taking
with him a horse and two mules ; he had taken them
down to the river to drink, and led them through to
the opposite side, in the face of both armies ; when
he reached the opposite bank, the French lifted him
on their shoulders, and leading the cattle behind him,
carried him up to their camp in triumph, cheering all
the way.

From this place, in consequence of orders to that
effect, we retired upon Salamanca, followed by the

enemy, and took up our position about a mile and
a half from that town, on the right bank of the river
Tormes, where we lay until the 22d July. On the
evening of the 21st it came on a dreadful storm of
thunder and lightning, which so terrified the horses
and mules, who were fastened to stakes in the camp,
that they broke loose and ran about in every direction, causing great confusion.

On the morning of the 22d, having recrossed the
Tormes, we took up our position in front of Salamanca, behind the village of Aldea Teja. The enemy,
who had manœuvered during the forenoon, about
two o'clock began to extend their left, and moved
forward on our position, which was now taken up, —
the seventh division on the right, the fourth and fifth
in the centre, while the first and light divisions on
our left were opposed to the enemy's right, and were,
with the fifth division, in reserve. The attack commenced by our division, in four columns, moving
forward supported by a body of cavalry, to turn the
enemy's left : we were led on by General Packenham,
(General Picton having gone to the rear sick a few
days before,) and completely succeeded ; for having
formed across the enemy's flank, we advanced under
a heavy fire from their artillery, overthrowing every
thing before us. The fifth regiment, in attacking a body
of infantry posted on a small height, were furiously
charged by the enemy's cavalry, and thrown into some
confusion : but ours coming up in time, not only
routed them, but cut off the retreat of their infantry,
who were taken prisoners, many of them dreadfully
wounded by our dragoons, some having their arms
hanging by a shred of flesh and skin, and others with
hideous gashes in their faces. In this manner driving
in their left, we came in front of where our artillery
were playing on the enemy ; but no time was lost, for
by marching past in open column, they continued to
fire without interruption, sending their shot through

the intervals between each company, without doing us any injury, although it created rather unpleasant sensations to hear it whistling past us. The enemy's shot and shell were now making dreadful havock. A Portuguese cadet who was attached to our regiment, received a shell in the centre of his body, which, bursting at the same instant, literally blew him to pieces. Another poor fellow receiving a grape shot across his belly, his bowels protruded, and he was obliged to apply both his hands to the wound to keep them in; I shall never forget the expression of agony depicted in his countenance. These were remarkable cases, but the men were now falling thick on every side. During the time we were thus successfully engaged, the fourth and fifth divisions advanced on the enemy's centre, supported by Sir Stapleton Cotton's cavalry, and drove them from one position after another with great slaughter; but they were in some measure retarded in their progress by a fresh body of troops being pushed forward on their left, from a height which the enemy had continued to hold in spite of the efforts of a brigade of our troops under General Pack. This accession of force was so powerful, that the fourth division was now brought up, and success was restored; but the enemy's right, which was reinforced by those who had fled from the left, and who had occupied the heights above-mentioned, still made a stand; the first and light divisions now had their turn of the battle, and attacking them with determined vigour, in a short time succeeded in turning their right. The flanks being now turned, the centre was attacked by the sixth division, supported by ours and the fourth; but the enemy made a brave and most determined resistance, and it was dark before the point was carried.

The French then broke up in great confusion, and fled through the woods towards the fords of the Tormes, pursued by the cavalry and first and light divisions, as long as any of them could be found together. Next morning the pursuit was renewed at day-break by the same troops, who, having crossed the Tormes, came up with the enemy's rear-guard of cavalry and infantry ; they were immediately attacked by our dragoons, and the French cavalry fled, leaving the infantry unprotected, who were charged by the heavy cavalry of our German legion, and the whole body, consisting of three battalions, were taken prisoners.

During the battle, the Spanish army, under Don Carlos d'Espagne, had remained at a respectable distance on a height in our rear without having been engaged ; they seemed to be perfectly contented with seeing us fighting for their country, without having a hand in it themselves ; and when we were successful, they threw up their caps in the air, and cheered as heartily as if they had earned the victory ; they had only one or two men wounded of their whole army, while ours lost nearly the half of its number in killed and wounded.

In this engagement twenty piece of cannon were taken, several ammunition waggons, two eagles, and six colours ; one general, three colonels, three lieutenant colonels, one hundred and thirty officers of inferior rank, and between six and seven thousand prisoners. Four generals were killed and General Marmont severely wounded.

The French continuing their retreat, our army, passing Alba de Tormes and Penaranda, continued their advance towards Madrid, some leagues from which, there was a severe skirmish between the French cavalry and some of our German dragoons. The Portuguese cavalry had been first engaged, but behaving ill, the Germans were obliged to take their place, and soon retrieved the day. When we passed the village where the skirmish had taken place, those who had fallen were lying on the road side, and our attention was drawn particularly to one of the French cavalry, who had received such a dreadful blow, that his head was completely cleft through his brass helmet. Passing on, we encamped about half a league from Madrid on the 11th of August, and in a short time our camp was filled with the inhabitants who had come out to see us, and in their own language, welcomed us as their deliverers. On the 12th, being ordered to march into the town, we were met by the inhabitants carrying branches of laurel, and playing on guitars and tambourines; joy beamed on every countenance, the ladies thronged round the British colours eager to touch them, and the air was rent with acclamations — " Viva los Engleses," echoed from every mouth. The windows were hung with embroidered cloth, and filled with ladies waving their handkerchiefs.

This was a proud day for the British army. Having marched up to the Placa del Sol, we took up our quarters in a large building; but our work was not yet finished. The French having fortified the Retiro, had left a garrison in it, whose outposts were established in the Prado and botanic garden; but that night a detachment having driven them in, broke through the wall in several places, and established themselves in the palace of Retiro, close to the exterior of the enemy's works, enclosing the building called La China. Next morning, the 13th, we were turned out and assembled on the Prado, with scaling ladders ready to attack the works, when they capitulated, and were allowed to march out with the honours of war, the officers their baggage, and soldiers their knapsacks, and surrendered themselves prisoners.

There was found in the garrison one hundred and eighty-nine piece of brass cannon, nine hundred barrels of gunpowder, twenty thousand stand of arms, and considerable magazines of clothing, provisions, and ammunition, with the eagles of the thirteenth and fifty-first regiments. Having relieved their guards, they marched out at four o'clock in the afternoon, two thousand five hundred and six men, among whom were two colonels, four lieutenant colonels, twenty-two captains, and thirty-five subalterns.

We were now peaceably quartered in the town, having time to look about us and recover from our former fatigues. No place could have been better adapted for this than Madrid ; the air was pure and healthy ; wine, fruit, and provision, good and cheap. Here we had food for observation in the buildings, institutions, and manners of the inhabitants, and we ranged about in the environs, and from one street to another, as if we had been in a new world. Madrid has been so often described by writers of ability, that it would be presumption in me to attempt it, even did the limits of this work allow ; but the delightful walks of the Prado, the gardens breathing perfume — the beautiful fountains — the extensive and picturesque view from the Segovia gate — the cool and delicious shades on the banks of the Manzanares — their women — their music and nightly serenades, gave it to my mind the charm of romance.

During the time we remained in Madrid, our troops were allowed free access to the museum, in the street Alcala, nearly opposite our barracks. In it there was a very valuable collection of natural history, particularly a lump of native gold brought from South America, which weighed many pounds, some enormous boa constrictors, and the entire skeleton of a mammoth. This, like the British Museum, was free to all visiters three or four days a-week.

Several times during our stay in Madrid we were admitted, gratis, to see the bull fights, the great national amusement of the Spaniards. The place of these exhibitons was a vast amphitheatre, with

three tiers of boxes ranged along the wall, the roof
of the building projecting so far over as to cover them
only, all the rest being open.   In the highest range
of these on the shade side, was the king's box,
gorgeously decorated, those on its right and left
being occupied by the principal nobility.   About a
dozen seats sloping from the lowest tier of boxes
formed the pit, where the common people were
admitted, and which varied in the price of admission,
according to the degree of shade afforded.   In front
of the pit was a passage of a few feet wide, separated
from the arena by a barricade between five and six
feet high.   The arena or space where the bulls were
fought was of great dimensions ; two main passages
opened into it through the barricade, one by which
the bulls were drawn off when killed, and the other
by which they entered, communicating with a place
where they were kept previous to the fight, that
resembled, in some degree, a large cage, having
spaces between the planks that covered it, where they
goaded and otherwise tormented the animals, to
render them more savage before they entered the
arena.   But besides these entrances there were
smaller doors opening into the passage, by which the
bull could be driven back into the area, in the event
of his leaping the barricade, this being no unfrequent
occurrence.

I only witnessed the sight once.   Lord Wellington
was present, and sat in a box on the right of the
king's, the royal box being empty.   The performance
commenced by a guard of soldiers marching into the
centre of the arena, forming a circle, and on a signal
by beat of drum, facing outwards, and marching up
to the barricade, where, placing a foot on a step, on
the next signal, they vaulted over into the passage,
where they stood during the exhibition.   The horseman who was to attack the bull, now entered, dressed
somewhat in the same manner as our equestrians or

rope dancers, armed with a spear, rolled round with
cord to within half an inch of the point, to prevent
the wound which he might give the animal from
proving mortal. With him also entered the men on
foot, whose office was to irritate or divert the attention of the bull from the horseman when in too great
danger. They were dressed in nearly the same
style, only carrying different coloured mantles or
cloaks.

The signal was now given for the performance to
commence. The footmen ranged themselves round
the barricade, while the horseman, placing his spear
in the rest, remained opposite to, and some distance
'rom, the door by which the bull was to enter. All
being thus prepared, the door was thrown open —
the animal rushed furiously out, his nostrils dilated,
and his eyeballs gleaming fire. A flight of pigeons
which were let off at his head as he entered the
arena, irritated him, and attracted his attention a
little ; but perceiving the horseman, he began to roar
and paw the ground, and rushed forward upon him.
The horse being urged to a gallop, he was met half-
way, and struck by the spear on the shoulder, and
fairly thrown on his hind legs, bellowing fearfully
with the pain of the wound. The horse had now
started aside, and when the animal regained his feet,
which he did almost instantaneously, he was surrounded by the footmen, who, whenever he made a
charge at one of them, threw a mantle over his head,
and while he tossed it, and roared to get rid of it,
danced round, planting arrows in his sides and neck
filled with crackers, which, by the time he got free
of the cloak, began to go off, and maddened him to
the utmost degree. His appearance at this time was
terrific. The horseman was now prepared for a second
charge, which being made, the bull was again
attacked by the footmen, who often ran imminent
danger, being pushed so closely that they were

obliged to leap the barricade. This alternate attack was continued several times, until the people being tired, the matador was called for, who entered on foot without any defence but a small sword. The men on foot still continued to irritate the animal, until it was roused to the utmost pitch of madness, when the matador placing himself in its way, in the midst of one of its most furious attacks, calmly waited its approach. Seeing the bull close upon him, we expected that the man would be gored to death—that there was no possibility of his escape. But the moment the enraged animal came within his reach, he darted the sword, quick as lightning, between the horns into the back of his neck, and he fell dead at his feet without giving a single struggle. The music now began to play, and amidst the deafening plaudits of the spectators, six mules gaily caparisoned entered, and having their traces fastened to the dead bull, dragged him from the arena.

Six bulls were thus despatched without much variation in the mode; but one of them, (of Andalusian breed,) remarkable for its strength and fierceness, having been missed by the horseman in his attempt to strike him, came on so furiously that he had not time to escape, and the bull running the poor horse up against the barricade, lowered his head, and bringing up his horns, tore up his belly in such a way, that part of his bowels protruded at the wound, and hung down to the ground. The horseman, who had with great agility drawn up his leg, was now supported from falling by those who were in the passage, his right leg being jambed in between the horse and the barricade. The attention of the animal was soon drawn off by the men on foot; and the man was no sooner released from his dangerous situation, than, mounting afresh the wounded animal, he endeavoured to push it forward to another charge, with its bowels trailing on the ground. This action, which deserved to be execrated as a piece of wanton cruelty, was lauded to the skies, and cries of " Bravo! bravo!" resounded from every quarter. But the poor animal only moved a few steps, when it fell down dead.

The bull was now enraged so much that nothing could divert him from his purpose, and having followed one of the footmen to the limits of the arena, fairly leaped the barricade after him. A scene of dreadful confusion ensued, those in the pit and passage flying in every direction. The danger was soon over, however, for opening one of the doors already mentioned, he was driven back into the arena, and despatched by the matador.

The last bull ushered in was baited by dogs. I do not believe that many of our men were much captivated with this amusement; it was rather considered a cruel and disgusting one. I cannot understand how it is so much encouraged in Spain, unless it be to serve the same purpose that we pay boxers to murder each other, namely, to keep up the national courage.

I have known some of those " bruising" fellows in the army,—indeed every regiment has its " bully;" but although they were always forward enough to abuse and tyrannize over their fellow-soldiers, who were not of the " fancy," I never knew one of them that displayed even ordinary courage in the field ; and it was invariably by fellows of this description that outrages, such as those perpetrated at Badajos, were committed.

While in Madrid, one of their state prisoners was executed for treason : I do not remember his rank or name, but the mode of execution was so singular, that it may be worth describing.

On the day appointed for his execution, a scaffold was raised in the Placa Real, or Royal Square. In the centre of this platform there was fixed an appa·

ratus, resembling a chair, only, in place of the usual back, there was an upright stake; to this there was fastened an iron collar, which by means of a screw behind, could be tightened or relaxed at pleasure. A vast concourse of people had assembled to see the criminal suffer. He was led to the place of execution on an ass, having his arms pinioned, a crucifix in his hand, and surrounded by priests. On mounting the scaffold, he was placed on the seat already described, bound firmly down, and the priest took his place in front of him, with a crucifix in his hand, and from his violent gesticulations, seemed to be exhorting him very earnestly. This ceremony finished, the garotte or collar was placed about his neck, and his face covered. The executioner stood prepared, and on the signal being given, as far as I recollect, one wrench did the business, having completely flattened his neck. In this situation he remained a considerable time, when the body was removed, and the crowd dispersed.

CHAPTER VI.

ABOUT the 24th of October, we marched from Madrid to Pinto, a distance of about three leagues; in consequence of the enemy advancing in great force in that direction. Here we remained until the 30th, when we were ordered to retreat upon Madrid, and passed our pontoons burning on the road side, having been set on fire to prevent them falling into the hands of the enemy.

We supposed at first that we would again occupy Madrid, but when we came in sight of it the Retiro was in flames, and we could hear the report of cannon, which proceeded from the brass guns in the fort being turned on each other for the purpose of rendering them useless to the enemy; the stores of provision and clothing which we had previously taken were also burned, and every preparation made for evacuating the place. The staff officers were galloping about giving directions to the different divisions concerning their route; the inhabitants whom we met on the road were in evident consternation, and every thing indicated an unexpected and hurried retreat: instead, therefore, of entering the city, we passed to the left of it. The enemy's cavalry by this time being close on our rear, and before ours had evacuated the town on the one side, the French had entered it on the other. We marched about a league past Madrid, when we encamped for the night; but next morning we proceeded on our retreat, nor halted until we reached Salamanca, having the enemy encamped close on our rear every night.

The French having taken up nearly the same position they had occupied on the 22d of July, on the afternoon of the 15th November we turned out of the town, and forming on nearly our old ground, expected an immediate engagement. We had been so much harassed in retreating from Madrid in the severe weather, that we felt much more inclination to fight than to go farther, but we were disappointed; and after performing some evolutions, we filed off on the road leading to Roderigo, and commenced retreating as night was setting in. I never saw the troops in such a bad humour.

Retreating before the enemy at any time was a grievous business, but in such weather it was doubly so; the rain, now pouring down in torrents, drenched us to the skin, and the road, composed of a clay soil, stuck to our shoes so fast, that they were torn off our feet. The night was dismally dark, the cold wind blew in heavy gusts, and the roads became gradually worse. After marching in this state for several hours, we halted in a field on the road side, and having

piled our arms, were allowed to dispose ourselves to
rest as we best could. The moon was now up, and
wading through the dense masses of clouds, she sometimes threw a momentary gleam on the miserable
beings who were huddled together in every variety
of posture, endeavouring to rest or screen themselves
from the cold. Some were lying stretched on the
wet ground rolled in still wetter blankets, more having
placed their knapsack on a stone, or their wooden
canteen, had seated themselves on it with their blankets wrapped about them, their head reclining on
their knees, and their teeth chattering with cold;
while others more resolute and wise, were walking
briskly about. Few words were spoken, and as if
ashamed to complain of the hardships we suffered,
execrating the retreat, and blaming Lord Wellington
for not having sufficient confidence in us to hazard a
battle with the enemy, under any circumstances, were
the only topics discussed.

A considerable time before day light we were again
ordered to fall in, and proceeded on our retreat.
The rain still continued to fall, and the roads were
knee deep. Many men got fatigued and unable to
proceed. Some spring waggons were kept in the rear
to bring them up, but the number increased so fast
that there was soon no conveyance for them; and as
we formed the rear guard, they soon fell into the
hands of the French cavalry, who hung on our rear
during the whole retreat. When we came to our
halting ground, the same accommodation awaited us
as on the preceding evening. By some mismanage-
ment the commissary stores had been sent on with
the rest of the baggage to Roderigo, and we were
without food. The feeling of hunger was very severe.
Some beef that had remained with the division was
served out to us, but our attempts to kindle fires with
wet wood was quite abortive. Sometimes, indeed, we
managed to raise a smoke. and numbers gathered

round, in the vain hope of getting themselves warmed, but the fire would extinguish in spite of all their efforts. Our situation was truly distressing : tormented by hunger, wet to the skin, and fatigued in the extreme, our reflections were bitter ; the comfortable homes and firesides which we had left were now recalled to mind, and contrasted with our present miserable situation ; and during that night many a tear of repentance and regret fell from eyes " unused to the melting mood."

About the same hour as on the preceding morning, we again fell in and marched off, but the effects of hunger and fatigue were now more visible. A savage sort of desperation had taken possession of our minds, and those who had lived on the most friendly terms in happier times, now quarrelled with each other, using the most frightful imprecations on the slightest offence. All former feeling of friendship was stifled, and a misanthropic spirit took possession of every bosom. The streams which fell from the hills were swelled into rivers, which we had to wade, and vast numbers fell out, among whom were officers, who, having been subject to the same privation, were reduced to the most abject misery.

It was piteous to see some of the men, who had dragged their limbs after them with determined spirit until their strength failed, fall down amongst the mud, unable to proceed farther ; and as they were sure of being taken prisoners, if they escaped being trampled to death by the enemy's cavalry, the despairing farewell look that the poor fellows gave us when they saw us pass on, would have pierced our hearts at any other time ; but our feelings were steeled, and so helpless had we become, that we had no power to assist, even had we felt the inclination to do so. Among the rest, one instance was so distressing, that no one could behold it unmoved. The wife of a young man, who had endeavoured to be present with her husband on every occasion, if possible, having kept up with us amidst all our sufferings from Salamanca, was at length so overcome by fatigue and want, that she could go no farther. For some distance, with the assistance of her husband's arm, she had managed to drag her weary limbs along, but at length she became so exhausted, that she stood still unable to move. Her husband was allowed to fall out with her, for the purpose of getting her into one of the spring waggons, but when they came up, they were already loaded in such a manner that she could not be admitted, and numbers in the same predicament were left lying on the road side. The poor fellow was now in a dreadful dilemma, being necessitated either to leave her to the mercy of the French soldiers, or by remaining with her to be taken prisoner, and even then perhaps be unable to protect her. The alternative either way was heart-rending; but there was no time to lose, — the French cavalry were close upon them. In despairing accents she begged him not to leave her, and at one time he had taken the resolution to remain; but the fear of being considered as a deserter urged him to proceed, and with feelings easier imagined than described, he left her to her fate, and never saw her again; but many a time afterwards did he deprecate his conduct on that occasion, and the recollection of it imbittered his life.

On this night the rain had somewhat abated, but the cold was excessive, and numbers who had resisted the effects of the hunger and fatigue with a hardy spirit, were now obliged to give way to its overpowering influence, and sunk to the ground praying for death to relieve them from their misery; and some prayed not in vain, for next morning before daylight, in passing from our halting ground to the road, we stumbled over several who had died during the night. Inadvertently I set my foot on one of

them, and stooped down to ascertain whether the
individual was really dead, and I shall never forget
the sickening thrill that went to my heart, when my
hand came in contact with his cold and clammy
face. On this day our hearts seemed to have wholly
failed us : to speak was a burden, and the most helpless weakness pervaded every individual ; we had now
arrived at that pitch of misery which levels all distinction of rank, and I believe no order would have
been obeyed unless that which was prompted by
regard to the common safety.

Dennis, round whom there used to be gathered a
host of his comrades, listening to his witticisms or
quaint remarks, and whose spirits I had never known
to fail, was now crest-fallen, and moved along with
the greatest difficulty. Nothing but death, however,
could altogether keep down his buoyant spirits ; for
if we got a minute's halt during the march, he made
such ludicrous remarks on the wo-begone countenances of himself or his companions, that, although
the effort was distressing, they were obliged to smile
in spite of their misery.

This day we halted sooner than usual, and the
weather being clearer, we got fires kindled,—still no
rations ; but we were encamped among oak trees,
and greedily devoured the acorns which grew upon
them, although nauseous in the extreme, the officer
commanding the brigade and our colonel joining in
the repast. In many respects the officers were in a
worse situation than the men, not having any thing to
change themselves, as their baggage had been sent on
before us.

If any thing could have given us comfort in our
miserable situation. it was having a kind and sympathizing commanding officer : he made many of the
weakly men throw away their knapsacks, and by
every means in his power he endeavoured to infuse
comfort and courage into their sinking hearts, braving

every difficulty in common with the meanest individual, and even rejected the superior accommodation which his rank afforded, while he saw the men suffering. It was in a situation like this where true greatness of mind could be displayed; and there must have been something innately great and noble in the mind which could thus rise superior even to nature. In my opinion, a much greater degree of real courage was necessary to brave the horrors of this retreat, than to face the fire of a battery.

During the night our situation was worse than in the day, for there was then nothing to divert our attention from our wretched state; and although we despaired of ever seeing it, we felt that indescribable longing after home, which every one must have felt in the same situation. It will be needless to detail our next day's sufferings,—they were of the same nature as the preceding, only more aggravated.

We were now drawing near Roderigo, where our baggage had been ordered; each day our hopes had been kept alive in the expectation that we would find provision at our halting place, but we were deceived. Now, however, these expectations were more likely to be realized. About dusk we took up our ground on the face of a hill near Roderigo, and the weather changing to a severe frost, was intensely cold. We had not been long halted when the well known summons of "Turn out for biscuit," rung in our ears. The whole camp was soon in a bustle, and some of the strongest having gone for it, they received two days' rations for each man. It was customary to divide it, but on this night it was dispensed with, and each eagerly seizing on what he could get, endeavoured to allay the dreadful gnawing which had tormented us during four days of unexampled cold and fatigue. In a short time, two rations more were delivered, and the inordinate eating that ensued threatened to do more mischief

than the former want. We went into quarters next
day, and many who had borne up during the retreat
now fell sick, and were sent to the hospital.

From this place we removed in a few days some
way into Portugal, where we took up our winter
quarters in a small village, called Fonte Arcada.

CHAPTER VII.

FONTE ARCADA, in which our regiment was
quartered, (the remainder of the division being distributed in the surrounding villages,) was situated on
the face of a hill, which formed one of an extensive
range ; at its foot ran one of the tributary streams of
the Douro, meandering through a fertile and tolerably
well cultivated valley. The village itself was built
on a bare and rugged mass of rock, and the frowning
ledge that hung over the town gave it a wild and
romantic air. The place had not escaped the
ravages of war, but being more out of the common
route, it had suffered little in comparison to others.
The houses had rather a mean appearance, with the
exception of three or four belonging to fidalgos, who
resided in the village ; but the situation was healthy.
And after we had cleaned it, (which we had to do
with every Portuguese village before we could in-
habit them,) we felt ourselves very comfortable, and
soon forgot all our former fatigue, which we did the
readier, that we had now a commanding officer who
interested himself warmly in our welfare.

Lieutenant-Colonel Lloyd had joined us from the
43d regiment. I have already had occasion to mention him, in describing the retreat from Salamanca.
No eulogium, however, of mine can convey an idea
of his merits as a man and soldier ; but it is deeply

engraven on the hearts of those who served under
him.

So harmoniously did he blend the qualities of a
brave, active, intelligent officer with those of the
gentleman and the scholar, that the combination
fascinated all ranks. His exterior corresponded with
his mind : he was somewhat above the middle size
—and to a face and head cast in the true Roman
mould, was joined an elegant and manly body. His
system of discipline was not coercive ; he endeavoured
to encourage, not to terrify — if there was a single
spark of pride or honour in the bosom, he would fan
it to a flame. His aim was to prevent crime rather
than to punish it, and he, rarely resorted to corporal
punishment. When he did so, it was only in the
case of hardened ill-doers, with whom no lenient
measures would succeed ; even then, he never
punished to the tenth part of the sentence awarded ;
and if the culprit sued for pardon, promising not to
be guilty again, he would say, " I take you at your
word, and forgive you, but remember your promise."

The men's interests formed his chief study, and
the complaint of the meanest individual was heard
and investigated with the strictest impartiality, without respect to persons. By the measures he took, he
made every individual interested in his own honour
and that of the regiment ; and I believe that every
man in it loved and honoured him. So successful
were his efforts, that he brought the regiment into a
state of order, cleanliness, and discipline, which could
never have been attained by any other means. He
was always the first in danger and the last out of it ;
and in camp, he went later to rest, and was sooner
up than the meanest individual composing his corps.

He was a native of Ireland, (Limerick, I believe,)
and a striking coroboration of the general remark,
that where an Irishman is a gentleman, he is one in
the most extensive meaning of the word : unfettered

by cold calculating selfishness, his noble heart and soul is seen in every thing he does—such was Colonel Lloyd.

The inhabitants here were similar to those we had met with in other villages in Portugal,—sunk in ignorance, dirt, and superstition; and although some of the fidalgos boasted that the blood of Braganza flowed in their veins, they did not seem to be a whit more refined or better informed than the plebeians. They were rigid attendants on all the religious ceremonies of their church, but religion with them appeared to be a mere habit,—it played on the surface, but did not reach the heart. When the bell rang at stated periods for prayers, each rosary was put in requisition; but this did not interrupt the conversation—they managed to pray and converse at the same time. As bigotry is always the attendant of ignorance, they were no way liberal in their opinions concerning us; and so contaminated did they consider us by heresy, that they would not drink out of the same vessel. But to tell the truth, I believe they did not understand the principles of the religion they professed, and the "Padre Cura" of the village (a gross and unspiritual looking piece of furniture) did not seem much qualified to inform them.

We remained here near six months, during which vigorous preparations were made for the ensuing campaign, but little occurred interesting or worth recording while quartered in the village, with the exception of a love affair in which my friend Henry was engaged, which is so tinged with romance that I could scarcely expect credence to the detail, were it not that all who were then present with the regiment can vouch for its truth. Henry, whose warm heart and romantic imagination often produced him remarkable adventures, here fell deeply in love. In fact, his head was so stuffed with the machinery and plots of novels and romances, that his heart, as Burns expresses it, " was like a piece of tinder ready to burst forth into a flame, from the first casual spark that might fall upon it." Fortune, however, had as yet guarded it from any such accident, and reserved for winter quarters and quieter times, the shaft which was to destroy his peace.

He had by dint of application to the principles of the language, and a talent for acquiring it, gained a tolerable knowledge of the Portuguese, and at this time he held a situation which exempted him in a degree from military duty, and left him time to associate with some of the inhabitants who were fond of his conversation, and felt friendly towards him. It was by this means he became acquainted with a female whose charms had captivated him. She was niece to one of the principal inhabitants, and about fifteen or sixteen years of age. In her he imagined he had found the long cherished ideal mistress of his soul, on whom he had lavished more accomplishments and perfections than would have made an angel in our degenerate days. I was, of course, his confidant, and certainly, of all I had ever heard or read of love's extravagance, I witnessed it in him. He could neither eat nor sleep ; every spare moment that he had was spent on a small eminence opposite the house where she lived, gazing at the windows, in hopes to catch a glance at her ; here he would sit luxuriating in all the wild uncertainty of hope, anticipation, and despair, which lovers commonly indulge in, and although his familiarity with the family might have gained him access to her company any time he pleased, he grew diffident of visiting them, and even shrunk from the idea of speaking to herself on the subject. He poured all his doubts and hopes in my ear, and he could not have found one to whom they were more interesting Of the same romantic temperament, I shared in all his sensations. Seeing the state of mind in which he was placed by his violent attachment, I recommended him strongly that he should endeavour to gain an interview, and speak to her on the subject; but he considered this impracticable, as the sight of her never failed to agitate him in such a manner, that it robbed him of all power of utterance. Thus situated, and willing to render my friend a service, through my interest with a family whom she was in the habit of visiting, I brought about an interview between the parties; and here, for the first time, I saw Maria. She was certainly a very pretty, good-humoured, lively girl, but in my opinion, very far indeed from the paragon of perfection which Henry was inclined to think her; but I felt not the magic influence of that power, which, like the philosopher's stone, can transmute the baser metals into gold. Little satisfaction accrued to Henry from this meeting, but it subsequently led to others in which the parties came to a mutual explanation, and he had reason to hope that he was not regarded by her with indifference. From this time their interviews were more frequent and less guarded; and visiting her aunt frequently, although he could not converse freely with Maria, still their eyes, which " looked unutterable things," were not sufficiently restrained, and the old lady began to suspect the truth; the tattle of the village confirmed her suspicions, and she forbade Henry the house. They had a few stolen meetings at her friend's in the village, but this also was discovered, and Maria was prohibited from leaving the house unattended.

I am almost persuaded that had affairs gone on smoothly, Henry would have come to his senses, and the attachment would have died a natural death. But these obstacles only served to increase his ardour and perseverance; for so well was Maria now guarded, that there was no possibility of seeing her. In this dilemma, he determined on applying to Donna Anna, the girl's aunt; from this application he had but little to hope, yet still he could lose nothing. Having thus resolved, he went boldly into the house, and without speaking to any one, lest they might frustrate his purpose, he traversed the passages, until he perceived Donna Anna in one of the apartments alone, employed at her distaff. He entered, his heart fluttering with suspense ; and after apologizing for his rudeness in thus intruding upon her, he proceeded to declare his love for Maria, and to beg her acquiescence to their union. The old lady seemed thunderstruck at his presumption, yet still Henry had so qualified his address to her, that she had no good reason to be angry, and after taking a few minutes to recollect herself, she replied, " that Maria was already betrothed to a very deserving young man, a cousin of her own ; but independent of this engagement, she could not give her consent. What had Maria to expect if she married a soldier of a foreign regiment ? In the midst of war, the soldiers themselves suffered much, but those hardships and sufferings must fall heavier on a delicate female who had never known any thing but comfort. No," continued she, " Maria has superior expectations. But supposing I considered you a fit match for her in every other respect, still your religion would be an insurmountable barrier —to enter into the bonds of matrimony with a heretic, she might as well ally herself to the devil ! I have no objection to your character, and feel a friendship for you, but I can never encourage you in your present designs, nor give my consent to a marriage, that would be productive of misery to at least one, if not to both parties."

The calm and decided tone in which she spoke, convinced Henry that he had nothing to hope for from her, and his heart grew too big for utterance. He tried to suppress his feelings, but they were too strong for him, and he was only relieved from their suffocating effect by a flood of tears. The Donna's heart softened to see his distress, yet she still remained inflexible to her purpose. Maria, who had seen Henry enter the house, having followed him to the door of her aunt's apartment, had overheard the conversation, and now, seeing her aunt's back turned towards the door, she watched him until he raised his eyes, when giving him a sign which infused new hope into his mind, she retired. Henry now took his leave without enforcing his suit any farther. I had been waiting his return, and when he told me the result of his visit, I encouraged him to hope that all might yet be well.

During the day he received a message by a Portuguese boy, who was servant with one of our officers, informing him that she was so closely watched, that there was no hope of her being able to see him, unless he could manage to get over the garden wall, which was exceedingly high ; if so, that she would meet him that night. Having returned an answer that she might expect him, he called upon me ; we reconnoitered the garden wall, and having noted where there was a ladder, and procured a rope which was intended for our descent, after waiting anxiously until within half-an-hour of the appointed time, we proceeded to the place where we intended to effect our escalade. The inhabitants having retired to rest, and the village silent, we got over without difficulty. We had waited for some time at the head of one of the side walks (the place appointed) concealed by the bushes, when we heard the gentle sound of footsteps. We did not move from our hiding place until the appointed signal was given, when, in an instant, they were in each other's arms.

Where the heart is pure, I am led to believe, that the zest of love is the higher, the lower the station of the lovers. No fictitious refinement interferes to check the cup of joy : so it was in the present instance. Still, however, our situation was perilous, and I urged the necessity of forming some plan to bring about the desired purpose ; but their hearts were too much fluttered with joy and hope, uncertainty and fear, to make the necessary arrangements, and they parted hurriedly without doing more than appointing a second meeting. The appointed time again arrived, and we reached the garden as easily as before, but Maria did not come for nearly an hour after the time agreed on, and we were beginning to think some accident had befallen her, when we heard her steps coming up the walk. She seemed much disturbed ; " You would wonder at my delay," said she, " but I am afraid they suspect me. My aunt did not retire to rest at the usual hour, and before she did, she came into my apartment, and held the candle close to my face, but I pretended to sleep soundly ; she then retired, and I embraced the opportunity of slipping out—but I cannot stay—she may return to my apartment, and if she does, I am undone."

" But can we come to no conclusion with regard to what should be done ?" said I. " You have no reason to hope that your aunt will ever consent to your marriage ; therefore your only plan is to escape with Henry, and get married by the chaplain of the division, before your friends can prevent it ; then, when they find that no better can be done, there is every reason to believe they will be reconciled to you."

" O it is impossible !" said she ; " I know them too well."

" Certainly," said I, " the sacrifice is great, but the alternative is to bid each other adieu for ever. You must now decide, or we may never have another opportunity."

" I cannot make up my mind to-night," said she : " I will meet you here to-morrow night at this hour, determined and ready prepared either to remain, or make my escape. Now farewell, for I am afraid that I am discovered."

So saying, she parted hastily from us, and returned into the house, leaving poor Henry in no enviable state; his fate hung upon her decision, she had spoken with uncertainty, and he looked forward to the next meeting as the die that would determine his future happiness or misery.

During next day, Henry's mind was in such a state of uneasiness and suspense, that I could, with great difficulty, bring him to make the necessary arrangements in the event of her escaping with him. It was necessary that he should apply to his commanding officer for permission to marry; and I advised him to disclose the whole matter to him, well knowing that such a character as he was would take an interest in his fate. Henry took my advice, and having called on Colonel L. disclosed every circumstance connected with the affair. Colonel L. listened with attention, and seemed much interested. The story in part was not new to him; he had heard it from some of the principal inhabitants. He reasoned the matter with Henry like a father; represented the difficulty which would lie in his path —marrying a foreigner of a different religion — the hardships she would have to endure — and the many difficulties which two people, marrying so young, would have to encounter. " But," said he, " I suppose all those things appear as trifles to you at present."

Henry owned that his affection was too deeply rooted to be moved by these considerations.

" Well," said Colonel L. " if you are determined on trying the experiment, and that she is agreeable, I have no objection to giving you permission to marry, but I cannot say you have my approbation."

Henry, however, it may be easily imagined, was not to be moved by sober reasoning.

The time of meeting arrived, and Henry, trembling with suspense and apprehension, accompanied me to the garden. We were not long there, when Maria arrived with a few articles of wearing apparel, which she had hurriedly collected.

" Well, Maria," said I, " have you decided — are you ready to accompany us ?"

" I don't know," said she, " I am so filled with apprehension, that I cannot think or speak."

" Say the word," said I, " all is ready."

" Oh, I don't know," said she. " Either let me return into the house, or let us leave this, or I shall die with fear : I am sure I have been observed. O Jesu, Maria ! there they come — I am lost."

So saying, she fled down the opposite path, where she was immediately seized by some of the domestics, who had been mustered for the purpose of surprising us. There was no time to lose, for resistance would have been useless ; and we too well knew the nature of the Portuguese, to depend much on their mercy. Hurrying, therefore, towards the wall, and having assisted Henry, who was rendered nearly powerless by the effect of his feelings, I made a spring and seized the top of the wall ; Henry was ready to lend me assistance, but before I could get myself raised to the summit, a sword aimed for my body, struck the wall so close to my side, that it cut out a piece of my jacket and shirt. Ere the blow could be repeated, I had fallen over on the opposite side, carrying Henry with me in my fall. I was severely hurt — but there was no time to lose, and we knew the alarm would soon be raised ; therefore, having conveyed the ladder to where we had found it, we hurried to our quarters.

Next day the Portuguese boy brought information to Henry that early that morning two mules had been brought into the court yard ; that Maria was brought out weeping, and mounted on one, her aunt on the other, and that two servants, armed, had accompanied them ; he was not allowed to follow them, and therefore could not tell what direction they had taken, but Maria had whispered to him, to give Henry her last farewell, for she never expected to see him again, as she was ignorant of where they were taking her. When Henry received this information, distracted with a thousand contending emotions, among which despair was predominant, he seized a bayonet, and rushed bare-headed from his quarters, traversed one road after another in search of her, making inquiry of every person whom he met, if they had seen her,— but she had been some hours gone. After travelling about from one place to another in this distracted state, and being taken for a madman by all who met him, worn out by the violence of his feelings, he became calm, and returned home in the dusk of the evening; but it was a calm produced by one master feeling having swallowed up the rest; despair had now taken possession of his mind, "The stricken bosom that can sigh, no mortal arrow bears." He walked into his apartment, and having taken up a musket, and loaded it, he placed the muzzle against his head, and was in the act of putting his foot on the trigger, when a soldier happened to enter, and seizing him, arrested the rash deed.

I had been placed on guard that morning, nor did I know any thing of what had occurred, until Henry was brought to the guard-house, where he was ordered to be particularly watched. I went over to speak to him, but he looked at me with a vacant stare, nor did he seem conscious of what I said. Sitting down in a corner, he remained with his eyes fixed on the floor for some time, then rising, he walked about with a hurried pace, while his countenance showed the burning fever of his mind; a fit of tenderness succeeded, and he raved of all that had happened, which I only could understand. To me it was a most affecting scene, for I had no hope that his reason would return, and I contemplated the wreck of his mind, as one would do the destruction of all that was

dear to him. I watched him attentively during the
night, and towards morning nature became so far exhausted, that he fell into a confused slumber. When
he awoke, the naked reality of his situation struck
him intensely. He perceived me, and stretching out
his hand, he burst into tears. In broken accents he
informed me of the death of all his hopes ; but his
mind was unstrung — he could not think connect-
edly.

At this time he was sent for to attend at the
colonel's lodgings. The noble character of our commanding officer was particularly shown in the sympathy and concern which he evinced for the unfortunate Henry : he entered into all his feelings, and
alternately soothed and reasoned with him, until he
had brought him to a calmer state of mind ; then,
after expressing the kindest solicitude for his welfare,
he dismissed him to his quarters, telling him at the
same time, that he would use his interest to gain the
consent of her relations to the match, and that
nothing should be wanting on his part to bring the
affair to a happy conclusion. This, in some measure,
restored the balm of hope to Henry's mind ; but, alas!
it was only a temporary relief, for although Colonel
L. faithfully kept his promise, and several of the
officers who were on good terms with the family
used their utmost endeavours in his behalf, it was all
to no purpose, — the more they pressed, the more
obstinate they became.

Things were in this state, when he unexpectedly
received a message from Maria, informing him that
she was closely confined in the house of a gentleman,
(who was a relative of her aunt,) about nine miles
from the town ; from the manner in which she was
guarded, she had no hope of being able to make her
escape, for there were people employed to watch the
avenues to the house, with orders if he approached it
to shew him no mercy ; that she saw little use in

giving him this information, but she could not resist
the opportunity which had presented itself, of letting
him know where she was. Henry gave way to the
most entrancing anticipations on receiving this information ; but when he communicated it to me, I considered the subject in a different light. I saw that it
was more likely to keep alive the commotion of a
passion which there was little hope of ever arriving
at its object ; I knew the attempt to go to the house
would be pregnant with danger, still I felt inclined to
assist him in another determinate effort to carry off
the prize.

Henry called on Colonel L. for the purpose of
procuring a pass. When he communicated his intention, he not only gave him the pass, but also a letter
to the gentleman of the house where Maria was,
(with whom he was well acquainted,) to serve as an
introduction. Thus prepared, Henry and I, in company with the boy already mentioned, set forward
after it was dark towards the place, taking a bye-road.
When we reached the house, we left the boy outside,
as he was known to the family, and entering, presented the letter from Colonel L. We were kindly
received ; and as it was late, the gentleman insisted
on us stopping all night — so far all was well. We
had been about an hour in the house when Maria
happened to come down stairs : she knew us immediately, but concealed her emotions, and coming near
the fire, she watched an opportunity until the servants
were engaged about the house, and then whispering
to us, asked our motive in coming there. " If they
know you," said she, " your lives are not safe."

I told her that our motive was by some means to
endeavour to effect her escape ; she replied, it was
utterly impossible, she was too well guarded. " Farewell, Henry," said she, " farewell for ever, for I
believe I will never see you again ; it would have

been happy for us both if we had never seen each other."

At this moment a female servant of Donna Anna's, who had accompanied Maria, came to speak to her, and recognizing Henry, she flew up stairs. Maria saw that we were discovered, and she cried to us, " Fly for your lives !" The whole family collected, were now descending the stairs, and Maria was hurried up to her room. The old lady of the house assailed us with the most abusive epithets, the men-servants gathered in, and every thing wore a hostile appearance. The gentleman, however, to whom the letter was directed, commanded silence, and addressing us, " I do not presume to say what your intentions may be towards my ward, but being convinced of the identity of the individual who has already caused us so much trouble, I am forced, even against the laws of hospitality, to retract my request of you to remain here to-night, and for the safety of those committed to my charge, I must insist on you returning immediately to your quarters. If you have come here for the purpose of decoying Maria from this house, I can tell you that whatever inclination she once might have felt for this foolish young man, she is now better advised, and does not wish to be troubled with him any more."

" Let me hear that from her own lips," cried Henry in a frenzied tone, "and I will give my word that I shall never trouble her again."

A short consultation was held by the family, and after some minutes delay, Maria was brought down stairs, trembling and weeping. But all their endeavours could not force her to repeat the words which they wished her to say. At length, Henry, as if inspired with more than his natural energy, exclaimed, " I find that every fresh effort of mine only causes you additional restraint and mortification. I must now cease to hope — they have cruelly parted us in this world, Maria, but we may yet meet. Suffer me," said he, "to take a last farewell, and I will trouble you no more."

This was spoken with such an impassioned voice and gesture, that it had a visible effect on those around. Maria, who had been restrained by the lady of the house, now broke from her, and fell into Henry's arms. While he pressed her to his bosom, a new spirit seemed to animate him — his eyes brightened — and putting his hand into his breast, where he had a pistol concealed, "Let us carry her off, Joseph," said he to me in English, "or die in the attempt."

"Then you will die before you reach the door," said I ; for the house was now filled with the retainers of the family ; and as if they suspected his purpose, Maria was torn shrieking from his arms.

Afraid that he might be induced to commit some rash act, I hurried him out of the house, and we returned home. I endeavoured to lead him into conversation, but he appeared not to hear me, nor did he speak a word during the journey ; he evinced no feeling of any kind — his mind seemed to be in a state of the utmost confusion.

Next morning the Portuguese boy brought him intelligence that Maria had passed through the village very early, escorted by her relations, on her way to a nunnery, about three leagues distant, where she was destined to remain until our army advanced.

This took place in a few days after, and they never met again. Henry's mind had been strained far beyond its pitch — it was now unnerved — and he fell into a state of listless melancholy from which he did not recover for many months.

CHAPTER VIII.

DURING the time the army were in winter quarters, great preparations were made for the campaign which was about to open, and we could now muster an army of about one hundred and thirty thousand men, namely, forty thousand British, twenty thousand Portuguese, and seventy thousand Spaniards, —the two former in the highest state of discipline, well clothed, and provided with stores of every description. The old camp-kettles, that were formerly carried on mules, were exchanged for lighter ones, which the men could carry on the top of their knapsacks ; and the mules now carried tents, which we had not been provided with prior to this period. In fact, the whole arrangements made reflected the highest honour on Lord Wellington.

The army commenced its advance on the 13th May, 1813, in three columns. The second division commanded by General Hill, formed the right, which was destined to advance along the line of the Tagus. The centre column, consisting of the fourth, sixth, seventh, and light divisions, under the immediate command of Lord Wellington, to advance by Salamanca. The left, consisting of the first, third, and fifth divisions, under the command of General Graham, to advance direct through Portugal, taking the line of Benevente for Burgos, and to be supported on the left by the Gallician army. The centre column came up with the French on the 26th May, and in a skirmish with their rear guard, took two hundred prisoners. A junction was here formed with General Hill, extending the line from the Tormes to the Douro. The left, to which our division belonged, passed the Elsa at Miranda de Douro on the 31st May, Lord Wellington being present, and advanced upon Zamora, when the French fell back upon Toro. Passing Valladolid, we continued our march upon Burgos, which the enemy evacuated on the 13th of June, having first blown up the works; thirty of the garrison perished by the explosion. The retreat of the French had been so rapid during this time, that our marches were often very severe, which, together with the heat of the weather, and occasional scarcity of water, caused many to get fatigued, and unable to keep up with their regiment. Here again the conduct of Colonel Lloyd was remarkable. By every means in his power he encouraged and assisted those who were weakly, taking their knapsacks from them, and carrying them on his own horse; sometimes having half a dozen on it, and a man sitting above all, while he walked on foot at the head of his regiment, in the most difficult parts of the road — at the same time, inducing the other officers to follow his example. Often when he saw an individual failing, through want of strength, he has taken off his liquor flask and given it to the poor fellow to drink, saying, "Don't let your spirits down, my man; you will soon get strength, and be able to keep up with the best of them; none of them shall have to say that you fell to the rear."

He had a most extensive and thorough knowledge of his profession, added to an acquaintance with most of the European languages. When he came into camp he was never a moment idle, either reconnoitering the enemy's position, or drawing charts of the roads, &c. He scarcely allowed himself to rest, and was always up an hour or two before the bugle sounded; but he would never allow the men to be disturbed before the proper time. " No," said he, " let the poor fellows get all the rest they can." But *then* he expected them to be alert; officers and men, without distinction, were obliged to be in their respective places at once without delay—all his motions were double-quick — and he detested nothing so much as laziness.

General Picton, who had joined from England a considerable time before, again commanded the division. To judge from appearance, no one would have suspected him of humour; yet he often indulged in it: his wit was generally, however, of the satirical kind. On this advance, a man belonging to one of the regiments of the brigade, who was remarkable for his mean pilfering disposition, had on some pretence lingered behind his regiment when they marched out to the assembling ground, and was prowling about from one house to another in search of plunder. General Picton, who was passing through, happened to cast his eye upon him, and called out, " What are you doing there, sir? Why are you behind your regiment?" The man, who did not expect to see the general in the village, had not an answer very ready; but he stammered out an excuse, saying, " I came back to the house where I was quartered to look for my gallowses," (braces.) " Ay, I see how it is," replied the general; "get along, sir, to your division, and take my advice—always keep the word *gallows* in your mind."

Having crossed the Ebro on the 16th, Lord Wellington took up his quarters a few leagues from Vittoria; and on the 19th we came up with the French, who had taken a position in front of that town, their left posted on a range of heights. Our army having closed up on the 20th, on the morning of the 21st, General Hill's division commenced the battle, by attacking their left on the heights of Puebla, and succeeded, after a most desperate and sanguinary contest, in gaining possession of them. When we descended the hill towards the river, the second division was warmly engaged, and the French commenced cannonading us from a small white village in front of Vittoria, where they had part of their army stationed. There was a brigade of our guns directing their fire towards this place when we were crossing the river along with the seventh division. Our attention was drawn to a young artillery officer who was with them, and who seemed to be very much frightened ; for every time that either our own or the French guns fired, he ducked to the ground. Some of the men felt inclined to make game of him ; but it only shewed that fighting needs practice before people can take things easy. It is likely that it was the first time he had been engaged, and I have no doubt but he would eventually get the better of that custom. Those who have not known it by experience, can form no idea of the indifference with which our soldiers entered a battle after being some time in the Peninsula. As an instance of this, we were at one time lying opposite to the enemy, in daily expectation of being engaged. One of our men, (a Highlandman,) having lost the small piece of ornamented leather which is worn in front of the uniform cap, on taking off his hat for some purpose, the deficiency caught his eye, and, looking at it for a few moments, he said, very seriously, " I wish to God there may be an engagement to-day, till I get a rosette for my cap."

After crossing the river, our division advanced in two lines upon the village where their artillery were posted under a tremendous fire, and succeeded, after an obstinate resistance, in dislodging them. The fourth and light divisions having also crossed the river, advanced upon the enemy's centre. The French had made sure of defeating us at this point ; and it was said that Joseph Buonaparte had erected a buttress on one of the spires, for the purpose of seeing them drive us back. But he was doomed to a severe disappointment ; for the second division having succeeded in driving the French off the heights, they commenced their retreat on the Burgos

road, but were intercepted by General Graham, with
the left of our army ; and after losing several villages
in succession, which they warmly contested, they
were at length compelled to abandon the main road
to France, (Joseph himself narrowly escaping,) and
take the road to Pampeluna, followed in pursuit by
the whole army ; and such was their haste, that they
were obliged to abandon all their baggage and guns,
with the exception of one gun and one howitzer.
One hundred and fifty-one cannon, four hundred and
fifteen ammunition waggons, one hundred other
waggons, fourteen thousand rounds of ammunition,
two million ball cartridges, and forty thousand
pounds of powder, with the baggage and treasury
waggons, said to be worth £630,000, fell into our
hands.

The enemy lost ten thousand killed and wounded,
and one thousand nine hundred prisoners. The loss
on our side amounted to about three thousand killed
and wounded.

When we reached the town, passing to the left of
it, we found their baggage to the right of the road,
lying in the greatest confusion. The columns passed
on, but some of the stragglers who fell out got
immense sums of money out of the treasury waggons.
Few of them were much the better of it, however. I
knew one man who got to the amount of £ 2000
here, who was going without shoes before we left the
country.. We passed on some distance beyond Vittoria, and encamped ; but many of the men returned
that night to the baggage, and got money and valu-
ables of every description. The camp that night
and next day was like a fair ; and the dollars and
doubloons were flying about in every direction.

The wounded were left in Vittoria, among whom
was a Captain G—— of ours, who subsequently lost
his life in a melancholy manner. During his stay in
Vittoria, while recovering from his wounds, he had

become acquainted with a young lady, and, it was
said, had seduced her. Her brother, who was an
officer in the Spanish army, having learned the circumstance, vowed revenge ; and one night, when on
guard, he took some of his men with him armed, and
forced his way into Captain G——'s quarters, who
was undressing himself to go to bed. Hearing a
noise, he seized his sword, and coming out into the
passage, he was attacked by the Spaniards ; but so
well did he defend himself, that they were fairly
beaten out of the house, and the door shut upon
them. They had not been long gone, however,
when they returned, and endeavoured to gain
entrance. Captain G—— had again left his apartment to see what was the matter, and was standing
in the passage with his sword in his hand, when they
burst open the door, fired a volley at him, and made
their escape. One of the shots took effect, and he
fell, mortally wounded. We were very sorry for
him, for he was an excellent officer ; and however he
might have been to blame otherwise, the base manner
in which he was assassinated excited the indignation
of the whole army. I never learned whether any
investigation took place, or any justice was rendered
by the Spanish government.

The rear of the French army entered Pampeluna
on the 24th, having previously lost their gun ; and
out of their whole artillery, they had now only left
one solitary howitzer. Never was an army so dis-
comfited. They were so confident of success, that
they had made no provision for a retreat.

Having left a garrison in Pampeluna, they proceeded to retreat by the road of Roncesvalles, and
we invested Pampeluna on the 26th. We were in
camp for a day or two here ; and during that time,
a party of our regiment relieved a Spanish picquet on
a hill above our encampment. It had rained during
the night, and the picquet's arms, which were piled

in front of the tent, had got a little rusty. Being fatigued, they had neglected to clean them. Colonel Lloyd, who was ever on the alert, particularly when near the enemy, having paid them a visit very early in the morning, took notice of their arms ; but, without passing any remark, he called the sergeant, who, thinking that he wished to inspect the picquet, ordered them to turn out. "Never mind falling in," said the colonel ; "I only called to ask why you did not make those Spaniards whom you relieved last night take their arms with them." The sergeant, who did not see through the sarcasm, replied, that the Spaniards did take their arms with them.

"And pray, whose arms are these?"

"The picquet's arms," replied the sergeant.

"Poh! nonsense! you don't intend to make me believe these arms belong to British soldiers. Send for the Spaniards, and make them take away their arms." So saying, he walked down the hill. Each man felt his honour implicated, and the colonel had not gone many paces when they were all busy cleaning their muskets. It was in this manner that he could convey severe reproof, and endear himself to his men at the same time.

From this place we marched across the country to Sanguessa, and on the march I was left on duty, which detained me behind the regiment. In my route to join them I had halted for the day with my party at a house a short distance off the road. There was a wood to the rear of the house, and we had not long taken up our quarters, when I perceived a lady galloping from it with great speed down a bye-path towards us. As she approached I observed that her dress was in great disorder, her face stained with blood, and she held a pistol in her hand, with which she urged on her horse. I was struck with surprise on seeing a lady in such trim, and did not know well what to think of her, when she reined up her horse at the door, and before I had time to assist her, sprung to the ground, and replacing the pistol in the holster, removed the saddle from her horse, and turned him loose to graze ; then sitting down, she drew forth a small pocket mirror, and began to arrange her dishevelled tresses. As a favour she asked me to procure her a little water, and when I had brought it —" Thank you," said she, " I believe I stand in need of this, for I have had a severe scuffle and a brisk gallop. I am on my way to join the Spanish army, and although eager to get forward, I could not persuade my lazy servants to dispense with their usual *siesta*, and when the fellows went to sleep I left them and pushed forward myself ; but I had not travelled far when I was stopped by three brigands, who, seizing my horse's bridle, demanded my money. Powder and shot are more plentiful with me than money in these times, and I drew out a pistol and sent a ball through the fellow's head who asked it — he fell, and I urged forward my horse ; but one of the villains still held by the bridle, and I was near unhorsed. Having another pistol left, I lost no time in making him relax his hold. My horse was now free, and sprung forward with me ; but a bullet from the surviving robber nearly stopped my flight, for it grazed my cheek here," said she, pointing to a slight wound which she was bathing with the cold water : " it was a narrow escape, certainly." I was not a little surprised at the *sang froid* with which she described the imminent danger she had been in, and could not sufficiently admire her courage and presence of mind ; but I ceased to wonder, when her servants coming up a short time after, told me that I had been conversing with the *heroine of Saragossa.*

In half an hour after they arrived, she again set forward. I had seen her before at Cadiz ; but I did not recollect her features. Every one has read or heard of her conduct at Saragossa; it will, therefore, be needless for me to recapitulate it here.

Having remained in camp at Sanguessa a few days, we returned, and were quartered in a small village, called Olaz, about three miles from Pampeluna, sending out working parties to the batteries which were forming against the town.

General Graham having pushed on by the sea side as far as Passages, and General Hill having dislodged the enemy on the right — the whole had now retired into France.

We remained in this place until the 25th of August, when Soult having hastily collected an army of forty thousand men, made a furious attack on the fourth division. Our division advanced to their support, but not being able to keep our ground against such a force as they had brought up, the whole were obliged to retreat precipitately that night upon Huarte, where a position was taken up by the army. On the 27th they made a desperate attack on the left of our line, where we had possession of a hill, which they made repeated attempts to gain possession of, but without success — for whenever they drove in our skirmishers, so as to reach the top, the regiments stationed to defend it came forward, and having poured a volley into them, charged them down the hill with dreadful slaughter.

On the 28th they again attempted it, but with like success. A desperate attack was then made on the fourth division, but they charged with the bayonet, and repulsed the enemy with immense loss. On the 29th Soult manœuvered to turn our left; but on the 30th, our army in turn attacked — the seventh division their right, our division their left, and the other divisions their centre — when they were defeated and fled in all directions, losing in their retreat many prisoners, among whom were a number of raw conscripts, who had not been four months enlisted.

During the time we lay in position, the French occupied a hill on one side, while our division were posted on a rise opposite, a small valley being between ; in this valley there was a sort of intrenchment formed, where our picquets lay. It could be of little use to either side, as it was exposed to the fire of both armies ; but the French, out of bravado, determined on taking it, and selected a party for that purpose. A brave fellow of an officer headed them, and came cheering down the hill ; our men did not incommode themselves in the least, until they were so near that they could take a sure aim, when those in the rear of the intrenchment starting up, saluted them with a volley of musketry that brought down an immense number, among others the officer, who was some way in front : whenever they saw him fall, they turned to the right-about, and ascended the hill, leaving him on the ground. We felt sorry for the fate of the brave fellow who had led them, and reprehended the cowardly scoundrels who had left him.

It is a peculiar feature of the British soldier, that his bravery does not depend on that of his officers, although, no doubt, it may be stimulated by the presence and example of a good one — I never knew it to fail through their bad conduct.

From this we followed the French by the road of Roncesvalles, and took up our encampment on one of the Pyrenees, above that village so much renowned in Spanish poetry. In our ascent we found a number of half burnt bodies lying on the mountain side, being those of the enemy who had been killed in the preceding engagement, and whom they thus disposed of. When we reached the top of the hill, we found ourselves enveloped in mist ; and during the few days we remained on it, it was so thick that we durst not move from the camp for water, without forming a chain of men to guide us back. From this place we removed, and were posted on the heights above the village of Maya, occupying the ground from which part of our advanced posts were driven back on the 25th ; the scene of action being marked out by the dead bodies lying about, and the ground strewed with the fragments of clothing, particularly the tartan dress of one of our Highland regiments.

Being relieved by other troops, we descended the mountain, and were encamped near the village of Ariscune. While here, one of the 83d regiment was shot for desertion ; he had deserted when we formed the advance at the Maya pass, and having come out with some of the French generals to reconnoitre our position, they were attacked by a picquet of our cavalry, when the French officers decamped, leaving the deserter behind. He was then taken, and being subsequently tried by a general court-martial, was sentenced to be shot. He blamed the tyrannical conduct of the officer commanding his company, and the pay-sergeant, for being the cause of his desertion,—that they had taken ill-will at him on some account, and rendered his life so miserable, that he was driven to the desperate step which ended in his death. Whether his statement was true, I cannot say, but his comrades were inclined to think it was.

During this time General Graham besieged and took St Sebastian.

While we were here, I was sent on command with a letter to General Hill, whose division now occupied the heights above Roncesvalles. In going from the one place to the other, I had to travel about six miles through a bye-path, on the ridge of one of the Pyrenees, and my imagination was struck in a peculiar manner by the awful grandeur of the scenery; yet I could not help feeling horror at the death-like stillness that reigned around me. I felt myself as it were lifted out of the world — I saw nor heard not any living thing but a huge vulture, who stood upright on a rock by the road side, looking at me as I passed, without seeming the least disturbed at my presence— he rather seemed to eye me as an invader of his solitary domain. I tried to startle him by making a noise, but he disdained to move; at length, when it suited his own pleasure, he slowly expanded his broad wings, and rising a few yards from the ground, hovered for some time immediately above my head, and then soared out of sight. Having ascended the mountain, I found the second division encamped on nearly the same ground that we had formerly occupied, and enveloped in mist as we had been. The place where General Hill and his staff were encamped was surrounded by a small intrenchment, inside of which the tents were pitched, and a kind of log-house built in the centre, to serve as a mess room. Judging from the proud and haughty bearing of some of our ensigns, in coming into the presence of the general second in command of the British army, I expected to be annihilated by his look, and I was ushered into the mess room to deliver my message with a palpitating heart; but I no sooner saw the humane and benevolent-looking countenance of the general, than my apprehensions vanished. Having read the letter, he questioned me concerning the health of the commanding officer, and asked me questions concerning our regiment, (of which he was colonel,) in the kindliest and most unaffected manner; then calling one of his servants, he ordered him to provide me liberally in meat and drink. Some time after, seeing me standing outside the tent, he called me, and asked whether the servants had paid attention to me. Next morning, on giving me a letter for my commanding officer, " I did not

intend," said he, " that you should have returned so
soon, but we are going to remove down to the valley,
and as it would be only taking you out of your road,
it will be as well for you to proceed ; but there is no
necessity that you should go farther than the small
village two leagues from this.   I will give directions
to my orderly dragoon to procure you a billet there,
and to-morrow you can join your regiment."   He
then ordered his servant to fill my haversack with
provision ; and when I was going away, he said,
" Remember now what I have told you, — don't go
farther than the village ; and here is something for
you to get yourself a refreshment when you arrive
there."

These circumstances have no particular interest in
themselves, to render them worth reciting, only that
they serve to shew the amiable disposition of a
general, whose character for bravery and skill is too
well known to the public to need any eulogium of
mine.   It was this feeling and humane disposition,
and attention to their interests, that caused him to be
so much beloved by the troops under his command,
and gained for him the appellation of father, —
" Daddy Hill" being the name he was called by in
his division.

CHAPTER IX.

FROM Ariscune we again moved, and occupied
the heights above Maya, from whence we advanced
in the beginning of October, and drove the French
outposts back into the valley, at the same time
burning their huts.   While engaged at this business,
there fell a tremendous shower of hailstones, some of
them measuring five inches in circumference.   The
regiment got partially under cover in a small chapel,

but those with the baggage were exposed, and many were hurt severely. On this day the left of our army succeeded in crossing the Bidasoa.

On returning from this affair, we ascended the heights above the village of Zaggaramurdi, where we encamped. From this part of the Pyrenees we had a view of France, and the position of the French army, which occupied a line, their right resting on the sea-port of St Jean de Luz, and the left on St Jean Pied de Port: here they had formed an intrenched camp, and had redoubts on each hill along the whole line.

We remained on this ground until the 10th of November, during which time the weather was severe—the wind often blowing with such violence that the tents could not be kept pitched.

From a precipice above our encampment, we could view the sea, and the towns along the coast. It was now three years since we beheld it, during which time our hopes and wishes had often fondly turned to our native homes; each fresh campaign and each battle was reckoned the precursor of our return, but "by expectation every day beguiled," we had almost begun to despair of ever beholding it again, when our recent successes, and the sight of the ocean which encircled the land of our birth, produced the most lively hopes and pleasing anticipations. A more than common friendly feeling was displayed amongst us; each saw in his comrade's face the reflection of the joy that animated his own heart. The mountain air braced our nerves, and gave us a bounding elasticity of spirit, which rose superior to every thing.

A few of us who were drawn together by congeniality of sentiment and disposition, used to assemble and wander up among the giant cliffs with which we were surrounded, and perching ourselves in a crany, would sit gazing on the ocean and ships passing, with emotions which I have felt, but cannot describe. Its expansive bosom seemed a magic mirror, wherein we could read our future fortune,—a happy return from all our dangers ; smiling friends, with all the early loved associations of childhood and youth, swam before our hope-dazzled imaginations, and we sat and sung the songs of Scotland while the tears trickled down our cheeks. He who has never heard the melodies of his native land sung in a foreign country, is ignorant of a pleasure that nothing can surpass. But we were not all doomed to realize those pleasing anticipations : many found their graves in the valley which we then overlooked.

Lord Wellington having prepared every thing for an attack on the French position in the valley, on the 10th of November, about two o'clock in the morning, we assembled, and having marched down to the foot of the hill, on a signal given by a gun firing, the attack commenced ; that on the enemy's left was made under the direction of General Hill, by the second and sixth divisions, supported by a division of Portuguese and Spaniards. Marshal Beresford commanded the centre, consisting of our division, the fourth and seventh, supported by a division of Spaniards.

The enemy having been driven from the redoubts in front of Sarre, we advanced upon the village. Our regiment being selected to charge a strong column that protected the bridge, Colonel Lloyd filed us off from the division, and led us on to the attack in the most heroic manner. Having succeeded in carrying it with considerable loss on our part, we returned and took up our place in the column. In a short time after, having passed through the village, the whole army co-operating, we advanced to the attack of the enemy's main position on the heights behind it, on which a line of strong redoubts were formed, with abattis in front, formed by trees cut down and placed with their branches towards us, serving as a cover for their infantry. Having exten-

ded our line at the foot of the hill, our division proceeded to the attack: Colonel Lloyd having pushed
his horse forward before the regiment, advanced
cheering on his men with the most undaunted bravery — but before he reached its summit, he received
a mortal wound in the breast, and was only saved
from falling off his horse by some of the men springing forward to his assistance. When this was perceived by the regiment, a pause of a moment was
made in the midst of their career, and the tear started
into each eye as they saw him borne down the hill;
but the next was devoted to revenge, and regardless
of every thing, they broke through all obstacles, and
driving the enemy from their position, they charged
them through their burning huts without mercy.
The troops to our right and left having carried the
other redoubts, the enemy were obliged to surrender
the strong position which they had taken; and in
the principal redoubt on the right, they left the
first battalion of their 88th regiment, which surrendered.

The troops under General Hill having succeeded
in forcing them from their positions on the right of
our army, our division and the seventh moved by the
left of the Nivelle, on St Pe, covered by the second
and sixth divisions. A part of the enemy's troops
had crossed, and advancing, gained possession of the
height above it. Our centre and right columns
were now established behind the enemy's right; but
night came on, and we were obliged to cease firing.
Having encamped, intelligence was brought up of
the death of Colonel Lloyd: he had been carried to a
house at the foot of the hill, where he expired in a
few minutes.

Thus fell the brave and noble Lloyd, in the vigour
of manhood and the height of his fame, for his worth
and services were well known, and duly appreciated
by Lord Wellington. Though young, his extraordi-

nary abilities had caused him to rise rapidly in the service, and had attracted the admiration of the army in which he served; while his humanity and wise system of discipline endeared him to those he commanded. Humble though thy grave be, gallant Lloyd, and though no sculptured marble rises o'er thy tomb, thine is a nobler meed: thy virtues are engraven on many a heart, which nothing but the rude hand of death can e'er efface; and though no pageantry followed thy remains to the grave, honest heart-felt tears were shed upon it.

I never witnessed sorrow so general as that produced by the intelligence of his death; our hearts were full — we felt as if we had lost a father — all his good qualities were recapitulated, and tears were shed in abundance during the recital.

Had any of those overbearing officers who carry all with a high hand and by dint of severity, witnessed the feeling displayed that night among the men of our regiment, they would have forsworn tyranny for ever. One individual only exulted in his death, and that was the captain of yellow and black badge celebrity, whom I have already had occasion to mention; he considered that Colonel Lloyd's promotion into our regiment had hindered his own, and as the goodness which some men cannot imitate causes their hate, so it was with him. When he received intelligence of Colonel Lloyd's death, snapping his fingers in a manner peculiar to himself, he exclaimed, " They have been licking the butter off my bread for some time, but I think I have them now."

This unfeeling expression becoming known in the regiment, caused him more detestation even than his former cruelty.

The enemy retired from the position on their right that night, and quitting also their position and works in front of St Jean de Luz, retired upon Bidart, destroying the bridges on the lower Nivelle. In the

course of the preceding day we had taken fifty-one
piece of cannon, six ammunition tumbrils, and one
thousand four hundred prisoners.

In consequence of the rapid movements of the
division, the baggage had not come up, and as
it rained heavy, we were rather uncomfortably
situated. Next day we moved forward a short distance, through dreadfully dirty roads, but the enemy
having retired into an intrenched camp before
Bayonne, we halted and again encamped, when the
baggage joined us. Some of them had been nearly
taken by the French during the preceding night; our
division being farther advanced than the enemy's
right, they were uncertain where to direct their march.
The corporal of our band, (a Glasgow lad,) coming
up that evening with the baggage, observed a poor
woman of the 88th regiment endeavouring to raise
the ass that carried her necessaries, out of a hole it
had fallen into. As it was getting dark, and the baggage had all passed, the poor woman was in a miserable plight, and begged of him to assist her. She
could not have applied to one more willing to succour
a person in distress, and setting to work, after a good
deal of trouble, he got the " borico" on its feet, but
so much time had elapsed that the baggage was now
out of hearing, and they were uncertain which way
to proceed. After travelling some distance, they
heard bugles sounding to their left, and they kept on
in that direction, until they found themselves in the
midst of some regiments of Spaniards, but who could
give them no information respecting the position of
our division. Pointing, however, to where they suspected them to be, our travellers continued their
route in that direction; but the poor ass was so
fatigued, that it lay down every now and then under
its burden. Assisting it on in the best way they could,
the road they had taken brought them between two
hills, on which they perceived the fires of different

encampments. When they arrived opposite them, they suspected from their relative position, that one must be the enemy, but which of them they knew not ; they were now in a dilemma, and to add to it, the poor ass tumbled headlong into a stream that ran through the valley, and their united efforts could not raise it. P——'s spirit of knight-errantry was now fast evaporating, and he was almost tempted to swear that he would never again be caught succouring dis-tressed damsels, when the woman, whose invention was sharpened by the exigency of her situation, pro-posed that she would creep softly up the hill, until she came within hearing of the soldiers in the camp, and from their language she would be able to learn whether they were our troops or the enemy. She then ascended the hill that she considered the most likely to be the encampment of our troops, leaving poor P—— sitting beside the half-drowned animal, to whose name he was inclined to think the transactions of that night gave him some claim. After waiting a considerable time in anxious suspense, he was begin-ning to forget his selfish considerations, in concern for the safety of the poor woman who had thus ven-tured on a forlorn hope, when his attention was attracted by some one descending the hill waving a light backwards and forwards, and shouting at the same time ; having answered the signal, the woman soon made her appearance, with a Portuguese soldier, whose division was encamped on the hill which she ascended, and they now learned that those on the opposite hill were the French. Having succeeded in raising the half-perished " buro," the Portuguese lifted the baggage on his back, and the others half dragging, half carrying the animal, they reached the top of the hill, but still no information could be got of the divi-sion. Considering it of no use to proceed farther, they seated themselves by a fire, but they had scarcely done so, when it came on a heavy shower of rain

which drenched them to the skin — there was no
remedy, however, but patience. Next morning at
daylight they again took the road, but they were
now more fortunate, for falling in with some of the
baggage they had parted with the preceding night,
they reached the division by the time we had encamped.

During our campaigns in the Peninsula, it is almost
incredible what the poor women who followed us had
to endure, marching often in a state of pregnancy,
and frequently bearing their children in the open air,
in some instances, on the line of march, by the road
side ; suffering, at the same time, all the privation to
which the army was liable. In quarters, on the
other hand, they were assailed by every temptation
which could be thrown in their way, and every
scheme laid by those who had rank and money, to
rob them of that virtue which was all they had left
to congratulate themselves upon. Was it to be
wondered at, then, if many of them were led astray,
particularly when it is considered that their starving
condition was often taken advantage of by those who
had it in their power to supply them, but who were
villains enough to make their chastity the price ?

From this encampment we advanced to Ustaritz,
where we remained until the 9th of December, when
we crossed the Nive. At the point we passed, we
met with little or no opposition, but some of the
army were warmly engaged. We then took up our
quarters in Hasparin. The day that we entered this
village, one of our men cut off his right hand, under
circumstances that may be worth relating.

For some time previous to this he had been low in
spirits, troubled with what some people call *religious
melancholy*, but which, at that time, was no very prevalent disease in the army. He scarcely ever spoke
to any one, and was in the habit of wandering out
from the encampment, with his Bible in his pocket,

and, seating himself in some place where he was not likely to be disturbed, he would sit for hours poring over it. While in Ustaritz, he conceived some ill will against the landlord of the house where he was quartered, and very unceremoniously knocked him down. Being confined for this offence, he remained a prisoner when we entered Hasparin. On the guard being placed in a house, he sat down, and having taken out his Bible, he commenced reading it. But suddenly rising, he laid the book down, and going over to a man who was breaking wood with a hatchet, he asked the loan of it for a few minutes. When the man gave it to him, he walked very deliberately into an inner apartment, and placing his right hand on the sill of the window, he severed it at the wrist. The first two strokes that he made did not finish the business, and he had nerve enough not only to repeat it a third time, but afterwards to wrench the lacerated integuments asunder, and throw the hand into the court below. He had been observed by some of the men in a window opposite, but too late to prevent the deed.

I assisted in leading him to the assistant surgeon's quarters, where the stump was dressed in a manner which I shall describe, and leave to the profession either to praise or censure, as they may feel inclined. The bone had been rather splintered than cut, and its sharp point protruded about two inches beyond the mangled integuments. Having prepared his apparatus he placed the patient on a seat, and after half an hour's poking with a tenacalum, he succeeded in taking up and tying the two principal arteries. He then nipt off the rough angles at the point of the bone, and forcing down the retracted integuments by straps of adhesive plaster, under which he had introduced some dry lint, he rolled the whole up with a bandage, and left him, congratulating himself, no doubt, on his dexterity.

The man, on being questioned as to his motive in thus mutilating himself, replied, " that he had only done what the Lord commanded, in a passage he had been reading, — If thy right hand offend thee, cut it off, and cast it from thee," &c. which injunction he had literally fulfilled, as his right hand offended him by knocking down his landlord. This was the only reason he ever assigned. As he went to the rear some time after, and did not join the regiment again, I had never an opportunity of learning whether the operation proved successful.

From the village of Hasparin we were removed about a mile, to the deserted palace of some Gascon nobleman, where we were quartered until the 6th of January, when we advanced, and drove in the enemy's outposts; but returning on the 7th, we did not again move until the middle of February.

While in Hasparin the weather was bad, and we were much harassed, marching a distance of two or three miles every morning to the alarm-post two hours before daylight, and remaining there until it appeared. The inhabitants of the province we were now in were different in dress and manners from both Spaniards and French, but their language (Patois) seemed to our ears harsh and discordant. The round bonnets of the men, and the dress and healthy look of the women, was much similar to the Scottish peasantry.

I am not certain whether it was here or in Ustaritz, —the latter, I believe,—that we had two men of our division executed; one hanged for robbing an officer's portmanteau, and another shot for presenting his empty piece at a sergeant of the mounted police corps, which acted as assistants to the provost marshall, and had been attached to the army since the commencement of the last campaign. Every one thought he would be pardoned, or at least his sentence commuted, as it was said there was some unnecessary provocation given by the sergeant; but mercy was not extended to him. We were often inclined to think that the provosts marshal were possessed of more power than they ought to have had, particularly as they were generally men of a description who abused it, and were guided more by caprice and personal pique than any regard to justice. In fact, they seemed to be above all control, doing what they pleased, without being brought to any account, and were often greater robbers than the men they punished.

After leaving this place, we came up with the French on the 23d of February, near the village of Sauveterre. A river ran between us and the town, over which there was a bridge that they had placed in a state of defence, their army occupying the opposite bank. On the morning of the 24th, our brigade were ordered some way down from the bridge, for the purpose of crossing a ford near a mill. Our light companies, covered by a party of the seventh hussars, first took the river, in a particular part of which there was a strong current, caused by the mill stream. This, together with the large round stones that formed the bottom, caused some difficulty in getting across ; but they effected it, and advancing up the bank through a narrow lane, lined a wall on the top of the height. The cavalry then returned, and the right of the brigade had crossed the river, when the enemy, having detached a strong force to oppose our progress, drove in the light troops so precipitately, that in retreating through the lane already mentioned, they were wedged in so closely that they could not move. A number then struck off to the right, and attempted to swim the river, but being carried away with the current, many of them were drowned. Of those who crossed at the ford many were wounded in the river, and losing their footing sunk to rise no more, among whom was a brave young officer of our regiment. The French had by this time come close down on them, and none would have escaped being killed or taken prisoners had not a brigade of guns been brought down to the edge of the river, and by a heavy fire of grape covered the retreat. On recrossing, the brigade withdrew under cover of some houses, and on the 25th the division crossed the river on a bridge of boats, the enemy having blown up the stone bridge, and retreated.

In the affair on the 24th a great number of our men were taken prisoners, exclusive of the killed and wounded. On the 27th, we came up with the enemy again at Orthes, where their whole army had taken up a position, their left resting on the village and heights of Orthes, and right extending to that of St Boes. The right of our line was composed of the third and sixth divisions, led on by General Picton; the light division, under Baron Alten, formed the centre; and Marshal Beresford, with the fourth and seventh, formed the left. The battle commenced by the latter attacking St Boes and carrying it; but by reason of the difficult nature of the ground, it was found impracticable to carry the heights. Their whole line was then attacked by the third, fourth, sixth, and light divisions, when the enemy were dislodged from the heights; and Sir Rowland Hill, who, in advancing to join the conflict, saw the French already routed, the more effectually to prevent their escape, pushed forward the second division and cavalry. Their retreat was well conducted at first, but it gradually became disorderly, and in the end a complete flight, many of the conscripts throwing down their arms and deserting.

The French had made a most obstinate resistance at the point which we had to carry, and kept up a severe cannonade on us, by which many of our men were decapitated, in consequence of their firing chain shot. In one part of the road where they had been driven from the fields, our cavalry had made a furious charge on them, and taken a number of prisoners. The road was almost rendered impassable by the number of arms lying on it. Near this place lay a sergeant belonging to our light brigade, extended by the side of a French grenadier, their bayonets transfixed in each other, and both dead. Passing Orthes, we followed the retreat of the enemy until we passed through another town, where part of their rear-guard lined the walls of a churchyard, situated a little above the town, and had brought out tables and chairs to stand on while they fired over upon us. In passing through this village, a shot from one of their cannon shattered the leg of an old midwife while she was crossing the street; the head doctor of our regiment, a skilful and intelligent surgeon, being passing at the time, having inspected the injury, found it necessary to amputate the limb, and although she was far advanced in years, in three weeks after, when we had occasion to pass near the village, she had almost entirely recovered.

Beyond this village, about two miles, we encamped by the road side, and had not been long encamped, when my friend the corporal of the band, whom I have already mentioned, arrived, bringing with him a child which he had found in a field under peculiar circumstances. As he and a musician of the 83d regiment were passing along the road, they were attracted by the piteous cries of a French officer, who lay severely wounded in a ditch a short distance from them; he begged for God's sake that they would give him a drink, and as I have already hinted, P——— always ready to follow the dictates of a benevolent heart, gave him some wine from his canteen. It was then dusk, but while he stooped to give the officer the wine, he perceived something moving beneath his cloak, and on drawing it a little aside, he found a fine boy, about four years ol', dressed in the English fashion, nestled in beside him. Taking him up in his arms, he asked him his name, when the child replied, " James." The officer entered into an expla-nation of the matter, and P—— understood enough of the language, to learn that the child came up the road during a heavy fire while our army and the French were engaged. The officer, who had been wounded a little before, seeing the poor child in imminent danger, and in the midst of his own suffer-ings, feeling interested for his fate, had enticed him off the road, and kept him amused until he fell asleep, when he wrapped him in the corner of his cloak. The officer expressed the utmost gratitude for P——'s kindness in giving him the wine, but he seemed to feel in parting with the child, nor did the child seem very willing to part with him. With the view, however, of finding out his parents, the child was brought home to the camp, and notice being sent to the different divisions of the army, in a few days the child's mother arrived. Her feelings on again finding her child, may be better imagined than described. She stated, that having come into the town in rear of where the army were engaged, the child had wandered from her knee while she was suckling a younger one, and that she had searched every part of the town for him without being able to get the least trace of the direction he had taken, or what had become of him.

Having children certainly increased the hardships that the poor women were fated to endure; but excess of suffering, which tore asunder every other tie, only rendered maternal love stronger, and it was amazing what hardships were voluntarily endured for the sake of their offspring. I remember one poor fellow of our brigade, whose wife died, and left an infant with him of a few months old, and although he might have got one of the women to take care of it, he preferred taking charge of it himself, and for many a day he trudged along with it sitting on the top of his knapsack. Sickness at length overtook him, and he went to the rear to hospital, carrying the child with him, but what was their fate afterwards I have never been able to learn.

Next morning we left our encampment, and returning by the way we had come, we passed a man of the division on the road side, who had been hung up to the branch of a tree a few minutes before. According to the current report in the division, he had entered a mill, and asked the miller to sell him some flour, but the miller refusing to sell it, he took it by force; and being caught in the act by some one, who reported the affair to Lord Wellington, he was tried by a general court martial, and sentenced to death. For a long time after his trial, he was marched a prisoner with the provost guard, and he entertained hopes of pardon; but on that morning, without any previous warning, while he was sitting at the fire with some of his fellow prisoners, the provost came in and ordered him to rise, when placing the rope round his neck, he marched him forward on the road a short distance, and hung him up on the branch of a tree. Examples, perhaps, were necessary, but we were inclined to think that the time was often unfortunately chosen; it was rather an awkward sort of spectacle to greet the eyes of an army the morning after a hard fought and successful battle; and the poor wretch's fate excited more commiseration that morning, than detestation of his crime.

Some of the men happened to make remarks on the subject, — " Pshaw !" said Dennis, who was listening to them, " I don't believe my countryman would do any thing of the sort. Sure it's only a dead man he has ordered to be hung up to frighten yees."

"He is dead enough now," said another. "Do you remember," said a third, "the tickler of a

circular that was served out to us after the dreadful
retreat from Salamanca,—was *that* your countryman's
doings ?"

" Troth, I don't know," said Dennis ; " but it
didn't go well down with us ; and if this is the sort
of payment we get for beating the French, the best
way is to go down on our knees, and promise never
to be guilty of the like again."

CHAPTER X.

IN consequence of the wet weather, we were unable
to proceed, and lay in camp near this place for about
three weeks ; and little of any moment occurred
during that time, except the capture of Aire on the
2d of March, by General's Hill's division.

On the 18th March, the enemy having retired in
the night upon Vic Bigorre, we advanced on the
19th, and came up with their rear guard, which was
posted in great force in the vineyards in front of that
town. Our division, under General Picton, advanced
up the main road to the attack, until the enemy's
artillery, which commanded it, forced us to strike
into the fields to the right and left, when we drove
them from one field to another, while they contested
every inch of the ground with the greatest obstinacy,
at every hedge and ditch giving us a volley as we
came up, and then retreating to the next fence.
While advancing upon one of these temporary
defences, a French soldier, through some cause, was
rather tardy in retreating, and our men were close
upon him before he started out of the ditch. His
comrades had, by this time, lined the fence farther
on, and being a remarkable object, a number of our
skirmishers directed their fire against him ; but he did
not seem much incommoded, for after running a few

paces, he turned about and fired on his pursuers;
and reloading his piece, continued this running fire
for some distance. His daring conduct having
attracted the attention of all, a great number joined
in trying to bring the poor fellow down, and the
shot was flying about him in every direction; but he
seemed invulnerable. At length, coming near to
where his own party was under cover, he walked up
to the edge of the embankment, and after firing at
the party who were in his rear, he clapped his hand
very contemptuously on his breech, and jumped down
into the ditch. Those to the left of the road, being
brought to a point by a river, were obliged to cross
the main road, where they suffered severely. A
sergeant of our brigade received a dreadful wound
here—a cannon shot having struck him, carried away
the fleshy part of the thigh, leaving the bone perfectly bare, to the extent of twelve or fourteen inches.
A little farther on, a lad belonging to the band of the
eighty-third regiment, lay killed. The band in general
accompanied the baggage, but he never would submit
to this; and when near the enemy, he always did
duty with the light company.

Having driven the enemy from the vineyards, in
retreating through the town they killed a number of
our men, from the various places they had got under
cover. One poor fellow of the fifth regiment received
a shot, which, passing through his temples, cut the
strings of his eyes, and we saw him sitting on a stone
with them hanging out of their sockets. The whole
of our army having assembled that night at Vic
Bigorre and Rabastains, the enemy retired in the
night upon Tarbes, and we came up with their
advanced posts in that town on the 20th; their centre
and left had retired, and their right was attacked by
the sixth division under General Clinton, while
General Hill attacked the hill by the high road from
Vic Bigorre.

The sixth division being successful, General Hill passed through the town, and disposed his columns for attack, when the enemy retreated in all directions, having suffered severely, while our loss was but trifling. Following them up the Garonne as far as Grenada, on the 8th of April a pontoon bridge was thrown across, and the eighteenth hussars, with a Portuguese and Spanish brigade, crossed, and drove in a body of the enemy's cavalry, taking about a hundred prisoners.

The town of Toulouse is surrounded on three sides by the canal of Languedoc and the Garonne. They had fortified the suburbs on the left of that river with strong field works; they had likewise formed works at each bridge of the canal, defended by artillery and musketry. Beyond the canal, to the eastward, and between that and the river Ers, there is a range of heights extending for some distance, over which pass all the roads to the canal and town from the eastward, which it defends; and the enemy, in addition to the outworks at the bridges of the canal, had fortified the heights with five redoubts connected by lines of intrenchments; they had also broken all the bridges over the river Ers within our reach, by which the right of their position could be approached. When the Spanish corps passed, the pontoon bridge was moved higher up, in order to shorten the communication with General Hill's division, and this was done so late on the evening of the 9th, that the attack was delayed till next day.

Our division crossed on the evening of the 9th, and next morning, the troops under Marshal Beresford attacked the enemy's right, while the Spaniards under General Frere assailed the centre; but the latter were soon repulsed, and being, with a heavy .oss, driven from the ground, were pursued to some distance. By the exertions of their officers, however, they were formed anew, when our light division, which was immediately on their right, took up their place. In the meantime, Beresford, with the fourth and sixth divisions, attacked and carried the heights on the enemy's right, and the redoubt, which covered and protected that flank, and lodged his troops in the redoubt. The enemy, however, still occupied the others. As soon as the Spaniards had re-formed, and were brought back to the attack, General Beresford continued his march along the ridge, and carried, with General Pack's brigade, the two principal redoubts, and the fortified houses in the enemy's centre. The enemy made a desperate effort from the canal to regain those redoubts, but were repulsed with considerable loss ; and the sixth division continuing their movement along the ridge, and the Spanish troops on the front, the enemy were driven from all their redoubts and intrenchments on the left, and the whole range of heights were in our possession.

While these operations were going on on the left, General Hill drove the enemy from their exterior works in the suburb on the left of the Garonne, within the old wall. Our division charged the works at the bridges, but, in consequence of their strength, were unable to carry them, and suffered severely in the attempt.

During the 11th, not a shot was fired on either side, and the French bands were playing the greater part of the day. Ours were also brought down, and a sort of conversation was kept up by the different tunes played. The French would listen attentively while ours played the " Downfall of Paris," and in turn gave us a reply of the same kind. Next morning, to our surprise, we found them gone. They had retreated during the night, leaving in our hands three generals and one thousand six hundred prisoners, with much stores of all descriptions.

On the evening of the 12th an express arrived

from Paris, to inform Lord Wellington of the peace; Marshal Soult would not believe it, but he agreed to a cessation of hostilities. We were now encamped at the outside of the town, where we remained for a few days. When advancing about three leagues, we met a messenger on his way to Toulouse, on a mission from the government, and it was now that we got full confirmation of the joyful news. Each heart beat light at the intelligence, but we could scarcely dare to believe it; we had been so often deceived, that we thought it too good news to be true. Nothing, however, was now talked of but home.

We were quartered in Le Mas, a short distance from Toulouse, where we remained until the order came for us to march to Blanchefort, situated in one of the sandy plains of the Landes. The land was incapable of cultivation, but they fed numerous flocks of sheep on it, and the shepherds were mounted on huge stilts to enable them to see for some distance around. The whole army being collected here, the different individuals who had formerly been acquainted, had an opportunity of seeing each other, and our meeting was the happier that we could now congratulate each other on the return of peace.

In marching from Toulouse to this place, we parted with the Portuguese army at Condom. They were then well regulated and well disciplined troops. The English mode of discipline had been introduced among them for some time, a number of English officers were attached to them; and acting always in concert with us, they were now little inferior to ourselves. A kind of friendship had thus arisen, and caused us to feel sorry at parting. On the morning that this happened, they were ranged upon the street, and saluted us as we passed, and their hearty "Vivas!" and exclamations of regret, evinced that they really felt: but a scene of a more affecting nature took place in the Portuguese and Spanish women parting

with the men of our army, to whom they had attached
themselves during the miserable state of their country.   The generality of them were not married, but
the steady affection and patient endurance of hardship
which they exhibited, in following those to whom
they belonged, would have done credit to a more
legal tie.   Being here ordered to return to their own
country with the Portuguese army, and strict orders
given to prevent any of them from proceeding farther,
the scene which ensued was distressing, — the poor
creatures running about concealing themselves, in the
vain hope of being allowed to remain ; but it was all
to no purpose : although they were willing to have
sacrificed country and relations to follow us, the
sacrifice could not be accepted.

From Blanchefort camp we proceeded to Pauilhac,
from whence, in a few days, we embarked in small
vessels, which took us down to the Corduan light-
house, where we were put on board the San Domingo,
74 gun ship, and after a pleasant passage arrived at
the Cove of Cork, where we disembarked.

Our regiment was nearly nine hundred strong
when we first went out to the Peninsula.   During
the time we remained there, we received at various
times recruits to the amount of four hundred, and
when we left the country, our strength was about two
hundred and fifty, out of which number not more
than one hundred and fifty remained who went out
with the regiment.

CONCLUSION.

I HAVE thus endeavoured as far as my recollection
served me, to give a simple and faithful description
of those scenes in which I was myself an actor, without partiality to any class.   If occasionally I have

drawn an unseemly picture, the fault was in the original, for I have no personal enmity to any individual in the service; and I beg it may be distinctly understood, that many of the abuses which I have narrated are only spoken of as things that have existed, rather than as a picture of the present state of the army. Thanks to his Royal Highness the commander-in-chief, little is now left the soldier to complain of.

When we look back twenty or thirty years, and consider what the army was then, and what it is now, the wonder will be, not that it is not in a better state, but that so much has been done to ameliorate the condition of the soldier. Then he was one of the veriest slaves existing, obliged to rise two or three hours before day to commence his cleaning operations. His hair required to be soaped, floured, and frizzed, or tortured into some uncouth shape which gave him acute pain, and robbed him of all power of moving his head unless he brought his body round with it. He had his musket to burnish, his cap and cartridge box to polish with heel-ball, and his white breeches to pipe-clay, so that it generally required three or four hours hard labour to prepare him for parade; and when he turned out, he was like something made of glass, which the slightest accident might derange or break to pieces. He was then subjected to a rigid inspection, in which, if a single hair stood out of its place, extra guard, drill, or some other punishment, awaited him. When to this was added the supercilious tyrannical demeanour of his superiors, who seemed to look upon him as a brute animal who had neither soul nor feeling, and who caned or flogged him without mercy for the slightest offence, we cannot wonder that he became the debased being, in body and mind, which they already considered him, or that he possessed the common vices of a slave — fawning servility, duplicity, and want of all self-respect ; to add to this, what was his reward when worn out and unfit for farther service ? — a pittance insufficient to support nature, or a pass to beg.

When we consider that, in the face of long established usages, and coadjutors of unbending and contracted views of human nature, the Commander-in-chief by his persevering exertions has almost entirely abolished those numerous vexations — when we see gentlemanly feeling and attention to the soldier's best interests encouraged among the officers of the army, and the change wrought in the moral and military character of the soldier by these means, — is it to be wondered at that every individual in the service is attached to the Duke of York, and looks up to him in the light of a father and a friend. Few generals of whom I have ever either heard or read, enjoyed the esteem and affection of the troops under their command, more than His Royal Highness.

The failings alleged against him by his enemies were severely visited upon him by many, who, had they examined their own conscience, could not have said they were innocent of similar errors, and who could not plead a kindly unsuspecting nature as an excuse. The country has long consigned to oblivion all remembrance of them ; but they have lately been sacrilegiously drawn forth by men, whom every well-regulated mind must blush to call countrymen — men who have not only made a jest of his sufferings and probable death, but grinned with fiendlike exultation at the prospect of a war which was to exterminate, and render miserable thousands of their fellow-creatures.*

* That such men should possess the confidence of the people of Ireland, that they should expect any assistance from them, or how the bombastic declamation and frothy venom, which they spew forth at public meetings, can have any other effect than to produce disgust, is to me not a little wonderful. The emancipation of the Catholics may be retarded, but it will never advance one step under the direction of men possessed of so much zeal, and so little judgment.

I hate that canting species of liberality which means free exercise of opinion only to those of the same mode of thinking, and that deals out unsparing censure on all those who (no matter how conscientiously) differ from them; such, however, is the conduct of some of our special pleaders for religious toleration. In his opposition to the Catholic claims, who will say that His Royal Highness did not act conscientiously? And if this is granted, however firmly he may be attached to his principles, it is evident he does not adhere to them with half the violence and pertinacity of those on the opposite side who raise the cry against him.

His character, however, can never be affected by vapouring declamation — the remembrance of his kindness, benevolence, and accessibility, (if I may use the term,) will outlive party feeling and animosity — all classes and sects will yet join in doing justice to the character of a prince, who, if he possess failings, they are those common to humanity, while his virtues raise him much above its ordinary level.

Since the preceding portion of this volume was sent to press, the melancholy event which was then feared has taken place, and the narrow tomb now encloses that heart which, while it continued to beat, embraced the interests and wellbeing of thousands. What I anticipated has already taken place — all parties join in eulogizing his worth and virtues. Rancour and fierce hatred have even been disarmed of their venom; but words can but very inadequately convey the feeling produced by his death throughout the army. They now naturally look round with intense anxiety, for the individual who is to succeed him. The Duke of Wellington, in point of military

ability, seems the most likely ; but, judging from the
past, I would say, he will not be to the army what
the Duke of York has been. He may concoct, arrange,
and put in practice, plans for their discipline and
equipment—he may lead them to victory, as he has
done before ; but his name will never be the key-note
to the warm and grateful feelings of the soldier, when
it strikes on his ear, to send the blood in tingling
currents from the heart to the cheek. Yet I may be
mistaken : when the country at large is progressing
rapidly in just sentiment and liberality of thinking,
and enlightened views in the government of every
department are taking the place of the more severe
and austere rules of the old school, it is doing injustice to the Duke of Wellington, to believe that he
will remain stationary. If he should assume the
command, he will have a glorious opportunity of
treading in the footsteps of his royal predecessor, and
of adding to his great military qualities all those
minor (but not less important) qualifications which
excite men's gratitude and esteem, and will enable
him to live in the hearts of those under his command
His claims to the character of a hero will then be
complete, and as such his name will be handed down
to posterity

SCENES AND SKETCHES
IN IRELAND.

A CONTINUATION

OF

RECOLLECTIONS OF THE EVENTFUL LIFE
OF A SOLDIER.

PREFACE.

FLATTERED by the approbation of the public in my former rude attempt to portray the scenes of my " Eventful Life," I am induced to lay before them the present volume.

I am aware that in my style and grammatical correctness they have much to censure, for which I can only plead the coat I wear. Peculiar circumstances deprived me of the assistance of a single individual in its correction ; for the errors, therefore, which have escaped my notice, I must entreat the indulgence of the public.

Under depressing circumstances, I have endeavoured to cultivate my mind : that I have not succeeded in attaining all the necessary qualifications to shine as an author, cannot surely, against one in my situation, be alleged as a fault. I have been accused of giving the former part of my narrative a romantic colouring. It may be a fault in style, and, as has been observed, may throw an air of doubt over its authenticity ; but, after all, it is perhaps its greatest charm. Had it not been for my romantic spirit, I might never have witnessed those scenes which I have attempted to describe, or, having seen them, they would not have made the impression on my mind, so necessary to paint them vividly.

It is needless to say any thing of the present volume; the public will judge for itself, independent of any representation of mine. Party feeling may induce individuals to rail, and others to praise; but the collective judgment of the public is the only true criterion. To its decision, therefore, I commit it. My pretensions are not high : if I have succeeded in drawing, simply and naturally, scenes which made a strong impression on my mind at the time, or infused into their recital the feeling that filled my own bosom, I am satisfied.

THE AUTHOR.

THE

EVENTFUL LIFE

OF

A SOLDIER.

CHAPTER I.

THE RETURN.

THE regiment I belonged to had been serving in the Peninsula from the early part of 1810, during that harassing and apparently interminable war; for campaign after campaign succeeded each other, and although we gained splendid victories in each, we generally found ourselves taking up our winter quarters on the same ground from whence we had set out.

At the close of 1812, after a weary and disastrous retreat from Madrid, we were again quartered in Portugal; here we remained for five months, during which the most active and energetic preparations were made for the ensuing campaign, which commenced in May, 1813. A series of successes almost unexampled enabled us to winter in France, and the battle of Toulouse in April, 1814, concluded a war which had drained the country of men and treasure.

With feelings which none can know but those who
have toiled through fields of death, we received the
order to embark for Britain, and it was with little
regret that we lost sight of the fair shores of France,
" with its bright beaming summers exhaling perfume."
Far dearer to our imaginations were the " humble
broom bowers" of our native land, " where the blue
bell and gowan lurks lowly unseen." On the voyage
homeward, hope smiled triumphant, dreams of joy
and bliss took the place of disappointment and despair. Yet often in sleep did my imagination return
to those fields of strife and rapine that we had left ;
the agony of disappointed hope again shed its chilling
mildew on my soul, and I awoke expecting to hear
the sound of the bugle or the roar of artillery ; but the
picture was reversed — " sorrow did not now return
with the dawning of morn."

Our voyage homeward was short and pleasant.
Ireland was our destination, and having anchored
in the cove of Cork, we proceeded to disembark in
lighters.

" You are welcome to old Ireland," exclaimed my
comrade Dennis, holding out his hand to me as
I stepped from the boat out of which he had sprung
an instant before, " welcome to the land of potatoes
and buttermilk. Didn't I tell you that we would live
to see this day ? May I never die if this isn't the
happiest minute of my life ! my heart's so light that
I think I could jump over the moon. Come along,
my gay fellow, we have been long together, 'and in
spite of wind and weather we will moisten well our
clay' — I mean bye and bye, when we get to our
billets. Did you ever drink any potheen, Joseph ?
Och ! there never was drink like it in the universe, for
if you wish to be in any mood at all, it 'll do the job
for ye. If you want to fight, potheen will make you
face the ould boy himself; if you have any notion of
making love, with a bumper or two of Inishone you

might malvader the heart of Diana; and if crying is
your game, it will make your heart as soft as prapeen.
Go to the first wake you can in this country, and
you'll see what wonders it works; it will do your
heart good to see how it makes the tears trickle down
their cheeks, and sets them a counting their pedigree
back to the time when Adam was a little boy; ay,
indeed, (but I must whisper it,) I have seen it make
a voteen of many an old woman that said her Pater-
nave dry enough at any other time. Och, pure
potheen's the liquor for me,—it beats brandy, rum,
and gin, out of all razon."

Whatever I might think of the extravagant praise
which Dennis had bestowed on his favourite whisky,
I certainly participated in his joyous feelings, and
felt an affection at that moment for every thing
living, from the half naked urchins that ran about
the cabin doors, down to the pigs, cocks, and
hens, that participated in their sports, food, and
lodging.

We were billeted that day in Cork, on a respectable tradesman,—a kind cheerful fellow, who exerted
himself to make us comfortable; and after a dinner
such as we had been long strangers to, he insisted
upon us joining him in a tumbler of punch.

" Come, my dear," said the landlord to his wife,
who was present, "be kind enough to sing us a
song."

" With all my heart," said she, and she began the
well-known song of " Erin go bragh." The air is
uncommonly plaintive and beautiful, but few who
have not heard it can conceive the expression and
pathos which an enthusiastic Irishwoman can throw
into it. Such was our hostess, and she poured out
her strains in a voice so delightfully sweet that my
heart thrilled to its core: no doubt association and
the state of our minds aided the effect, but I never
felt so much pleasure from music. Recollections of

former scenes and feelings crowded on my memory, and my eyes filled with tears. Dennis sat entranced in his chair, trying to swallow the emotion that he was ashamed to shew, while his eye was fixed on the singer as if on some heavenly vision. She had herself caught the infection, and as she repeated

" Ah ! where is the mother that watch'd o'er my childhood ? "

her voice faltered, and the tear trembled in her eye. Dennis could contain himself no longer: he covered his face with his hands and wept aloud; a pause ensued, but it was a pause occasioned by revealings of the soul, too purely intellectual for expression.

Silence was broken by our hostess.

" Poor fellows !" said she, " I see the dreadful scenes you have witnessed have not hardened your hearts: they still beat true to nature."

" Oh," said Dennis, " there's more in that song than you have any notion of; many's the time I sung it when I was far from home, and when I little expected to see old Ireland or my poor mother again—surely it was an Irishman that made that song."

" He has all the warm feeling of one," said I, " but I believe he is a townsman of mine, Dennis."

" Never mind," replied he, " his heart is an Irish one—and that's the best part of him."

From the various circumstances connected with it, I am sure I never spent a happier evening, and next morning we parted with our kind hosts with as much regret as if we had known each other for years.

From Cork the regiment marched to Fermoy; having been on duty, which detained me some hours after the corps, I set out alone to perform the journey. When about half way, I overtook a countryman travelling the same road, with whom I entered into conversation. We had not gone far together when my attention was attracted by a wild cry, which seemed to be borne on the wind from some distance ; it burst on my ear like the cry of a person in distress—then, gradually sinking to a low moan, it ceased for a few moments, when again the despairing shriek swelled to the utmost pitch of the human voice,—again it sank to the plaintive murmur, and melted into air. There was something uncouth in the notes, but they were expressively wild and melancholy, and I felt myself powerfully affected without being able to account for it. I stopped for a moment to listen, and asked my companion the meaning of what I heard.

" Oh, it's some poor creature going to his long home," said he, " that they are keening over."

We had not gone far, when at a turning of the road, the melancholy procession opened on our view, —a countryman driving a car, on which was placed a coffin. One solitary mourner, (an old woman,) clung to it with one hand, while the other was raised in a despairing attitude ; her gray hair hung in disheveled tresses about her face and shoulders, and intense grief was depicted in her haggard countenance. My companion requested me to wait a moment, while he turned back a short way with the corpse. " Well," said he to me when he returned, " many 's the funeral I have seen ; but never one like that,—they haven't a single neighbour with them. when the poorest creature would nave half the parish, but that comes of the boy's own behaviour—God be merciful to his soul !"

" Why, what harm did ne do ?"

" So much that I believe his poor father and mother will never be able to hold up their heads again : he was the means of bringing two of his own relations to the gallows, that but for him might have been alive and well to-day : they were all three laid up for taking arms from a gentleman's house near this, and there was no clear proof against them, but they wheedled over this boy that's dead now, to turn king's evidence, and save his own life ; but he never did a day's good after, and he died the other day of fever, and not one of his neighbours would attend his wake.—God help his poor people !"

On reaching Fermoy, I found the regiment in barracks, where we remained only a few days, when we received the route to march to Wexford, a town on the west coast of Ireland. On reaching a village that lay in our route, the place being small, and the inhabitants poor, we were but indifferently supplied with billets. Poor Dennis had been rather unwell for a day or two previous, and I hastened to find out our quarters, that we might have an opportunity of lying down. Having inquired for the person we were billeted on, we were directed to a low roofed cabin, where a tall masculine-looking old woman was standing in the door-way.

" Come away, honies," said she, with an arch mischievous expression of countenance, " you are welcome, I was just waiting for yees."

" Thank you," said I, stooping down to enter the cabin, which was so filled with smoke that I could see nothing of the interior. By the help of the crone, however, we got ourselves seated by the fire, which was made in the centre of the apartment, the door of which served for chimney, window, and all.

Dennis feeling himself very sick, expressed a wish to lie down, and I asked the landlady to shew him our bed, for although I saw none, I thought she might have some other apartment.

" That I will, I'll be after making a fahl for the poor boy in a minute. Get up out o' that," said she, angrily, to some one who lay on a bundle of straw, in a dark corner of the room, enveloped in something resembling an old great coat.

"Oh! don't disturb any body for us."

"Troth and it's myself that will," and seized a stick that was lying by the fire to chastise the object she had addressed.

Seeing the miserable appearance of the hovel, I had made up my mind to seek other quarters, and was proceeding to remonstrate, but before I could, the old woman had inflicted the blow; a grunt followed, and presently an enormous pig, carrying the half of the straw, and the ragged coat on his back, came running towards the door, and in his struggle to pass me, threw me over. Ill as Dennis was, he could not help laughing, and the old woman, instead of condoling with me on my misfortune, exclaimed, "What a smashing sodger you are, to let the pigs knock you down."

"Come away, Dennis," said I, "if this is a specimen of your country, you have much reason to be proud of it."

"Och! is that the way you are going to leave me?" said the old hag, when she saw us moving off.

"Troth is it," replied Dennis, "for I would be sorry to disturb any of the decent family."

We luckily procured a lodging in a public house near the cabin, and having mentioned our reason for changing our quarters—

"Judy is too many for ye," said our host; "she's no friend to the sodgers any how: she lost two brave boys in the rebellion, and was a right rebel herself I have seen the day when she would have thought no more of knocking down a man than of eating her breakfast. It's not many years since, when we had a fair here, the boys were seemingly going to disperse without a bit of a *row*, and bad luck to me if she didn't take off her jock, and holding it by the one sleeve, trailed it through the fair, crying out to her own party, that the blood of the O'Briens had turned into butter-milk, or they would never let the faction

of the Murphies home, without a blow being struck.
' Come, you chicken-hearted rogues !' said she, while
she brandished a stick in her hand, 'let me see the
thief's breed of a Murphy that will dare to put
his foot on my jock.' The boys only laughed at first,
but some one in the crowd, out of contempt, threw
a dead rat which struck her on the face ; this enraged
her so, that she knocked down the man nearest her,
and in a twinkling there was a fight that beat any
thing ever was seen, and she was there to the last.
But the devil himself's but a fool to ould Judy."

CHAPTER II.

PARTY SPIRIT.

WE arrived at Wexford, the station allotted for
our regiment. It had been for some time the head
quarters of the rebel army during the disturbances of
1798, and the scenes said to have been acted in and
near it during that unfortunate period, being im-
pressed on our minds, we entered the place with
strong prejudices against the inhabitants. From a
people implicated in what was termed a foul, unnatural rebellion, against a mild and equitable government, what could soldiers expect but treachery and
fixed enmity ? How were we deceived when we
found them the most urbane, good-humoured people
we had ever been amongst. This is remarkable,
thought I ; surely it must have been some strange
infatuation, or some galling wrong that goaded these
people into rebellion ; and when we had been a short
time there, I sought a solution of the enigma from a
person with whom I had become acquainted, from
being billeted in his house, when we first came into
the town.

" In the first place," said he, " I need not tell
you what every body knows, that it was only the
Catholics that rebelled. You wonder at them not
shewing their rebellious spirit: now," said he, " do
you know the reason? they durstn't. When they had
the power, they shewed us poor Protestants what
they could do; did you never read or hear of the
burning of Scullabogue, the piking on the wooden
bridge there beyond, and all the bloody cruelties
they committed in every part of Ireland?"

" I have," replied I, " and that is the very reason
I am surprised at the peaceable temper they now
display."

" It was driven into them by the lash and the
gibbet," said he; " but if they durst put out their
horns, you would soon see them at their old tricks;
devil a Protestant but they would pike and throw
into the Slaney. Do you think that we could live in
safety here an hour, if it wasn't for the military?
God help ye! you think because they put on a smooth
face to ye, now when they can't better themselves,
that they are every thing that's good; but you may
take my word for it that every mother's son of them
are perfect Judas's, and when they look smiling in
your face they are wishing for an opportunity to cut
your throat. Och, man! does not their priests tell
them that they are to keep no faith with heretics?—
They talk about emancipating them — By my soul! I
would as soon emancipate a roaring lion; if ever that
takes place, the reign of bloody Mary would be
nothing to what would follow; you would soon see
the Pope over here with his inquisition, and not one
Protestant they would leave in the country in six
months. I hope I will never live to see the day
when the Papists will be put on a footing with us:
nothing will ever save the poor Protestants but to
keep the hold while they have it, and resist the Pope,
the Papists, and the devil, up to the knees in blood,

as every true orangeman is in duty bound. You should join our orange club, man—sure, two of your officers have joined us."

I was carried away with this declamation, which he accompanied with violent and emphatic gesture, and really began to think the Catholics the guilty beings that he represented them ; still I could not but consider them miserably situated, when they were alike distrusted and reviled — in arms against the government, or living as peaceable subjects. On more mature deliberation, I did not feel satisfied with the round assertions he had made, and I sought opportunities of mixing with people of the Catholic persuasion. I am sorry to say that those whom my rank in life enabled me to mix with, did not give me very favourable opportunities of judging; they seemed to feel the same rancour against the Protestants, which my friend had evinced against them, without being able to give a very satisfactory reason for it. They had an idea that the Protestants were insolent tyrants, that the Catholics were oppressed and injured by them, and therefore had a right to hate their oppressors.

Some time after this, I became acquainted with a very intelligent Catholic, and anxious to hear what he could say in answer to the assertions of my Protestant friend, I several times attempted to lead our conversation to that point, but he seemed to feel averse from the subject.

" Remember," said he to me, one day, " that it is rather a dangerous thing to express our political opinions in this country. I might," said he, in a half joking manner, " get heated on the subject, and spout treason ; and who knows but you might lodge informations against me, that would get me exhibited in front of the gaol, as an example to my deluded countrymen, or sent to cool my heels in New South Wales. You laugh, but the time is scarcely yet

gone by, when your report of my disaffection to the
government would have got me elevated to the first
lamp post, without either judge or jury. But to shew
you I place some confidence in you, I will put my
neck in your power, by repeating my opinion on the
subject. Believe me, whatever your friend may
have said to the contrary, that the rancour and hatred
of Protestants and Catholics, so apparent in this
country, does not lie so much in the difference of
their creed, as in prejudices artfully engendered and
kept alive by political and religious intrigue, aided
no doubt by the ignorance of the people themselves.
You are a young man, a native of a happier kingdom, and of a different persuasion, and cannot, therefore, enter into the feelings of this oppressed and
insulted nation ; nor can those who have not felt the
legalized tyranny which is practised on us form any
idea of what this miserable country has suffered.
Victims to political corruption on the one hand, and
religious rapacity and bigotry on the other; by
the one we are deprived of our rights as men and
subjects, and by the other robbed of our means of
subsistence, to support in luxury and idleness a
church establishment of which we are not members,
the clergymen of which in their own persons exercise
the office of priest and judge, to whom, if we consider ourselves aggrieved by their extortions, we are
obliged to appeal for redress ; but this is nothing to
the continual dropping torment which we are doomed
to endure from our subordinate oppressors, who are to
a man what are termed Protestants, — tithe proctors,
excisemen, constables, pound keepers, all are Protestants, and contrive at every step to put us in mind
of our political bondage ; and when we are goaded
on by our merciless drivers until we grow frantic,
they term the writhings of tortured and insulted
nature, rebellion.

" The rebellion which rendered this county noto-

rious, has been called a rebellion of the Catholics.
It is false ; it was first begun in the north of Ireland
by Protestants— Presbyterians if you will. A grand
political scheme was then in agitation,— the withdrawing the semblance of a government from this
country. Great opposition was expected. This
rebellion, properly managed, would afford a pretext
for the measure, and prepare the way for the important change. The conspiracy might have been crushed
at the outset ; but instead of that, it was allowed to
spread its ramifications through the whole island.
This it did more rapidly than was at first imagined,
and as Samson of old, when deprived of his eyesight,
and brought out to make sport for the lords of the
Philistines, made a dreadful end of their amusement,
our rulers ran some danger of being involved in the
commotion which ensued.

"'Divide to govern,' seems to have been the
Machiavelian policy by which this unhappy country
has been always ruled. As the only measure to save
themselves was to create distrust between those
implicated, the Catholics were stigmatized as the
movers of the rebellion, and their end to overturn
the Protestant religion. This had the desired effect ;
the Protestants, for their secession from the cause,
were invested with the office of hunting us down, —
how they performed their task, is in this country too
well known. As those who commit wrong are more
implacable and unforgiving than those injured, the
Protestants have ever since nourished a deadly hatred
towards us, and knowing the tenure on which they
hold their power, dread that we should ever be
placed on a par with them.

" Would your countrymen suffer what we have
done without trying to shake themselves free of the
yoke ? — no, they would not. When an attempt was
made to saddle Episcopacy upon them, to a man
they resisted the attempt ; and the consequence was,

that, like us, they were hunted as wild beasts, their houses were burned, their property robbed, their women violated, and themselves brought to the torture and the gibbet. They bore it all, animated by a determined spirit, and, aided by good fortune, they triumphed; and now in possession of dear-earned privileges, you look back with pride and exultation on what they achieved. But what is in you esteemed a virtue, is with us a crime. Poor Ireland has not been so fortunate; her efforts to assert her birth-right, through the want of unanimity amongst her children, have been unsuccessful, and are still stigmatized as rebellion, while yours are lauded to the skies. Remember, I do not attempt to vindicate the insurrection of that period, which was at best but an insane project, and even had it succeeded, would have produced no permanent advantage to this country.

" Above all other people, you ought to feel most sympathy for us; but if I mistake not, the measure of our emancipation meets with more virulent opposition in Scotland than in any other place. I repeat it again, that our creeds do not cause the deadly hatred which exists between the Catholic and Protestant in Ireland. See how peaceably they live together in England and Scotland, where they do not feel the irritation which excites us here. Nothing will ever restore our unhappy country to a state of quiet, but removing the disgraceful bonds with which we are weighed down to the earth. An enthusiasm pervades the country to emancipate the West Indian negroes; let them first remove the taint from their own constitution, let them eradicate the plague-spot from themselves, and then, with a clear conscience, they may go on and prosper; until then, their exertions in that cause will appear hypocritical and absurd —But I am talking to you as if you were interested in the matter. I forget that soldiers have nothing to do with politics, and far less soldiers who are here to keep the peace among the wild Irish."

The conflicting statements here given may serve to give a tolerably correct idea of the state of party feeling in Ireland ; at present I refrain from making any observations of my own on the subject.

CHAPTER III.

ARREARS.

WHEN we had been a few weeks in Wexford, we received about six months' pay, of which we had fallen in arrear while in the Peninsula, amounting to a considerable sum each man ; and as it could scarcely be spent by individuals like us, who had been exiled from home and all its enjoyments for a number of years, without some spreeing, the commanding officer wisely resolved to relax the reins of discipline a little. In such cases I have always found that severe restraint creates the evil that it is meant to prevent ; but when humoured in some degree, the ebullition passes over,— foolishly enough certainly, but in general harmlessly. Nothing is more natural than that men's judgment should be carried away by their animal spirits on such occasions, and those who purse up their mouths and treat the matter as a crime, know nothing at all about it.

Our poor fellows, when they got their money, in the joy of their hearts, played such fooleries as could challenge comparison with any ship's crew that ever came into port. It would be an endless task to portray every extravagance they ran into ; all joined, however, in a greater or less degree, in paying their addresses to the whisky ; each heart then became unveiled, and a very common observer could have told the ruling passion of each individual in the regiment. Some shewed their devotion to the fair sex, by hauling in every female with whom they had the slightest acquaintance, and treating them to gowns, caps, or any thing they chose to ask. Others gratified their ambitious longings by hiring horses, coaches, gigs, or jaunting cars, and riding into the country or about the town. Dennis and I were in the throng, no doubt, and on receiving our cash sallied forth in quest of adventures. Dennis could not brook the idea of entering a common public-house on that day. " We have not long to act the gentleman," said he, " we nay as well make a good use of our time ;" so saying, ne led the way to the head inn, and with the utmost pomp bawled out " waiter !" — The waiter made his appearance. — " Bring us a bottle of wine." — The waiter smiled, and looked as if he thought him mad.— " Go along, sir, and do as I order you," said Dennis ; " you stare, you spalpeen, as if you never saw a gentleman before." The waiter made his escape, and having consulted with his master, brought the wine. We had scarcely seated ourselves when two of our officers entered,—the one was a good fellow, generous, brave, and feeling ; the other was the reverse. " Mr G." said Dennis, addressing the former, " will you be kind enough to drink with us ?"

" Certainly, my good fellow, it is not the first time you and I have drank together ; I do not forget the time you gave me the last drop out of your canteen, on that long day's march going up through Spain, when every one was dying with thirst, and no water to be had."

Having drank to our health, and the glasses replenished, Dennis took up one, — " Long life to you, Mr G. you are a noble, brave officer, and I could shed my heart's blood for you by night or by day ; I wish I could say as much for many a one in the corps," casting a significant look at the other officer.

I whispered to Dennis, " You had better ask him
to drink."

" Devil a sup," said he, loud enough to be heard.
Mr J. felt galled to the soul, and colouring with rage
he walked out of the room, accompanied by the
other officer, who seemed to take no notice of what
Dennis had said.

" You were too rude," said I ; " you provoke the
man to be your enemy."

" Is it my enemy — sure he is every body's enemy,
and any thing that Dennis could say or do, would
not change him for better or worse. Don't you
remember the death of poor H—b—s—n, how could
any body like him after that ? I wouldn't have his
conscience for worlds.* But come, comrade, let's into
the city — By the powers, I had almost forgot myself,
I promised to call on Peggy Doyle. Let me see,
what will I buy for Peggy ?"—but that moment a carriage came rattling down the street, filled outside and
inside with our comrades, and ribbons and handkerchiefs streaming from all parts of it. " By the
hokey !" cried Dennis, in a yell of transport, " let's

---

* The story Dennis alluded to was certainly a dreadful one. Poor H.
joined us a short time before we advanced through Spain, and being but a
weakly boy, when we commenced the march, he was unable to keep up with
the regiment. He reported himself sick, but the doctor finding that he complained of nothing but weakness, accused him of scheming, and scratched his
name out of the report ; this did not give him more strength, and he fell out
the next day's march. The officer of whom Dennis had expressed his dislike,
being riding in the rear of the regiment, swore at him dreadfully, and
threatened to turn him over to the provost and have him flogged if he would
not keep up, but his threatenings were of no avail. Next day he was again
reported sick, again accused of scheming, and sent to march with his company,
and, as on the preceding day, was unable to keep pace with his comrades.
He was given in charge to the rear guard, and Mr J. ordered two men of the
guard to drag him along, and another to go behind him and prick him on
with his bayonet ; but all this cruelty was unavailing — they were obliged to
give up dragging him, and leave him behind. During this time he had never
complained, but his heart was broken. When he was left he crawled off the
road into a field, and, tired of a world in which he had met with such cruel
treatment, loaded his musket, and taking off his stocking, put his toe on
the trigger, and blew out his brains.

scale the garrison." In a moment we were mounted, and poor Peggy Doyle was consigned to oblivion.

The town was now in an uproar ; carriages, sociables, and jaunting cars were in requisition, flying past in every direction, with our men clinging to the outside of them, to the manifest danger of their necks and limbs. Every thing seemed to have received an impulse unusual to it, and participated in the flying motion, — the old women shouted, the children capered, the dogs barked, and the very pigs, instead of lying lazily before the doors, were galloping about the streets with their tails cocked.

Some of the boys had tarried so long at the whisky, that all the vehicles of any speed had been taken up ; but their invention was soon at work ; common cars were hired by them, and driven furiously along, to the great torment of the poor hacks. One fellow, who had been too late for even a common car, and determined at all events to ride, jumped into an empty buttermilk churn* up to the neck, and paid the woman handsomely to drive him along. " Och, it's yourself that has the taste, Slobber-daddy," cried Dennis, " you were always fond of the slurry."† He had scarcely spoke the word, when the wheel of our carriage came in contact with that of the car, and in a twinkling we were all sprawling in the mud, in glorious confusion. Nobody was hurt, however, the buttermilk hero excepted, who had broken his nose when emptied out of the churn. Up we were again in a moment, dashing along, regardless of old women, children, and corners, until the poor horses were so jaded that they actually stood still. It was now near evening, all the public houses soon filled, and drinking and boisterous mirth of every description was kept up during the night.

* In Ireland the buttermilk is brought into the towns in the churn, fastened on a common car.
† A cant term for buttermilk.

Next day the same scenes were renewed, the same
wanton prodigality in spending the money which had
been so dearly earned. On this day Dennis was
determined that his sweetheart should not be forgotten ; but it may be as well to exonerate him from
falling in love too hastily, by stating that Peggy and
he had been acquainted when children, and were dis-
tantly related to each other. She had removed to this
place along with her mistress, during the time Dennis
was abroad. They had accidentally met — their joy
on meeting was as great as it was unexpected, and a
kind of courtship had been kept up between them
from that time. A gown-piece and a handsome
shawl were now bought for her, and Dennis having
delivered it, we were going farther into the town
when we met John ——, a particular friend of ours,
though not in the same company, whom we had not
seen since the commencement of the riot.

"Where on earth have you been, John ?" said I ;
" we have been hunting every place for you, and you
were not to be found.   What's the matter with you,
man ? you look very demure ; why don't you join in
the general joy ? come along into the town."

" I hope you will excuse me," replied he, " I cannot
go now."

We insisted on knowing his reason ; he tried to
evade giving any, but at length he said, " he had no
money."

" O, what consequence is that ?" said Dennis, " we
have some.   But what has become of your back pay,
have you lost it ?"

" No."

" And what the deuce have you done with it ?"

John blushed and hesitated a moment, " I have
sent it to my mother."

" What—all ? without keeping any thing to drink ?"

" Yes," said he, " I durst not trust myself to send
it if I once began, and in my sober senses I thought

it a pity to spend a shilling uselessly of that which
would do her so much good."

" Long life to you, Jack !" said Dennis, shaking
him by the hand, " you're a noble boy ; but come
along with us, you are not going home to mope in
the barracks, and nobody there but yourself; you shall
share with us while we have any thing."

" No," replied John, firmly, " that I cannot do ; I
thought on all these things before I sent the money ;
I know I shall be lonely enough while these times
last, but I will never drink at any other person's
expense, in such circumstances. No, no, the first
letter I get from my poor mother, after she receives
the money, will repay me for all I have done, a thousand times."

We parted from him with reluctance, but we knew
it was of no use to press him farther. Dennis and I
adjourned to a public house, where, having got a
room to ourselves, he called for a sheet of paper and
pen and ink.

" What do you want with the paper ?" said I.

" I wish you to write a bit of a letter for me. Do
you know, that when John was telling us about sending
the money, I could have cried, so I could, to think
that the whisky or the noise should put my old
mother out of my head ; and I owe John my blessing
for putting me in mind of her. Now, there's nothing
like striking the iron while it's hot ; so just write me
a bit of a line. I'll send — let me see, (dividing the
notes from the silver,) I'll send the bits of paper, and
keep the tenpennies, and much good may it do the
poor old creature."

I wrote the letter accordingly, and having enclosed
the money, Dennis got up to go to the post office.

" Will you not drink before you go ?"

" No, indeed, it wouldn't go down." He was off,
and returning in a few minutes, —

" Hand us the glass, now," said he, "for my throat's clear, and my heart's light."

Many of the lads were now beginning to feel the bottom of their purse, and put on a sober face, but few of them, I believe, derived so much pleasure from a review of the manner in which they had spent their money as did my friends John and Dennis.

By the end of a week things were restored to their usual routine ; but the kindly feeling generated between us and the inhabitants did not so soon cease, for during the many months we remained there, we were on the very best terms with them.

CHAPTER IV

COLONEL LLOYD.

ABOUT three months after our arrival, we were sitting by the barrack-room fire one night, talking of our campaigns, a subject which was deeply interesting to us all.

" Here we are," said Dennis, " round a good fire in the heart of Paddy's land ; last year at this time we were lying on the Pyrenees, starving alive, with the tents blowing down about our ears. But we had then what would make us forget every thing else — we had Colonel Lloyd commanding us — God rest his soul! he was too good to live long. Do you think his friends will not bring home his remains? Upon my soul, if I had the means, if I would not travel every foot to the heights of Zara, and bring them to Ireland ; I am sure he would rest easier in his own native place."

" Why are you so anxious about his body," said

I, " when your creed forbids you to believe his soul
safe— Colonel Lloyd was a heretic, you know."

" Och, bother !" said Dennis, " all the priests in
Christendom would not make me believe that. Troth
if he isn't in heaven, deuce a one of themselves are
there ; and if I thought he would not get there
because he was a Protestant, I would deny my
religion for ever."

My comrades continued to talk of his goodness,
for it was a theme they never tired of, but I was
abstracted. To-morrow, thought I, it is just a
twelvemonth since he closed his gallant career.
Never will I forget that day. We turned out about
two o'clock in the morning to storm the French
intrenchments ; as was his usual custom, he was on
the ground before the regiment formed, mounted on
his gray horse, which had carried him in many
engagements. On reaching the foot of the hill on
which we were encamped, we halted and waited the
signal gun to advance. Daylight had broke, and the
eastern clouds were tinged with that glorious colour
which no painter can copy or no tongue describe.
The French were in our view, and, " like greyhounds
on the slip," we were waiting the signal to begin the
fight, with that fearful anxiety which is more intolerable to bear than the greatest danger, and to
which action is relief. Colonel Lloyd was at our
head, with his face turned towards us, lighted up with
its usual benignity and confidence. He looked on us
as if he had said, I see you are all devoted to me ;
and the high resolutions he was forming on this conviction could be seen working in his countenance ;
his eye was " wildly spiritually bright," and the
reflection of the gorgeous sky beaming on his fine
features gave them an expression almost superhuman.
I am sure there was not a man in the regiment who
could not have died for him, or with him, at that

moment. A few minutes after, and the battle raged from right to left of the British line. His bravery exceeded all encomium, but it was the "last of his fields;" he met his death-shot in ascending to the attack of a redoubt in the last line of intrenchments. He lived only a few minutes, and the only words he uttered were, — "I am dying, I am dying, I am dying!"—but his feelings might, with truth, have been portrayed thus : — "I perish in the noon of my fame ; I have bought honour and distinction with my blood, but when they are within my grasp, death, with his cold hand, intercepts them, and cuts me off from the world for ever. 'O Glory! thou art an unreal good.'" Mingled with these reflections came, no doubt, thoughts of kindred and friends, whose face he was doomed never to behold ; but the scene soon closed, and all that remained of the young and gifted Lloyd, was the inanimate mould which had enshrined a soul as generous and brave "as e'er burst its mortal control."

My praise of Colonel Lloyd may appear, to some, hyperbolical ; but I have no end to serve—he is himself gone, and his relations, if he have any living, I know nothing about. In giving vent to my feelings in portraying his character, I am sensible I only give a faithful transcript of those of my comrades who then composed the corps, and whose devotion to his memory proves how susceptible soldiers are of feelings of love and gratitude to those who treat them as they ought to be treated — with kindness.

Furloughs were now granting to a certain number of men to go home to see their friends. Dennis, on the faith of some former promise, got one, but I was not so fortunate. He was quite delighted at the idea of going to see his mother and relations, and the evening previous to his intended departure he was very busy packing up his things.

"Now," said he, when he had finished, "I will start very early to-morrow morning, and I think I will be able to manage the journey in four days."

"Here's some one asking for Dennis," said a comrade.

An old woman, habited in a gray cloak, with a handkerchief on her head tied under her chin, entered the room, and looked round inquiringly at each face, until she found the one which was too deeply imprinted on her memory ever to forget. Then, springing forward, she caught Dennis in her arms, and almost smothered him with kisses.

"Och, my poor child!" said she, "do I live to see you once more? Jewel and darling! but this is a blessed day for your poor mother."

Dennis was perfectly bewildered—so much taken by surprise that he could not utter a word for some minutes; at length he said —

"In the name of God, mother, what brought you here?"

"Indeed, I just came to see yourself astore; and wasn't that reason good enough? and I would have come for that same, if it had been twice as far, although I walked every foot of the road."

"Well, well," said Dennis, "that beats Banacher and Balinasloe! Haven't I my knapsack packed to set off home to-morrow? and here you have made all this journey for nothing, dragging the old limbs of ye."

"What matter, child? can't we go home together? we'll be company on the road."

They actually set off in a day or two after, taking the first stage by the coach. The poor old woman, although between sixty and seventy years of age, had travelled upwards of a hundred miles on foot to see her son.

Soon after this, several parties going to Scotland on the recruiting service, I had an offer, if I chose, to go on that duty, but I refused it, as did many others to whom the offer was made. Few soldiers like it, being associated in their minds with something mean and dishonest; and the fact that those men who possess laxity of principle, and are but otherwise indifferent soldiers, are generally the most successful on that duty, strengthens the idea; and it is well known that men so employed, whatever might have been their previous character, return to their regiment much worse soldiers than when they left it. It is too often the practice of those so employed, to consider all stratagem fair, and so that they enlist men for the service, they care little whether the means taken are legal or not. Many, I know, argue, that when men are wanted, we should not be too fastidious in the means used to procure them; and they quote the impressment of seamen, —that stain in our constitution, which our strenuous efforts to emancipate the West Indian negroes renders deeper and deeper. But one bad action can never be vindicated by another; and I cannot see how any cause can be really benefited by duplicity and cunning; on the contrary, it must hurt it, for it raises suspicion where there is no real grounds for any. I am sure it would facilitate the recruiting of the army, to give up all undue means to entrap men by plying them with drink, or telling them lies. I am persuaded that there are thousands to whom a military life would be far preferable to what they are employed at — many of whom would enlist, were it not that a suspicion is excited in their minds, that all is not right, by the finessing and over-anxiety displayed by those employed on the recruiting service. The liberal feeling and good sense which pervades the majority of the officers in the army at present, have rendered the situation of a soldier now quite another thing to what it was when I first entered it. This has been brought about by the increasing intelligence of the nation, but also in a great degree by the disposition evinced by the commander-in-chief. "One tyrant makes many"—of the reverse of this we have a bright example in His Royal Highness the Duke of York. He is in truth the SOLDIER'S FRIEND, and the whole army look up to him with confidence. I can have no aim in flattering him: if he did not deserve this encomium, he would not get it from me.

CHAPTER V.

MY NATIVE LAND.

I HAD received several letters from my parents since my return; they were both well, and urged me to procure a furlough and go home to see them. It was some time before I could accomplish this; but at length it was effected, and having taken a seat on the coach, I set off on my journey home. On reaching Dublin I luckily found a vessel prepared to sail for Irvine, and securing a passage, I embarked next morning. The wind being favourable, we set sail, and were soon fairly in the Channel, holding on our course; the breeze continued steady all that day, and by night we had run a long way down the coast.

Feeling little inclination to sleep, about midnight I came on deck. Considering the season of the year, it was a delightful night; the moon shed her silver radiance o'er reposing nature, like the smile of a fond mother over her sleeping infant, and as I gazed on her, sailing through the blue expanse of heaven, with her attendant train of myriads of sparkling orbs, I felt my mind soar beyond this earth and all its concerns.

> Who ever gazed upon them shining,
> And turn'd to earth without repining,
> Nor wish'd for wings to fly away,
> And mix in their eternal ray.

While I leaned over the ship's bow, watching the moonbeams dancing on the glassy bosom of the deep — my ear soothed with the rippling of the vessel, as she urged her way through the waters,—I felt as if shut out from the world, and emancipated from its laws and control. At sea is the place for reflection and contemplation — there the memory, as if secure in her privacy, unlocks and draws forth her secret treasures, and broods over them with miser care.

Before me the softened outline of the distant coast of Scotland could be seen, its rugged points bursting through the gauzy film with which they were enveloped ; but the well known rock of Ailsa stood forth in bold relief, its giant mass towering proudly above the waves, alike defying their fury and the hand of time. The sight of that rock, which the emigrant associates with the farewell to his country, called forth in my bosom a tide of recollections. When I last saw it, I was returning as now, from one of my wild adventures in search of happiness and fame ; the result of both were nearly equal — misery and disappointment : the last, however, had been the most severe lesson, and I was now, like the prodigal son, retracing my way from a far country, where I had been glad, literally, to feed on the husks which formed the food of the swine. My past life glided in review before my mind, and I could not help exclaiming, What a fool have I been ? I have bartered every privilege which was my birthright, in the pursuit of wild and vain dreams of renown and happiness. Setting aside the misery and hardship I have endured, has not the last six years of my life been a blank ? That period of time employed in my education at home, what might I not have been ? but my doom is fixed, I have sealed it myself — There was distraction in the thought.

That day I landed at Irvine, and resolved to pursue my journey homeward without stopping. As

I travelled along, I felt that tumultuous fluttering and overflowing of the heart, and buoyancy of tread, which every sensitive being must have felt on revisiting the land of his birth, after years of separation from all that was dear to him. The sun was setting when I reached the wood of Curcarth. It had been the haunt of many of my childish wanderings ; there I had often roved, unconscious of where I was going. My soul, awed with the deep shade that the trees cast around, I trod as if on holy ground, while the ceaseless hum of its insect inhabitants, mingled with the wail of the cushat, cherished the deep pensive feeling which the scene had excited in my bosom. It was here that I first learned to commune with my own heart, and my imagination first soared into the realms of faëry. Near its margin was the stream, on whose banks I have lain listening to its murmuring, my gaze fixed on the world, portrayed in its transparent bosom so beautiful, so bright, I could scarcely believe it was not some world of spirituality, some realm of bliss. The scene was changed — winter had stripped it of all its attractions — the blast howled through the leafless trees — and the stream that had meandered so sweetly through the verdant plain, was now roaring down its channel with impetuous force. The scene was changed ; but he who looked on it was not less so.

> Morning of life ! too soon o'ercast,
>   Young days of bliss, too dear to lose ;
> Ah ! whither have thy visions past
>   That brighten'd all my childish views ?
> For never yet when poets muse,
>   Or maidens dream in bowers alone,
> Were glorious visions more profuse.
>   Ah ! whither have those visions gone ? *

I was roused from one of memory's sweetest dreams, by the distant sound of bells — they were

---

* This expression of my feelings may appear, to some, like bombast or affected feeling — I care not. I appeal to those who have felt an enthusiastic love of nature : if it touches a responding chord in their bosoms, I am satisfied.

those of my native city — I had often heard them at the same hour — they spoke of wo, devotion, and joy, and scenes long gone by. In this softened state of feeling I entered the town, and, heedless of the throng, I hurried on to the home of my parents — reached the house — threw myself into their arms, and the first tumult of feeling over, I sat at the fireside, with my father on the one side, and my mother at the other, gazing affectionately upon me, while I talked of all I had seen, and all I had felt.

Being tired after my journey, my mother suggested the propriety of my going to rest; and the tender hand that had often smoothed my pillow, again performed that office. I could not help comparing my situation with the nights that I had lain exposed to the storm, with the cold earth for my bed; and I felt a lively impulse of gratitude — worth a thousand formal prayers — to the Divine Being, who had watched over, and protected me through every danger, and brought me in safety back to my home and my parents.

While my mind was occupied in these reflections, my mother again entered my chamber to see if I wanted any thing. "Are you asleep, Joseph" — my eyes were shut, and I did not reply. She stood over me with the light in her hand gazing on my weather-beaten countenance. "My poor wanderer!" she ejaculated, "what must you have endured since I last saw you. Danger and death has surrounded you, fatigue and hunger attended your steps; but yet you have been kindly dealt with, mercifully preserved. I return thee thanks, thou Almighty giver of every good, for thy bounteous mercy to my poor boy — O guide him to thyself!" She stooped to kiss my forehead — her warm tears fell upon my face — my emotions became too strong for concealment, and afraid that she had disturbed my sleep, she softly left the room.

Those who have felt the rude storms of adversity, and the endearing kindness of a mother, will appreciate my feelings on this occasion.

CHAPTER VI.

STORY OF WILLIAM.

WHILE in winter quarters, in the latter end of 1812, a detachment of recruits joined us from the depot at home, some of whom were attached to our company. Among them was a lad of the name of William Young, a native of Glasgow. His conduct and character were so strikingly different from that of his comrades, that he soon became an object of remark. He might then be about eighteen or nineteen years of age, prepossessing in his appearance; but his countenance was " sicklied o'er with the pale cast of thought," — something seemed to lie heavy at his heart. When not on duty he was in the habit of wandering much by himself, and, unless when he could not avoid it, he rarely spoke to any one. When the weather did not permit him to ramble, he occupied himself in reading a small pocket Bible, which he always carried about with ,him, and often, while thus engaged, the tears could be seen trickling down his cheeks. Those of course were considered symptoms of religious feeling, and as such were ridiculed by the more brutal and illiterate part of his comrades; it was, however, confined to them, for there is a sacredness attached to even the appearance of religion in the minds of those who have been brought up by religious parents, that however lax their own morality may be, prevents them from turning it into ridicule. Their hearts still cherish the recollection of the holy feelings which have been excited in their younger years, and

untainted at the core, sigh to think they do not now feel
as they were wont, that purity and happiness which
by association must ever be connected with their
religious observances. I felt interested in him, and
soon acquired his confidence so far, that he confided
to me the outlines of his story, up to the time of his
enlisting. There seemed, however, to be a feeling of
self-contempt mixed up with his grief, that prevented
him from entering particularly into the circumstances
which led to that step. What I learned was, that he
had left a widowed mother and a sister behind, who
had depended in a great measure upon him for support; that the Bible, which he was in the habit of
reading, was the gift of his mother when they parted;
and although he felt pleasure and consolation from
scanning its contents, there were other feelings connected with it which often led his thoughts far from
what he was reading, and raised emotions in his mind
that brought tears from his eyes. Without seeking to
pry into what he seemed inclined to conceal, I endeavoured by every means in my power to turn the
current of his thoughts into some other channel, but
my efforts were unavailing; the destitute manner in
which he had left his mother seemed to prey upon
his mind, and although he conformed himself well
enough to the duties he had to perform, yet he still
remained the same melancholy abstracted being as
when I first knew him.

We had advanced some way into France, when one
evening we were walking together, and talking of the
possibility of our soon seeing home, as we had now
some reason to expect peace.

" I hope," said he, " that I will live to return to
my poor mother; but if it should be my fate to fall,
and yours to survive, there is one request I have to
make."

" What is that?" said I.

" That you will send home this Bible to my mother,

I have fastened a lock of my hair at a place she will remember, and think with pity and forgiveness of me when I am no more."

" Don't let such melancholy reflections get the better of you," said I ; " still hope for the best. I trust we shall both see our native land again, but should there be any necessity for it, and I survive, I will faithfully perform what you wish."

A few days after, the battle of Orthes was fought. At night, when the companies were mustered, poor William was missing : he had been detached with the sharp-shooters in the morning, to cover the advance of the column, and had been killed by a grape shot in the early part of the day. We were far past the place where he had fallen, and I could not return even had there been any chance of finding him among the numbers of dead and wounded that strewed the field. But he had given his Bible in charge to an officer's servant, with whom he was acquainted, to place among his master's baggage, as a place of greater security, from whom I received it, previous to our embarkation at Paulilhac, for Ireland. Between the Old and New Testaments, on the blank page, was fastened a lock of his hair, so disposed as to encircle the following passages, which were copied in a small hand, with the chapter and verse of each annexed :—

" Refrain thy voice from weeping, and thine eyes from tears, for there is hope in thine end, saith the Lord, that thy children shall come again unto their own border."

" Fear not, thy Maker is thine husband."

" Commit thy fatherless children to my care."

" Call upon me in the day of trouble, I will deliver thee, and thou shalt glorify me."

THE INTERVIEW.

HAVING brought the Bible home with me, I had now the melancholy task to perform, of delivering it to his aged mother. Accordingly, when I had been a few days at home, I sought out her dwelling. She was absent when I first called ; but I left the book, with a note, explaining the nature of my visit, and promising to return next day.

Agreeable to promise, having again called at her house, I rapped at the door, but no one answered, and lifting the latch, to try whether it was locked, it opened, and I discovered the old woman sitting at a table, with the small Bible that I had brought, open before her, at the place which had been so particularly addressed to herself; her eyes were red with weeping, and she was so absorbed in grief, that she did not observe my entrance. Sensible that I had intruded rather abruptly, I attempted to withdraw ; but she happened to lift up her head, and seeing a soldier in uniform, she rose hastily and came towards me : " Are you the kind lad that was here yesterday with this," (pointing to the Bible.) " I dinna ken how to be thankfu' enough to you for being the bearer of my puir Willie's dyin' bequest. Come in an' sit down.—I was in a manner prepared for't, by the kind considerate letter you sent me, and I thocht that I cou'd have borne't wi' some fortitude ; but the sight o' my dear laddie's hand-writing, and the lock o' his hair, has opened a' my wounds afresh. But I would be hard hard hearted if I didna grieve for the loss o' him that was aye sae guid an' kind to me. Oh ! the sight o' that Bible brings things to my mind that maist dries up my heart a' thegither ; and if it wasna for the comfort that's in't, (that I ha'e often experienced) wad drive me out o' my senses. It was bought on the day o' my weddin', and was carried wi' me when I first entered the Lord's house, after being joined heart an' han' wi' a man that has left few like him behind. For twenty years, in joy an' in trouble it was my companion; and, alas! weel do I mind it, frae this book I read the blessed an' faithfu' promises o' God to my dear husband in his last hours; an' when the pangs o' death were on him, an' he held my nan in his, takin', as I thocht, an everlastin' fareweel o' me, when my heart was burstin' wi' grief, the assurance gi'en me there that I wad again meet wi' him, gied me consolation in the midst o' my distress.

" When my boy listed, and was leaving me, I gied him this Bible, charging him never to forget the reading o't, for there he wad find comfort in the hour o' trouble."

" And it gives me pleasure," said I, " to inform you that he followed your advice."

" O ay! I am sure he did," replied she, " I canna doubt but his heart was right."

" His listin' was a sair heart-break to me, for he had aye been sae guid an' sae kind, an' was the only stay that I had. Did he ever tell you what was the reason o' him listin'?"

" No," said I.

" No, no, he was owre proud-spirited for that, puir fellow; but he is no the first that a silly woman has driven to ruin; an' it's a waesome thocht to me that a heart like his shou'd hae been thrown awa' on a worthless tawpy, that didna care a preen about him."

Having expressed a wish to hear the story to which she alluded, she proceeded:

CHAPTER VII.

THE MOTHER'S STORY.

" When my gudeman died, I was left wi' twa
bairns, a boy an' a girl. We had six in family, but
Willie and Mary were a' the Lord was pleased to
leave wi' us. It was by dint o' hard wark that I cou'd
keep them in meat an' claes, an' gi'e them schoolin';
but they were guid bairns, an' when Willie cam in
frae his school, an' sat down by my wheel side, an'
asked me to let him read the bonny lesson for me
that he had learned out o' that Bible, I cou'dna been
happier if I had been possessed o' a' Glasgow. They
baith grew up fond o' me, an' fond o' ane anither, an'
Willie improved sae much in his education that I got
him engaged in a warehouse as a clerk, where he gied
great satisfaction to his master; and when he cam
hame at night, instead of spending his time like idle
glaiket creatures o' his ain age, he wou'd sit an' read
for his sister an' me, or else be busy at his drawing,
or sometimes he wou'd play the flute, while Mary
sang, and I wad sit wi' my heart at my mouth wi'
perfect joy. Oh! thae were happy days — little did
I then think that I wad now be sittin' mournin' the
loss o' a' that I thocht worth livin' for. Yet I had
a mistrust about me, that I was owre happy for 't to
last lang; but oh I didna think I was to drink the
cup o' affliction sae deep as I hae done."

The old woman's feelings here became uncontrollable, and the tears trickled down her furrowed cheeks
in quick succession; but, recovering herself in a few
minutes, she clasped her hands, and, looking up to
Heaven with pious resignation, she said, " ' Thy will

be done,'—' TheLord gave, and the Lord taketh away, blessed be the name of the Lord,'—I hope I'll soon meet wi' them, where we'll ne'er part again."

She continued : — " Willie had been about three years in the warehouse, an' his maister had such a respect for him, that he gied Mary an' me as much sewing as we cou'd do at hame.

" It was about this time that we got neebors in the house but an' ben wi' us, — kind an' sober fo'k they were, an' we were unco freendly wi' ane anither. They had ae dochter that their hearts were bund up in, owre muckle bund up for her gude. She was as bonny a lassie as ye cou'd hae seen in a day's walkin', an' free an' light-hearted ; but she was sae much dawted by her fayther an' mother, an' her beauty sae roosed by ither fo'k, that stronger heads than her's micht been turn'd wi't.

" For company's sake she used to come in an' sit wi' her wark beside Mary, an' they turn'd unco fond o' ane anither, an' at nicht when Willie cam hame, they wad sing while he play'd the flute ; an' at length we seemed just like ae family.

" In a short time I cou'd see that Willie was mair ta'en up wi' Jessie, an' she wi' him, than I cou'd hae wished ; if she happened no to be in when he cam hame, he was dowie an' restless, an' cou'dna content himsel' at his books or his drawin' the way he used to do. I was vexed to see this for twa or three reasons : in the first place, they were owre young to think on marryin' ; an' in the next, she wasna the kind o' woman I wad hae wished Willie for a wife. She was owre fond o' dress, an' folk admiring her, to suit his sober douce temper ; an' I saw that it wad be a sair struggle for his heart. But as what was done cou'dna be mended, I resolved to lippen to Providence, hoping that every thing wad turn out for the best. They now began to meet out o' the house, an' the langer they were acquainted, I could see that

Willie's heart was the deeper in love; but Jessie didna seem to keep up wi' him in that respect. She had owre great a likin' for hersel' to spare much to him; her affection for him raise an' sank wi' every turn o' her flighty head,—ae day she wad be dyin' wi' kindness about him, because he had on some dress that took her fancy, an' she wad parade wi' him round the town; anither time she wad refuse to walk wi' him, because his hat or his napkin wasna in the fashion. I often wondered that Willie put up wi' a' her fancies; for he wasna easy imposed on wi' other folk, but wi' her he seemed as if he was bewitched.

THE COQUET.

" About this time, Jessie, wha had been at a dancing-school, was to be at a practisin' ball, an' gied Willie an' Mary tickets. Puir things, nane o' them nad ever learned to dance, for besides no being very sure aboot the propriety o' the thing, I thought that dancing wasna very necessar' in their station o' life; but their curiosity had been raised sae much wi' Jessie's description, that they were keen to gang, and although I wad been better pleased that they had staid at hame, they had aye been sae guid that I couldna think to deny them.

" Jessie cam in for them that night, busked up like ony lady, wi' her white gown a' flounces an' spangles, her neck and arms bare, and her head dressed out wi' artificial flowers, and her white satin shoon tied up in her pocket napkin, to put on when she gaed into the ball-room. I could scarcely believe my ain een — I glanced at her, and syne at Willie — he looked as if he could have fa'en down and worshipped her — and for a moment I was proud to think that my son should hae sic a sweetheart; but when I thocht on what micht be the upshot o' a' this, I couldna help sighin' an' sayin' to mysel', 'I wish this mayna end in breakin' my puir laddie's heart.'

"Weel, they gaed to the ball, but it was a waesome ball to Willie : he was obliged to sit lookin' on, while she was skimmin' through the dance wi' ither lads. This he bore wi' some patience, but when she rose up to dance some new-fashioned dance, (a waltz I think she ca'd it,) and he saw a strange lad's arms twined aboot her in a manner that he would have thocht it sacrilege to attempt, he couldna bear longer—his head grew confused, and the measure o' his vexation was filled up by a lad coming owre an' asking Mary to stand up to dance wi' him; poor Mary was obliged to tell the truth. 'Canna dance !' said the lad in surprise. Willie didna wait for ony mair,. but takin' Mary's han', 'Come awa,' said he, 'we canna stay here to be affronted.' I was surprised to see them come hame sae soon, and asked him the reason : he made some trifling excuse ; but when he gaed to his bed, Mary told me the hale story.

"Next day he was dowie an' thochtfu', his pride was hurt, an' he was jealous o' Jessie, but he didna speak. When he cam hame at night she was in, an' before he had time to speak, she cried out, 'O Willie, what gart ye gang awa an' leave me ; I waited lookin' for you through the room when I wanted to gang hame, but I couldna find ye. Ye wad be vext seein' a' the rest dancin', an' you no able : what a pity you canna dance, Willie ; if ye could, I'm sure naebody should be my partner but yoursel', for I couldna see onybody there that I liked sae weel.' This was plenty, Willie's een brightened, an' he took her hand — 'Will you be sure to keep your promise, Jessie, if I learn before the next ball?' 'As sure as I have life,' said she. He looked at me. I kent what he meant. O ay, Willie, you have my consent to gang to the school, an' tak Mary wi' ye — it's no against the dancin' itsel' that I have sae much objection, as

what it leads to. My mind tell'd me I was doin,
wrang, but I couldna help bein' pleased to think it
was makin' him sae happy. Weel, to the dancin'
school they gaed, an' books, an' drawin' an' every
thing was laid aside. He was clever at ony thing,
but his mind was so much set on this, that he couldna
but learn fast, and by the next ball he was able to
dance wi' Jessie himsel'. But, poor fellow, a' his
endeavours seemed vain, for Jessie was asked that
night to dance wi' a lad who was the brag o' the
country side. He was a fine lookin' chiel, I believe,
but puffed up wi' vanity. The twa gaed through
some new fangled dance by themsel's, — every body
roosed them to the skies, and they turned the prouder
the mair they heard themsel's praised. Instead o'
comin' owre beside Willie when it was finished,
Jessie sat down beside her new partner. Willie, you
may be sure, was unhappy enough before, but his
heart was like to burst within him when he saw her
hearkening wi' delight to some nonsense the chiel was
sayin' to her. He could thole nae langer, and he
gaed owre to her and asked if she would stand up wi'
him the next dance ; but she answered (in a way as if
she was ashamed of being seen speaking to him)
that she was engaged. Willie said nae mair before
the lad, but he sat patiently until the ball was ended,
thinking he might have an opportunity of speaking
to her on the road hame ; but her new lad saw
her into her father's door. That night Willie didna
close an eye, and my heart was like to break for
him, the way he sighed the hale nicht lang. Like
maist folk, when they do wrang, they think they
have the best right to be offended, so Jessie didna
look near our house the next day, until Mary gaed
in for her. ' What ailed you at Willie last night?'
said Mary, willing to bring about some explanation ;
' I fear you vext him unco sair by leavin' him to
dance wi' yon ideot.' ' 'Deed then,' replied Jessie,

' he needna fash to be vex'd about it, for I wadna tie mysel' down to please him or ony ither body; does he really think, because I consented to be his partner at the ball, that I obliged mysel' no to dance wi' ony body but him ?' ' It was na because you danced wi' ony ither body,' said Mary, ' although he had your ain promise for that, but because you left his company a'thegether, that he wad fin' vex'd.' ' Tuts, I canna be fash'd wi' him aye rinnin' after me frae place to place, and aye sittin' beside me.' ' You didna aye think sae,' said Mary, looking her in the face; ' but although you couldna be fashed wi' him, there was ither folk there, far inferior to him, that you could sit beside till the last minute.' Wha is't you ca' inferior to him ? I am sure the lad I was wi' is a far bonnier lad, and a far better dancer, than ever he'll be in his life.' This observation o' hers brought the tears in my een, for I saw my poor laddie's heart was gien to ane that wad tread it under her feet, and laugh while she did it.

" For twa or three days after this, he gaed about like a ghaist; he couldna tak' his meat through the day, nor his sleep at night, and I was fear'd that he wad bring some trouble on himsel'. He had tried twa or three times, I understood, to get a word o' Jessie by hersel', but she refused to see him. Mary had seen her ance or twice walkin' wi' her new sweetheart. Willie had heard this, and ae night he watch'd her until she parted wi' him, and met her comin' through her ain entry. I happen'd to be gaun out, but seein' a glimpse o' twa folk in the passage, I stopped short and o'erheard Willie say, ' Jessie, I wish to speak to you.' ' I have nae time to speak to you,' said she, pressing to get past him. ' I'll no keep you lang, and as it is likely it may be the last time I'll request it, I hope you'll hear me.' ' Weel, what hae ye to say.' ' I find by your manner of speakin' that it'll no be necessary to say much.

I only wish to know whether, considering what has passed between us, you have any excuse to make for your conduct to me of late?' 'No; what business have I to make any excuse to you? Let me go.' 'O Jessie, your words would signify little, if I didna ken that your conduct was like them. Like a fool, I ance thought your heart was a' my ain. You have deceived me, Jessie, broken my heart; but I canna wish you ill. May you never have your conduct to me returned on your own head. Although you have deserted me, you will never find one to love you as I have done; but I don't say this to make you feel for me, or to bring back your lost affections. You never could be to me what you have been, and I wouldna lay my heart, broken as it is, again at your mercy, for any consideration. Farewell, Jessie, I wish you every happiness.' She appeared to be affected, for I could hear her sabbin'; but she didna mak' ony reply.

" Although he pretended that he was heart-hale again, I cou'd see that the battle my poor laddie was fightin' in his ain breast was owre hard for him. Two or three days after he was beyond his usual hour o' comin' in to his dinner, and I fand mysel' unco uneasy about him, for he was aye particular to the hour. It was sax o'clock before he cam hame. 'What keepit ye, my laddie?' says I, 'ye're far ayont your time.' 'I was busy,' says he, careless like,—and I didna think ony mair about it. Next day he cam hame in the middle o' the day, 'What's wrang now, Willie?' says I, 'are ye no weel, that you are hame at this hour?' He sat for a lang while without saying a word, and then burst into tears,—'O no, mother! I'm no weel, nor have na been weel this mony a day; but there will soon be an end o't, for I'm gaun to leave the town.' 'My goodness! laddie, whare are ye gaun? what do ye mean?' 'I canna hide it ony langer, mother; I am listed for a soldier,

and I have to march this night to join my regiment.'
'Listed!' said I, and the word stuck in my throat,
'O! no Willie, that canna be sae;' but I could see
by his face that it was owre true—he wasna guilty o'
telling lees. 'O! then, for Godsake, for my sake, if
ye dinna wish to send your auld mither to her grave,
gang and gie them back their siller. I 'll sell every
thing I hae to get ye free. O haste ye, William, and
pay them the smart.' Willie shook his head,—' It 's
owre late for that.' 'Then ye 're lost, my bairn —
my a' that I have for your father — my only dependence! O! and where is your regiment?' 'In Portugal.' I didna hear ony mair, my head grew dizzy,
the cauld sweat broke on my face; I thought I was
dyin', and I was happy at it.

"I minded naething mair until I wakened as it
were frae a sleep, and looking up saw Mary and
Willie hanging owre me greetin'. My mind during
the rest o' that day was a' confusion; I mind something about soldiers comin' for Willie, and me takin'
fareweel o' him, and gieing him this Bible, and seein'
his sister clasped in his arms; but there was something cauld at my heart, I had lost my natural feelin'.
I fand as if I had swallowed laudanum. In the
middle o' the night I wakened frae a fearfu' dream —
I had seen my Willie torn frae me, and stretchin' out
his hands to me for help; but he was dragged frae
my sight — again he appeared to me, pale and
bluidy, and his claiths dreepin' wat. I sprang forward to catch him in my arms; but before I could
reach him he fell on the floor; the scream that I gied
wakened me, and I fand mysel' standin' at my bedside, for I had jumped out in the distress o' my mind.
I had nae clear notion o' ony thing; but I had a
confused thought that there was something wrang wi'
my Willie, and I staggered into the wee room where
he sleepit—I hearken'd to hear his breath, but a' was
hush'd — I grew fearfu' anxious, and to satisfy mysel'

I stretched my hand on the bed, to feel if he was there; but there was naebody in't — the claes were na ruffled, and the cauld feel o' the quilt affected my heart, as if it had been squeezed between twa pieces o' ice. I sunk on the bed — What can a' this mean? said I to mysel', and the truth gradually opened on my mind. O ay, it's owre true, — ye're gane, Willie, — ye've left me; — what for did you no tell me before ye took sic a rash step? O Willie, will I never see you again? — What mischief that glaiket heartless hizzie has done. May she be made to suffer — but I stopped mysel' in the rash wish — there was nae need for 't — poor wretch, she was fast fillin' the bitter cup for hersel'

"I was sittin' in this way, mournin' for my bairn, until I had forgotten where I was, when I was started by somebody sabbin' by my side. 'In God's name, wha's that?' 'It's me, mother,' said Mary, 'are ye no comin' to your bed?' 'O ay, my bairn; I wish the Lord may keep me in my natural senses, for I find my head no right ava.' Mary tried to comfort me, but, poor thing, she needed comfort as much as mysel'. I need scarcely gang farther wi' my story, my heart never raise aboon't.

"About a week after he left us, we had a letter frae him, wi' an order for ten pounds in 't. It was his bounty. He said he was weel and happy, and begged that I would buy claes for mysel' and Mary wi' the siller. Although I was proud of his affection and his mind-fu'ness, yet before I would have used a penny o' that siller, I wad have starved. I couldna consider 't in ony light but as the price o' his bluid. Mary saw what was passin' in my mind when we read the letter—her feelings were the same as mine.—'I'll tell you what we will do, mother,' said she, 'we'll put the siller in the bank, and we'll work hard, and put something till't if we can, and by the time that he comes hame again, he'll hae forgotten a' this business between Jessie and him, and we'll buy his discharge, and get him hame beside us again.' I couldna help claspin' my kind hearted lassie to my bosom. 'Weel, Mary, my dear, we'll just do that, and we'll maybe be a' happy yet.

"The next letter we had frae Willie, he was in France wi' the army; he had joined his regiment the day before a battle, and escaped without scaith. The neist we had frae him, he was in high spirits; 'the war,' he said, 'couldna be lang o' bein' ended, and he would see us again.' We were quite uplifted. We had added sae much to the ten pound we had in the bank by our hard workin', that it was now near-hand twenty, and we were plannin' how we would surprise him by gettin' his discharge, when he cam hame.

"We had gien up our house, intendin' to remove to anither quarter o' the town, to be awa frae Jessie and her friends; but that wasna necessar'. Jessie had been courtin' wi' the lad that she had gien up Willie for, ever since he had gaen awa. It was reported for a lang while that they were to be married; but when a' thing was prepared, and the day appointed, he set aff, and wasna heard o' for some weeks. They were in an awfu' way about it, but at length they got word frae a near friend o' his, that ne had sailed for America wi' his wife, having married anither lass twa or three days before he sailed. This was dreadfu' news to poor Jessie, she couldna haud up her head after't, and her father and mother removed to a different part of the country, takin' her wi' them — I hae ne'er heard what becam o' them since.

"Weel, as I was sayin', we had every thing planned out, and waitin' anxiously for anither letter. We had heard by the papers that the allied troops were marching for Paris; every day brought fresh news, until at length we saw the mail-coach rattle

past our door wi' flags fleein'.   Peace, peace, was in
ilka body's mouth — every body that had friends in
the army were rinnin' frae door to door congratulating ane anither, and every body was overjoyed.

"Orders were gi'en for an illumination. 'That
I'll do wi' a' my heart,' says I, 'for I hope my
laddie's on his passage hame.' 'O mother!' cried
Mary, 'here's the postman wi' a letter for you.' My
heart lap to my mouth — I ran into the room and
tore't open—' this will be gude news frae Willie. O
Mary, read it, for I'm sae flurried that I canna read.'
'Preserve us,' says she, 'that's no Willie's writing.'
'Never mind,' says I; 'read, read.' She read on
hurriedly to hersel', but while she read, her face
turn'd ghastly pale — the letter drapped frae her
hands — 'O! mother, he's kill'd,' — and she sank
down before me, without me havin' power to help
her.

"Oh!" said the old woman, passing her hand
across her forehead, "I canna think about that day,
but my head turns, and I'm no mysel'."

CHAPTER VIII.

DENNIS.

MY leave of absence flew swiftly by, and I had
again to bid my friends farewell, and return to my
regiment. When I arrived, I found my comrade
Dennis, along with some others, standing in full
marching order, with his arms carried, and his face
within a few inches of the barrack wall, in which
position he was sentenced to remain during three
successive days, from sunrise to sunset, for being
absent when the roll was called at tattoo. This was
a new invented punishment, intended as a mild
substitute for flogging, but, in my opinion, more

severe and injurious to the health. Our moral physicians seem to consider bodily pain as the grand panacea for all errors of the mind. It is strange how precedent or prejudice should guide men of information on these points ; it proceeds either from indolence, which prevents them thinking at all, or their passions are so much stronger than their reason, that they act contrary to their better judgment. The latter is the most common of the two.

The fault of poor Dennis, had it been inquired into, did not deserve the severe punishment with which it was visited. His sweetheart, Peggy Doyle, had been seized with typhus fever, which was at that time prevalent. The common people in Ireland have a dread of fever almost incredible. The nearest relations of the sick will often refuse to visit them, and many times the suffering individual is almost totally deserted, unless there be some devoted wife, child, or mother, whose affection is stronger than the fear of death. Poor Peggy had caught the infection from a family, one of the girls of whom was her particular friend; the whole of the family, consisting of five individuals, were unfortunately ill at the same time, and Peggy, finding that no one would attend them, heedless of all selfish considerations, had given up her place to become their nurse. The father and a little boy died, but the two girls and the mother became convalescent. During this time she had been often assisted by Dennis, who shared cheerfully with her in the labour and danger to which her disinterested benevolence had exposed her. While they were ill, she had remained perfectly healthy, but the disease was working in her blood, and her friends were scarcely able to crawl about, when their kind nurse was stretched on the bed from which they had just risen, with every symptom of the disorder more aggravated than that from which they had recovered.

This was a heart-breaking business to poor Dennis; every moment he could spare he was at her bedside, and the night on which he had been absent from roll-calling, she was so ill, that, in his anxiety for her, he had forgot the hour of tattoo, and the reports were given in before he reached the barrack. I exerted the little influence I possessed to get Dennis forgiven, and was successful, and to prevent any misunderstanding, I got leave for myself and him for the night. When this point was gained, I accompanied him to see poor Peggy, but being insensible, she did not know me; she did not rave, but there was a deadly stupor in her eye. Poor Dennis was affected to the heart, but he endeavoured to bear it with fortitude. The girls were still too weak to endure the fatigue, and were in bed, but the mother sat beside us. It was evident that life was now fast ebbing—her eye became more glazed, the livid circle round her mouth became deeper, and her respiration more laborious. We had been sitting in silence for some time, watching the progress of dissolution, when we were startled by the melancholy and lengthened howl of a dog, outside the door. I cannot, need not, attempt to describe the effect it had upon us.

" Ah ! that's a sure sign," said the old woman, when she recovered herself, " the poor child will soon be gone."

I am not very superstitious, and I strove to dispel the emotion I felt by going to discover the dog. I found him seated on the street opposite the door, with his face turned towards it. He was well known to the regiment, for he frequented the barrack-square, and whenever the bugles sounded, he emitted the same kind of howl he had done that night. The knowledge of this in a measure quieted my mind, but I could not altogether rid myself of the strange impression created by the incident. Having returned to Peggy's bedside, I found her much worse ; the death-rattle was in her throat, and a long and distressing moan every two or three minutes, told how dreadful was the struggle.

The old woman awakened her daughters. " Rise, my dear girls," said she, " and pray for the soul of her who is losing her life for your sakes."

By the time they got up she was in the agonies of death.

" Fall down on your knees, my childer," said she, " and pray to God to smooth her way to heaven."

We sunk down with one accord by the bedside, and while they offered up their fervent prayers, her soul winged its way to a world where her benevolent deeds would be appreciated and rewarded. Poor Dennis had held her hand in his for some time before she died, and he did not relinquish it, until the old woman came over to him and said, " O Dennis, astore, she is gone !" when he started to his feet, and gazing intensely on the corpse for a few minutes, he stooped down and imprinted a last kiss on her cold and livid lips, which but a few days before had glowed in all the vermilion of health ; then turning about, he sat down in a corner of the room without saying a word.

After a pause of an hour, during which they were busily employed in offering up prayers for the soul of the deceased, — " Come, my dear," said the mother to the elder girl, " we may as well get her laid out while she is warm, for I believe she hasn't much to travel.* Boys, you had better go home and try and get some rest."

Dennis was for guard next day, and could not

---

* It is generally believed among the common people of this part of Ireland, that when the soul leaves its earthly tenement, the first thing it does is to travel over every spot of ground that the body did while living ; during which time the tie between it and its mortal remains is not entirely severed ; and for that reason they will not touch the body for a certain time after life is extinct.

accompany me ; but when I returned I found the old
woman and her daughters, weak as they were, had
not been idle. The bed on which Peggy had lain
was removed and burnt, the walls of both apartments
white-washed with lime, and the floor strewed with
mint and lavender. On the room door, which had
been unhinged for the purpose, and placed resting on
two chairs, was stretched the dead body, covered
with a white sheet all but the face, which now wore
a composed smile. Three candles lighted were placed
at her head, ornamented with cut paper. Though
the morning had been stormy, the younger girl had
gone out and collected such flowers as the season
afforded, — the snowdrop, the primrose, and the ever-
green, and strewed them on the corpse.

The same dread that prevented the neighbours
from visiting her in her sickness, restrained them
from attending her wake ; but it was so much the
better — none but true hearts mourned over her —
no tears were shed but those of affection — there was
no boisterous or disgraceful mirth, such as I have
witnessed on similar occasions. A few neighbours,
more friendly than the others, ventured into the outer
apartment, and remained during the night ; but the
old woman and the two girls sat alternately, and
sometimes together, at the head of the corpse — and
apostrophizing the inanimate clay, they ran over
every endearing quality that she possessed, adverted
to the happy moments they had passed in her company, and with the tears trickling over their cheeks,
chaunted the plaintive airs which she was partial to,
and had often joined them in singing.

There was something in the scene so impressive
and solemn, and in the simple tribute of affection to
the remains of their friend so touching, that it was
impossible to witness it without the heart whispering
" it is good to be here." Having gone out for a few
minutes to warm myself at the fire where the neigh-

bours were sitting, I overheard one of the women repeating an irregular rhyme.

" What is the meaning of that ? " said I.

" It's a rhyme," replied she, " that a poor innocent who frequented this used to repeat, and we happened to be talking about her."

I expressed a wish to hear something concerning her ; and in a detached and irregular manner she told me the following story : —

Molly Kelly was the daughter of a small farmer in an adjoining county. She had been seduced by a young man of the same neighbourhood under pr mise of marriage, which he delayed to fulfil so long, that Mary, finding herself in a situation she could not long conceal, disclosed the secret to her mother. Knowing that her father was of a stern unforgiving temper, she endeavoured to keep it from his knowledge, but it was soon found necessary to tell even him. In his first transports of rage, he threatened to take her life, and her mother was obliged to conceal her from his fury ; she endeavoured to excite his pity for the unfortunate girl, but all she could get him to do was to restrain his anger until he saw whether the young man would marry her, who was accordingly sent for, but he refused in the most insulting terms. This was communicated by the heart-broken mother to Mary, who at the same time warned her of her father's anger, and advised her to go to a relation's house at some distance, until he could be brought to forgive her ; this Mary at first refused to do, but her mother urged her departure, and she at length consented.

Having reached her friend's house, she remained there until within a few days of the delivery of her child, when she left it without giving any intimation, and wandered as far as her precarious situation permitted. She was seized with the pains of labour in a cottage where she had gone in to rest herself, and was delivered of a daughter before she left it. The people were kind to her, and administered every thing to her comfort their circumstances admitted; but poor Mary's distress of mind enhanced her danger: she was seized with violent inflammation and became delirious. The disorder, however, at length subsided, and she gradually recovered her health, but her reason was gone for ever.

Her situation was taken notice of by some kind-hearted people, and they meditated taking the child from her; but she was so harmless, and so fond of the babe, grew so uneasy and even frantic when any one attempted to take it, and besides had so much natural nourishment for it, that they allowed it to remain with her.

For nearly a twelvemonth she roved about from one place to another subsisting on charity, when the child caught the small-pox; at first she did not seem to understand that it was sick, but when the disorder came to a height, she felt uneasy at seeing the pustules which covered its skin, and one day she carried the poor infant to a stream and endeavoured to wash them off with a wisp of straw. Some person passing discovered her thus employed, and interfered to save the child, but it was too late,—it had expired in her hands; and she would not part with it until it was forcibly taken from her to be buried.

From this time the disorder of her mind assumed a different character. She would not enter a house, but slept about old walls or barns, and mourned continually for her child. Some one thought of giving her a large doll by the way of quieting her mind, and the experiment was so far successful; she lavished the same fondness on it, dressed it, and nursed it, as if it had been a living child; but she still avoided going into the houses, unless when the weather was very severe; then she would seek some favourite house, and chaunt over the rhyme at the door, that heard the woman repeat on my coming out of the room :

" Open the door to pretty Polly, for this is a cold winter night;
It rains, it hails, it blows, and the elements give no light."

Her petition was never in vain, for they were all fond of poor Molly ; but her constitution could not long withstand the constant exposure to the weather ; her health gradually gave way, and one morning the wretched victim of seduction and parental cruelty was found dead by the side of a ditch.

CHAPTER IX.

CHANGE OF QUARTERS.

WE had been about nine months here when we got the rout to march to Kilkenny, a distance of about forty miles, where we were destined to relieve the forty-second regiment, ordered on service. We parted with the people of Wexford with regret, and on their part with every demonstration of sorrow. Many of our men had married while in the town, and every thing during our stay conspired in a degree to identify us with the inhabitants.

We were escorted some miles by half the people of the town. A meeting was called of the magistrates and principal inhabitants, and an address drawn up, flattering alike to our feelings and pride, which was published in the principal newspapers. Thus we entered Kilkenny in the best possible disposition to be on friendly terms with its inhabitants, but we soon found that we had got a different kind of people to deal with. The sneers and oblique hints, the evident wish to quarrel, which they evinced when any of our men came in contact with them in the public houses, convinced us that we could never expect to be on the same terms with them as we had been with the inhabitants of Wexford.

The county being almost continually in a disturbed state, it was found necessary to have a large force distributed throughout its extent, to counteract their lawless schemes, and caused the duty to be particularly unpleasant. On our part it was not a little enhanced by the envious egotism and gasconading of the corps whom we relieved, — a corps that has been flattered by the country into a belief that they are the flower of the British army. To hear themselves speak, they were the saviours of the nation, — their exertions, wherever they had been engaged, had turned the tide of battle in our favour, — and, without the gallant forty-second, the army would be like a watch without a main-spring.

How the country could have been so long the dupe of high-sounding pretension, I do not understand. It could never be from the general appearance of the corps, for of all the Highland regiments in the service, they are the most despicable, or, to use an expressive Scottish term, *shauchlin*, in point of appearance. Is it for their superior discipline? all who have seen them in quarters or in the field, know that the reverse is the fact. Was it for their superior courage? this I deny: they have often got into scrapes by their want of steadiness, and when they did so, they fought desperately, no doubt, to recover themselves; but if a man, through his own imprudence, were to set his house on fire about his ears, his hazarding a jump of two stories to escape the flames, could scarcely be cried up as a very heroic action. Trace them from their origin as a police corps in the Highlands, through Egypt, the Peninsula, in fact wherever they have been, and what have they done to merit the particular distinction above every other corps in the service, which they pretend to ? Nothing — absolutely nothing : they are a complete verification of the proverb, " If you get a name of rising early, you may lie in bed all day." No doubt much of the popular feeling relating to them has been revived and cherished by certain writers, who have thrown the charm of romance round an age distinguished by tyranny and unrelenting barbarity, on the one hand, and brutal ignorance and superstition on the other,—whose taste might be questioned as much as that of a painter, who would throw gorgeous drapery around a hideous skeleton.

It must have confounded every person of any judgment to see the nation carried away with this mania, until they were dancing in masquerade, from the peer to the half-starved mechanic, doffing their warm comfortable breeches, to sport a pair of extenuated spindleshanks in a kilt, and those who could not afford to buy one, throwing a piece of tartan over·their shoulders, or wearing a bonnet filled with ostrich feathers, and dubbing themselves Highland societies, under the name of Celtic, &c. &c. although perhaps they never saw the Highlands, unless at the distance of forty or fifty miles. These things are now dying away, and, if we except the casual appearance of some frail dandy, who has failed to attract attention by any other means, and who does so to put himself into the mouth of the public, philabegs are banished to their native hills. You may now find buckles and ostrich feathers in every broker's shop, articles which, by the by, the real clansmen never heard of until they came down to the Lowlands to see their dress and manners caricatured ; if they ever wore feathers, they must have been crow feathers, and their shoe-buckles, I believe, were as scarce as those for the knee.

I have no animosity to Highlanders, as a body ; there are many brave and intelligent men amongst them, who would disdain to seek any adventitious

aid from the mania of the day, and I willingly allow
them credit for what they deserve in common with
the rest of the army ; but the behaviour of a regiment
is so much influenced by the officers, or officer, commanding, and the men who compose it are so often
changed during war or foreign service, that a judgment formed of them at one time would be erroneous
at another. I have never seen any difference worth
observing between the courage of English, Irish, or
Scotch; and in a profession like ours, where the natives
of the three kingdoms are so intimately mixed, any
comparison of the bravery of either country must be
artificial in the extreme. The following is a specimen
of the mode in which the *gallant Highland Watch*
acted towards us : —

They wore long frills to their shirts, that reached to
the first or second button of their jackets, which were
on all occasions ostentatiously drawn out ; but these,
in compliance with the regulation, our regiment did
not wear. This having been remarked by the inhabitants, they asked the reason, and the one currently
alleged by the forty-second was, " O ! she 'll lose her
frill for rinnin' awa'," and this *lie* was propagated by
them at the time they were pretending the greatest
friendship for us, and expressing their hope that
(should we go abroad) we might be in the same division with them.

Any comparison of the merits of the two corps
might appear invidious ; but I believe we had no
reason to shrink from it. Had it been the reply of an
individual, it would have been unworthy of remark ;
but those regiments who have been quartered with
the forty-second must be well acquainted with their
boasting illiberal manner.

Trifling as they may appear, these things certainly produced a feeling which added to the discon-
tented state of the people, and we could perceive,
before we were many days in the place, that our

situation amongst them would be very uncomfortable ; and we had not been long there, when one of our sentries upon the hospital at the head of the town, had his hamstrings cut by some person who had been lurking about his post. Whether this proceeded from individual enmity, or a dislike to the soldiers in general, is a thing which must remain in doubt ; but it excited a mutual animosity, and caused strict orders to be issued to the sentinels not to allow any person to approach within a certain distance of their post, without coming to the charge ; and not long after, an inhabitant, the worse of liquor, passing by one of our sentries, and disregarding the caution given him, obstinately persisted in forcing himself upon the sentry, and received a wound which eventually proved mortal. Thus, new cause of hatred was produced and kept alive, by circumstances which sprung from a jealous feeling on either side. We very naturally blamed the inhabitants as being the aggressors, and referred to our conduct in Wexford, of which the inhabitants had borne honourable testimony. The people of Kilkenny, on the other hand, execrated us as savages, who cared nothing for human life. This feeling might have died away, but a melancholy occurrence took place, which kindled it anew.

In consequence of the disturbed state of the surrounding country, the men coming in to head quarters for the pay of the detachments, were obliged to carry arms for their personal safety ; and one of the sergeants coming in for that purpose, accompanied by one or two of his own men, and an inhabitant of the village where the detachment was stationed, went into a public house, for the purpose of getting some refreshment. Having sat until the liquor exerted its influence on their heads, one of the soldiers quarreled with the inhabitant, and they stood up to fight. The sergeant who was naturally hasty and choleric, rose up with the pistol which he carried in his hand, to separate them. In the scuffle the pistol was fired, and the inhabitant fell, mortally wounded; the alarm was given, a crowd gathered round the house, and the infuriated mob would have torn the sergeant to pieces, had he not been protected by the constables and conveyed to jail.

It was an unfortunate affair, and was made the most of by the mob. I knew Sergeant Brody well — perhaps I was one of his most intimate friends; he was then about twenty years of age. In point of duty he was strictly correct, and much esteemed by his officers; his education and intelligence were far beyond that commonly possessed by soldiers, and altogether he would have formed an agreeable companion, were it not that his good qualities were tinged with petulance and impatience of contradiction, arising, no doubt, from a consciousness of his abilities, added to a temper naturally irritable and fiery.

I happened to be on duty when the deed was done; but next day I was admitted to see him. His mind was overwhelmed with horror, and he pressed my offered hand in silence, while he looked doubtfully in my face, as if he asked, Can I expect you to feel for me? — do you not consider me a monster? I understood him — " I do feel for you," said I; " I feel all the awful exigency of your situation; but I will not forsake you — command me in any thing that can serve you."

" This is more than I expected," he replied, " but I cannot now speak to you, my mind is in the most gloomy confusion; but I hope you will come to see me when you can." And on my assurance that I would, we parted.

He never entered into any particulars of the unfortunate affair, even to me; but his feelings were too agonizing for concealment. Every indulgence was given him consistent with his safety, which he could expect; and being allowed to visit him, I generally saw him every day. As the assizes approached, he summoned up all his energy for the event—death seemed a dreadful thing, no doubt, should such be his sentence; but the idea of a public execution was to him worse than a thousand deaths. On this subject he often spoke to me, and with such fearful emphasis of manner, that I expected the horrible idea would unsettle his reason. Some days previous to his trial, however, when I visited him, a wonderful change seemed to have taken place in his mind; he talked of the event with composure—every wild passion of his soul seemed swallowed up in a melancholy softness; he talked of his friends, of what the world would say of him after he was dead, and seemed to derive pleasure from speculating on the nature of the immortal world he thought himself on the point of entering. Yet at times I could observe a triumph in his eye, when he adverted to the attendant circumstances of an execution, and he once or twice even hazarded a jest on the subject. All this was so utterly at variance with his former feelings, that I did not know what to think of it. When we were parting, I mentioned that as I was going on guard next day, probably I would not have an opportunity of seeing him before his trial.

"I am sorry for that," said he, "for I have something important to say to you; but I may as well say it now—Do you see no difference in me since you saw me last?"

"More than I can account for," said I.

"He took my hand, and looking me earnestly in the face, "Do you really think," said he, "that I have made up my mind (if such should be my sentence) to consign myself to the hands of the common executioner—If you think so, you do not know me; they may condemn me, but they shall never make a gazing-stock of me. I have struggled with nature, reason, and religion, until my brain is nearly turned. I have only one alternative, and that I shall embrace." We were here interrupted by the turnkey locking up the cells ; but I needed no farther explanation of his determination.

I could not see him next day ; but I determined to write to him, and sat down when I got home for that purpose ; but what could I say ? When I imagined myself in his situation for the purpose of trying the question, I was obliged to own that I would have been in danger of forming the same resolution ; — still, however, I endeavoured by every argument I was master of, to sway him from his purpose ; but when I gave the letter next morning to a comrade, for the purpose of conveying it to him, I felt it was of no use.

The second day after, when I got off guard, I hastened to the court-house : his trial had commenced, — the house was crowded, and the greater number of the officers of the regiment were present. The evidence adduced proved clearly that he had fired the shot ; but no malice or forethought of the crime was established : so far from that, the prisoner and the deceased had been on the best terms. Several officers came forward and gave him an excellent character — the Jury retired, and during the interval, I am certain there were many there who felt the dreadful suspense nearly as much as the prisoner — they again appeared, and gave in a verdict of manslaughter — a weight was relieved from my heart, — he was sentenced to nine months' imprisonment. Will it be believed, that on my next seeing him he seemed to feel disappointed? Such is the strange inconsistency and vanity of human nature, that after working his mind up to the pitch necessary to take away his own life, and throwing a colouring round the deed that had strongly excited his imagination, he felt a kind of regret that the sacrifice was not now necessary.

It is needless to enter more at large into his story : he survived his imprisonment, but he could not endure the stigma which was attached to his character. In an evil moment he deserted — was afterwards apprehended and drafted to a corps stationed in the Grecian Islands, where he soon after died, leaving an example of the awful consequences which may proceed from one unguarded burst of passion. Few men in the regiment had better prospects — a common mind might have regained in a great measure its equilibrium ; but how often is it the case, that when a mind of sensibility and genius errs, " it falls, like Lucifer, never to rise again."

CHAPTER X.

DETACHMENT.

In the course of duty, I was one of a detachment sent to a village about twenty miles from headquarters, where the inhabitants were in a disturbed state. From the accounts given us by the constables when we first went there, we were led to believe that the whole country was in arms, ready, when the word was given, to massacre all opposed to their schemes. But we soon found that their fears or their prejudices had magnified the cause of alarm to a wonderful degree. Before we became acquainted with the true state of affairs, they made us complete hacks, calling us out to their assistance in every drunken squabble which took place, often through their own insolent behaviour.

I remember one night we were turned out in a great hurry by one of the constables, who rode up to our barrack, with his horse sweating and his face pale with terror. He laid off a dreadful story of his coming home from the fair of T——, and on the top of a hill, about two miles from the town, he had unexpectedly come upon about two hundred Shanavests in a field, holding one of their nocturnal meetings, who, when they saw him, shouted out and fired half-a-dozen shots at him; that he, seeing it of no use to face so many, set spurs to his horse and fled, followed by a whole troop of them, to the very end of the village.

Having turned out, we set off at a double quick pace towards the scene of action; on reaching the foot of the hill, where he said the boys were assembled, we loaded, fixed our bayonets, and were gallantly led up to the attack by the constable himself.

" Easy, easy boys," said he, " we 'll be on them in a jiffy — don't fire till I give you the word, and you'll see we'll surround them and take them all prisoners." So saying, he crept softly on some way in front. The night was very dark, and we could see nothing distinctly; but when within about fifty yards of the top of the hill, we were startled by a tremendous clatter of feet upon the stones of the road, followed by the cry of " Murder, murder! Fire, fire!" We had not been accustomed to waste our ammunition uselessly, and waited a second or two to see what we had to fire at; but one of our party (a recruit) snapt his musket on the alarm; luckily for the constable, it missed fire, for it was directed at him as the only object that could be seen. In less time, however, than I could relate it, the cause of our alarm rushed past in the shape of a horse, that had sprung from the field upon the road as we advanced. Having reached the spot pointed out by the constable, nothing could be seen but a few heifers grazing about, quite unconscious of having disturbed the peace. We

certainly did not feel well pleased at being turned
out at such an unseasonable hour to no purpose, and
we taxed the constable roundly with imagining the
whole story,—but he swore by all that was good, that
every word of what he told was truth. Next morning, however, we were convinced that our surmises
were correct, for on inspecting the field where the
Shanavests were said to be assembled, not a single
foot-mark could be seen, although the ground was
moist from previous rain ; besides, it was well known
that the constable had taken a sup too much at the
fair, for when he left it he was scarcely able to sit
his horse.

For some time we were regularly called out by
these fellows, when they went to distrain a man's
goods for rent or tithes, until we were more like the
bailiff's body-guard than any thing else. But after
being made fools of in this way two or three times,
our officer remonstrated, and arranged matters so,
that we were not obliged to go out without a special
order from the magistrate. This relieved us from
the petty affairs more immediately under the cogni-
zance of the constable ; but still we had enough to do
in following the magistrate, who seemed to consider
a hunt after his countrymen even more amusing than
one after the fox. Had the people been peaceably
inclined, his conduct would have goaded them on to
outrage. He was continually up to the ears in
business — some momentous matter always in hand.
Every trifling riot was magnified into a deep-laid
rebellion—if a cabin or a hay stack was set on fire, a
whole village was burned—if one man was wounded,
a dozen were killed ; and so on, always magnifying
the event in proportion to the distance. His conduct
put me in mind of those amateurs, who, when they
want to bait a bull, aggravate it to the necessary
pitch to create them sufficient sport, and then allege
its madness as a pretext for treating it cruelly.

On the other hand, there were magistrates, who, going to the opposite extreme, rendered themselves useless to the country. One of this description lived near us, and from having no strength of mind, or reliance on his own judgment, was alternately the slave of either party, repealing now, what he had enacted before — ordering men to be apprehended one day as criminals, and on being threatened by their party, releasing them the next,—he was despised by all, and trusted by none. There were not wanting magistrates who, to an active and effective execution of their duty, added discrimination and a conciliatory spirit ; but I am sorry to say that their efforts were often neutralized by the blundering hot-headed zeal, or the timid inanity of their colleagues in office.

Although the alarmists made the most of every trifling circumstance that occurred, yet it cannot be denied that some very barbarous actions were committed by the associated bands of Shanavests and Caravats, always directed, however, against individuals who showed themselves forward in oppressing them, or who took the land at a rack-rent over their heads. Nothing could be more absurd than to say they had any regular political aim in view. In their combination, the two parties seemed to have a jealousy of each other, and often fell out at their hurling matches, and beat each other soundly ; and there were a good many spies among them in pay or the magistracy, who gave information of all their proceedings. While we were there, they had a quantity of arms, which they had forcibly taken from people in the neighbourhood, who, being loyalists, were authorized to keep them. A smith belonging to their faction kept them in repair, but when payment came to be asked for his trouble, instead of money they gave him a " good licking" for his presumption. Barny did not like this mode of clearing scores, and, to be revenged, gave in a list of the

names of all who had arms in their possession to the
magistrate. This list was stuck up at the cross-roads,
along with a summons, to deliver them up, or stand
the consequence. Some did comply, but the greater
number evaded the order by secreting them. Barny,
however, would not let them slip that way : he conducted us to an old drain, where we found upwards of
forty stand of blunderbusses, fowling-pieces, and
pistols ; but two-thirds of them were so much out of
repair that it would have been dangerous to use
them. Poor Barny, from the time he had lodged
the information, was obliged to take up his quarters
with us, and eventually had to bid " his native land
good-night" for his share in the business, and I daresay did not venture back in a hurry.

In general their aim was revenge, not plunder
but a few of the most hardened and daring of them
were regular robbers and house-breakers—a gang or
six or seven of whom were apprehended while I was
there, and sent into jail. At the ensuing assizes they
were tried ; one or two got off through want of
evidence, and others were transported for life.
happened to be present when the trial of one of them
came on, who, from his activity and forwardness in
their depredations, was considered a ringleader. I.
I recollect right, there was some murder connected
with the robbery with which he was charged. I do
not now remember the exact particulars of his trial
but I cannot forget the boldness and audacity of his
conduct while at the bar. Evidence after evidence
was examined, and although there was much circum-
stantial proof of his guilt, yet there seemed to be a
connecting link wanting, without which it must fall
to the ground. One evidence (a woman) had been
repeatedly called, but she did not appear ; and the
eye of the prisoner beamed triumph and defiance.
The public prosecutor stood up to close his case.

" He was compelled to own," he said, " that it had

been but imperfectly made out, and he would therefore not trouble"— At this moment a bustle was
heard in the court.

"Make way for the witness," said the crier, and
she stood before them. All were surprised ; but I
cannot convey an idea of the effect her appearance
had upon the prisoner ; he stood as if turned into
stone, his face grew deadly pale, and he reeled back
from the bar, while, with a convulsive fetch of his
breath, he uttered, "I am sold." She went on with
her evidence ; it was clear and conclusive, and filled
up every blank. The prisoner had recovered himself, and stood listening to her story with his livid
lips strongly compressed, his hands clenched, and
the cold sweat standing on his forehead. When she
concluded, he caught her eye as she turned to descend
from the table, and gave her a withering look, full of
deadly revenge, and summoning up his remaining
energy for the effort, he uttered a curse upon her,
with an emphasis worthy of a demon, and sunk back
in the dock. He was sentenced to death.

There is little time allowed in Ireland between
sentence and execution, and this he employed in
steeling his mind to every feeling. On the morning
of his execution, his relations from the country were
admitted to see him ; they had drank whisky before
they came in, to drown their grief, and a scene took
place between them and the dying man, which, were
I to attempt to draw in the ludicrous light it was
presented, would not .be credited. The drop was in
front of the jail, and his relations accompanied him
to the foot of the stairs he had to ascend : as they
parted with him, "Here, Murthy," said he, shuffling
off his shoes, "take them—no hangman rascal shall
get my shoes."

His friends now came to the front of the jail, and
were allowed to remain on the green plot, between
the soldiers and the drop. When the unfortunate

man approached the door, from which he was to plunge into another world, he pushed hurriedly forward, with the intention of addressing the multitude; but he was drawn back until the rope was placed about his neck, which being done, he advanced boldly to the edge of the platform, and in the face of the clearest evidence of his guilt, and former abandoned course of life, he cried out to the spectators, " I am innocent of the crime for which I suffer."

A murmur burst from the crowd, responsive of their belief in his asseveration, when one of his half-intoxicated relatives cried out, —

" Ah, poor Andy, and his shoes off too !" and sunk down upon the grass, but immediately rising and raising his arm, he cried out to the unfortunate wretch, who was now standing on the fatal drop — " Die hard, Andy—Andy, jewel, die like a man."

The next moment Andy spurned the handkerchief indignantly from his hand, and was lanched into eternity amid the prayers of the surrounding multitude, who, I have no doubt, considered him a martyr to the vindictive spirit of the laws.

CHAPTER XI.

EUGENE M'CARTHY.

While on detachment at this place, I became acquainted with Eugene M'Carthy, a young man, whose education and intelligence far exceeded the generality of the people in the village. He was the most liberal minded Catholic I ever met with : his views of the world and its manners were clear and unprejudiced, and to him I am principally indebted for what I know of the real state of Ireland ; for party-spirit exists to such an extent, that it is almost impossible for a stranger to learn any thing of it, unless through some prejudiced and distorted medium. There was something congenial in our habits and pursuits, which led us to associate ; and in answer to the question from me, how he had managed to cultivate his mind more than the rest of his neighbours ? he gave me the following history of his life.

" My father possessed a farm of an hundred acres, about five miles from this, which we still hold. My mother and two sisters, one older, and the other younger than me, composed his family. Being active and industrious, he managed his little estate in such a way that we were enabled to live comfortably and respectably. He was a man of strong sound sense, though in point of education not much above the common, his attention being more turned towards the improvement of his farm than his mind; but he was very anxious that his children should be well-informed. Our village school was none of the best, and had it not been for my mother, we would have made little improvement. She was a native of Dublin, where she had received an excellent education, and having a natural taste for literature, she found little pleasure in associating with her neighbours — thus concentrating all her pleasures in her little family. She led us to the source from which she had derived so much pleasure, and early imbued our minds with a thirst for knowledge, which she took care to gratify by every means in her power. But her system of teaching was not that of the schools, unless in learning to read : we had no formal tasks—her book was nature, which she first led us to admire, then to examine, and when our curiosity was raised, she drew speech from stones, sermons from brooks, and good from every thing. The phenomena of nature, as they occurred, furnished subjects for explanation and illustration. The growth and construction of a flower—the change of seasons

— the succession of day and night — the thunder,
whirlwind, and tempest, — were all pressed into her
service ; and when our young imaginations were
excited, she seized the important moment to impress
their nature and use on our minds. Thus we were
every moment insensibly acquiring knowledge, not
by formal study, or by being pent up in a room,
poring over a book for six or eight hours a-day,
getting question and answer by rote like a parrot,
but by our judgments being brought into action.
Books, however, were not excluded : when our
curiosity was once excited, and we felt inclined to
acquire more information on any subject, we were
referred to those which contained it, and by its being
made the theme of a subsequent conversation, our
doubts were solved, and our perplexities removed.
The filial affection which this mode of education
cherished, I shall feel to my latest breath. Her
instructions were the pleasure of our lives, the with-
holding them the greatest punishment. We looked
up to her as our guide, our comforter, and friend on
all occasions.

" One day I was questioning her with childish
simplicity about the horizon, and the form of our
earth, as they had been the subject of some of my
reveries ; and never shall I forget the flood of delight
that flowed in upon my soul, when, with the ball I
was playing with, suspended from a thread, she conveyed to my mind an idea of its form and motion.
In morality her system was much the same : after
having taught us its general principles, she left us to
the freedom of our own will. She used to say, such
and such consequences attend on our good and evil
actions, your minds will tell you which are most conducive to your happiness ; thus, when we committed
an error, she did not endeavour to avert the consequences, but seized on that opportunity to describe
the pleasure a contrary conduct would have afforded

Her pious exhortations, however, were never formal
she watched the favourable moment for making an
impression, when our hearts were uplifted by some
unexpected good, or lighted up with pleasure from
the appearance of nature; she then led us up to
nature's God, and expatiated on the wonders of his
power, and attributes, until we spontaneously bowed
in wonder and adoration. She is a Catholic, but not
a bigotted one—she does not believe that other sects
will be damned, if their hearts are sincere, and their
actions good; and although she is regular in the
duties of her church, she does not substitute them
for the more important ones of mercy and justice.
Under the guidance of such a mother, is it to be
wondered at, that I am better informed than our
neighbours?

" However, my education did not rest here. From
my earliest years, I was destined by my father for
the church, in accordance with a foolish vanity prevalent in Ireland, which induces parents often to
bring up some favourite son for the priesthood, to the
injury of the rest of the family; and it is remarkable
with what fond delusion they rely upon this individual for both worldly and spiritual benefits: the child
so set aside is treated with as much deference as if he
were already in office, and his brothers and sisters
are slaved to procure the means for his subsistence,
as a gentleman at college.

" My mother did not take the same view of the
subject as my father: she thought there was no want
of priests, and she considered that I might be as good
a man, and as useful to society, in some other situation of life; but her objections were overruled by my
father, who was determined in his purpose.

" From a preparatory school about forty miles from
this, I was sent to Maynooth College, where I had
been about two years, when I was summoned home,
in consequence of my father's illness, and arrived

only in time to witness his last moments. My mother was in great distress of mind, and urged me strongly to give up my studies, and remain at home; but I needed little solicitation, for I had no taste for the life of a priest. I had been too early taught the sympathies, charities, and pleasures of domestic life, to prefer celibacy and seclusion in their stead; so I left college and settled at home.

"I have been residing in town for these two months back, in consequence of my uncle's absence in England, whose business I have to look after; but I expect him home in a few days, when, I trust, you will accompany me to see our little farm, when I will introduce you to her whom I have been describing, and I am sure you will say that I have not done more than justice to her character."

Accordingly, when Eugene was relieved from his trust, I accompanied him out to B——. At the foot of a small avenue of trees, leading up to his house, we were met by a large Newfoundland dog, who came bounding down to meet his master, followed by Billy M'Daniel, who was a kind of *fac totum* on the farm.

"Welcome home, master! Are you come for good and all to us? It's the mistress, and Miss Ellen, and Catherine, that will be glad to see you. Your servant, sir," turning about to me—"Get down, Cæsar, and don't be dirtying the gentleman's clothes; but he's so proud to see yees all, that he doesn't know what to make of himself."

"Well, Billy," said Eugene, "how's the hay getting on?"

"Mighty well, sir, never better; we finished the low meadow this morning."

We had now reached the lawn in front of the cottage, where we were met by his mother, "Welcome, child," said she; "is your uncle come home, or is this only a visit?"

" My uncle arrived yesterday; but he is still so
busy that he will not be able to get out to see you
until next week—Give me leave to introduce you to
a friend of mine, whom I have brought out to see
how the *wild Irish* grow in the country—he has had
a specimen of it in the village.

" Any friend of Eugene's is always welcome to
me," said she, " but a soldier in particular; my
favourite brother belonged to that profession; he was
an officer in the eighty-eighth regiment; but, alas! he
is now no more: he fell at the battle of Talavera.
Was your regiment in Spain?"

" Yes," replied I, " but it had not arrived in the
Peninsula when the battle of Talavera was fought."

" Come, mother," said Eugene, seeing the tear
standing in her eye, " Let us drop all conversation
about ' war's alarms' now — Have you got any thing
for us to eat? remember we have had a brisk walk.
Where's Ellen and Catherine?"

" They are out in the garden weeding," said she,
" but when they hear you have returned, they will
not stop long."

She had scarcely done speaking, when in bounced
a sprightly girl about fourteen years of age, and
throwing her arms about his neck, " You are welcome
back, Eugene," said she, " we've been pining the life
out of us since you left home; but you are going to
stay now, are you not?"

The elder girl now came in, and advancing, without any affected reserve, shook my proffered hand
warmly, and welcomed me as the friend of her
brother. The Irish infuse their soul and spirit into
every thing they do, and nothing can be warmer than
their welcome; they set your mind at ease in a
moment, and convince you so strongly that they are
in earnest in their professions, that you feel yourself
like one of themselves, before you are half an hour in
their company. After we had got some refreshment,

we were joined by the family, who had now completed the labours of the day, and I had an opportunity of observing the character of each.

Mrs M'Carthy might then be about forty years of
age : she was still a fine-looking woman, although the
traces of time and care were beginning to shew themselves in her countenance — the rose had fled her
cheek ; but there was an eloquent expression in her
eye at once mild and commanding, that kept pace
with the varied emotions of her soul, and a dignity
in her manner which bespoke a mind conscious of its
own powers.

Catharine was a Hebe blushing with health and
spirit, sporting in the morning beam of life, without
a thought or care to disturb her happy frame of mind.
But Ellen had more of the collected sedateness of
womanhood in her manner : she might then be about
one or two and twenty ; her person in height was
above the middle size, but exquisitely formed ; and
her glossy black hair fell in natural ringlets about a
face, which, although it could not be called regularly
beautiful, had so much soul in it, that even at first
sight you could not behold it with indifference ; but
when her dark eyes were lighted up with feeling,
whether " shining through sorrow's stream," or flash-
ing with enthusiasm, the effect was alike irresistible,
— and she was an enthusiast in every thing belonging
to Ireland. She prided herself on the national character, vindicated its weakness and follies, and dropped
a tear o'er its misery.

" The poor Irish are called degraded and wicked,"
said she, " by those who exert all their influence to
make them so ; but relax the iron grasp that holds
them to the earth, let them be instructed, and you
will see what they will become. Where they have
had an opportunity, have they not signalized themselves in every department ? Where will you find
poets, orators, warriors, and statesmen like them ?"

" My sister is an enthusiast in every thing Irish,"
said Eugene; " but after all there are exceptions to
her rule,—we have had Irish statesmen who betrayed
their country, Irish warriors who were no heroes,
and poets who never drank of the Castalian fount."

" Oh ! I do not go to such an extravagant length
as to take in all ; but look at the names that fame has
written in golden letters on her annals."

" Have we not a Wellington, a Grattan, a Sheridan,
and a Cast——?" said Eugene.

" Name him not," said she hastily, putting her
hand on his mouth.

" At present," said Mrs M'Carthy, " we see all his
actions through the haze of prejudice — posterity will
judge better of his character, and say whether he
deserves the odium which has been cast upon it."

" By the bye, you served with our countryman,
Wellington, whose fame has sounded through the
world, — what character does he hold among the
soldiers ? "

" That is a question I am scarcely prepared to
answer ; but I will give you my own opinion, which
may after all be nearly the sense of the army on the
subject. I admit that he has many of the qualities
which constitute a great general, such as valour,
prudence, discrimination, &c. but there is one which,
in my opinion, he fell short of."

" Indeed !" said Mrs M'Carthy, " what is it ?"

" He had not the art of gaining the men's affections,—he never identified himself with his army,
and being either above or below human sympathy,
he was the same cold stern individual when they
performed feats of valour as when they committed
faults. In short, he was a being removed from all
our associations, who might be admired at a distance, feared or respected on the spot ; but never
loved."

" You seem determined to put me out of conceit

with my countrymen," said Ellen; " I need not speak
of Moore, our great national poet, you will have some
drawback on his fame also."

" He has been accused," said Mrs M'Carthy, " of
loose and voluptuous sentiment. I can say nothing
of the minor poems, said to be his, for I never read
them ; but in reading his Lalla Rookh, and his Irish
Melodies, I have caught a portion of the inspiration
and enthusiasm which he must have possessed when
writing them."

" His own apology for his venal errors," said Ellen,
" who can withstand ?

> Then blame not the bard if in pleasure's soft dream,
>   He should try to forget what he never can heal :
> Oh ! give but a hope — let a vista but gleam
>   Through the gloom of his country, and mark how he 'll feel !
> That instant his heart at her shrine would lay down
>   Every passion it nursed, every bliss it adored, &c.

" Whatever may be his faults, his deep and fervent
love of country, his enthusiasm in the cause of
liberty, and the magic strains in which he ' pours
the full tide of a patriot's song,' must endear him
to every Irish heart — must endear him to the
world."

" I 'm afraid my sister will make an Irishman of
you, before you leave us," said Eugene.

" On that subject her opinion is mine," said I,
" and I am sure it would be no ordinary gratification
to Thomas Moore, to hear his praise poured forth so
eloquently from the lips of a fair countrywoman.
The works of Moore and Byron excite my feelings,
in reading them, more than those of any modern
poet ; different in their style, yet each in that style
excelling all others. I cannot find a better simile to
express my opinion of their powers, than one drawn
from the fairy legend of O'Donoghue. The poetry
of Moore may be compared to the band of youths
and maidens who skim over the lake, to the sound of

heavenly music, scattering flowers on every side,—
that of Byron to the spectre chief, who, mounted on
his resistless spirit horse, prances through the foam-
crested waves."

" Well," said Eugene, " I suppose you have heard
enough of Ireland for one night ; we may as well
retire to rest, for we rise earlier here than you do in
town.   This is a busy time with us, and we must be
all at work by four in the morning."

" At work," said I, " so early ?"

" Yes," said Eugene, " for although we generally
spend our evenings in this manner, we find it necessary to assist in the labours of the farm during the
day. Many of the higher class of society laugh at the
idea of individuals who earn their bread by manual
labour, possessing refined taste or imagination ; they
consider it as incongruous and unnatural.   Not content with engrossing all the pleasures of sense, they
seek to rob them of those which a cultivated mind
afford ; and any attempt of their poorer brethren to
soar into the regions of science or imagination, is
met by them with the most supercilious contempt and
sneering ridicule.   The novel writers of our day
have contributed much towards this false and unjust
association,—all their *dramatis personæ* are dukes,
lords, and squires, rich as Crœsus, with nothing to do
but gad about the country.   In proportion to the
mental powers, intellectual cultivation has the same
effect upon the poor man and the rich, — the want of
it equally debases them.   But knowledge does not
altogether depend on going through a certain routine
of education.   The man of keen observation, who
has his eyes and ears open, and compares and draws
conclusions from all that comes within his notice,
who thinks for himself, and reasons fearlessly on all
subjects, that man will gain knowledge under very
unfavourable circumstances."

When I got up next morning, I found them all

a-field working at the hay. It was a beautiful morning, and Eugene conducted me round his little estate, which was finely situated, compact, and advantageously laid out. The cottage lay on the top of a small rise in the centre of the farm ; before it was a lawn of about an acre, skirted on each side by trees, beyond which lay his pasture-ground and meadows, divided from the adjoining farm by a stream, whose margin was fringed with the birch, the hazel, and the willow. Behind the cottage was his orchard and garden ; the house itself consisted of one story, with what is commonly called the loft, formed into bed-rooms, the windows being raised in the neatly thatched roof; outside it was dashed and white-washed, and around the door and windows was trained a profusion of honeysuckle, whose flowers shed a delightful fragrance through every apartment. The interior corresponded with its appearance outside ; without any gaudy superfluity there was every thing conducive to comfort, and the greatest regularity and neatness was apparent throughout the whole. But all this was nothing to the pure affection that reigned in the bosom of its inmates towards each other. Whatever trouble Eugene's mother might have had with her family when young, she was now richly repaid ; they hung on every word she said as if it were the precepts of an angel — they anticipated every wish, shunned every subject which would cause her disquiet, while she treated them with all the affection of a mother and all the confidence of a friend.

The surrounding commotions touched them not. Mrs M'Carthy was almost adored among her neighbours for her benevolence, and, what they termed, her *true Irish spirit ;* and Eugene, though a young man, had more influence over the members of the lawless associations in his neighbourhood than almost any individual in the county, which he never failed to exert on all occasions when it was in his power to prevent their atrocities.

After breakfast,—" Come," said Eugene, " as I have nothing very particular to do, I will conduct you over the classic ground in the neighbourhood, and as Ellen possesses the *amor patria* in so eminent a degree, she will accompany us, and describe all its beauties, lay open the arcana of every fairy mount, read you long lectures on the *good people*, their midnight gambols and mischievous freaks ; shew you the stream over which the *Banshee* raises her ominous howl, as a prelude to the death of a M'Carthy, or describe the form and properties of *Cluricaunes, Phookas, Fetches,* &c. &c. for she is deeply learned in fairy lore."

" Never mind him," said Ellen, " few people delight more in hearing these fairy legends than Eugene himself."

Having set out on our ramble, about a mile from the house, near a small village, (if a few cottar houses deserved the name,) we passed a well, over which hung a bush covered with white linen rags. Having expressed my surprise at such an unusual thing, " This is one of our holy wells," said Ellen, " to which the country people resort, who are troubled with sore eyes, each bringing a linen rag to wash them, and leaving it as an oblation, hanging on the bush."

On reaching the houses, Eugene stopped us in front of one, the roof of which had fallen in.

CHAPTER XII.

THE VILLAGE SCHOOL.

" This is all that remains of our village school.
Here, in his noisy mansion, sat Phil. Sullivan,
wielding his birch as if it had been a sceptre, while
his little subjects were ranged around on benches
formed of sods, that you may still see along the wall.
The fire, when any was required, was made in the
centre of the apartment, the fuel being furnished by
each scholar daily bringing a turf with him. The
door was formed of stakes interlaced with *wattles*, a
loop of which thrown over a crooked nail served the
purpose of a lock, and a rude table that the master
sat at was all the desk in his school. As they came
in at the door, the urchins were obliged to make their
best bow, by drawing back the left leg, catching the
tuft of hair that hung over the forehead, and bringing
their stiff necks to the precise mathematical curve
that constituted politeness; while Phil. sat in the
middle, sometimes talking English, sometimes Irish,
to suit himself to the comprehension of his pupils.
As a specimen of the manner in which he accomplished this, I will give you a journal of my first day
at school.

" While the more advanced scholars were conning
their tasks, he taught the younger tyros the alphabet
—' Come up here, Pat Geehan,' said he to a red-
headed boy, dressed in a gray frieze coat, which came
down to his heels, and a pair of old leather breeches,
that, only reaching half-way down his thighs, exposed
his red measled legs, —' Come, stand up here on the
table, and let the boys hear how well you can say
your letters.' — Pat mounted with great confidence ;

but when his phiz, by being raised into the light,
became more distinctly seen, ' Ubbaboo, tearin' murder !' exclaimed Phil. ' where have you been wid that
face ? why, man alive, you 've been kissing the prata
pot ; and your hair, too, stannin' up for a price, like
the bristles of a fighting pig. Is there no water in
the stream ? and it would have been no great trouble
to draw your fingers through your hair any how.' —
Pat very composedly lifted up the tail of his coat,
and, spitting upon it, gave his face a wipe that left it
streaked like a branded cow —' There now,' said Phil.
' blow your nose, and hold up your head like a
gentleman. What 's this, avick ?' said he, pointing to
the first letter of the alphabet — Pat scratched his
head —' You don't know what it is ? —small blame to
you, for your mother keeps you running after the
cows, when you should be at your larnin' ; but look
up at the couples of the house, and try if you can't
remember it.'—' A,' said Pat.—' Well done ! What's
the name of the next one ?' Pat hesitated again.
' What do you call the big fly that makes the honey ?'
—' B.' —' Och you're a genus, Pat, ready made.'
So on he went illustrating in this manner, until he
came to the letter O. Having tried Pat's ' genus' with
it two or three ways to no purpose, Phil. was getting
out of patience —' What would you say if I was to
hit you a palthog on the ear ? (suiting the action to
the word,) —' O !' cried Pat, clapping his hand upon
the afflicted spot, which rung with the blow. — ' I
knew you would find it,' said Phil. — By the help of
this admonition Pat struggled through the rest of the
letters, — 'Well, you may sit down now, and send up
Mick Moriarty.' — Mick was rather farther on than
Pat — he was spelling words. After spelling two or
three tolerably well, he came to the word ' what' —
' Well what does w-h-a-t make ?' — Mick was not
sure about it — ' W-h-a-t,' said Phil. ' sounds *fat ;*
but,' (conscious of his own error in the pronunciation)

' when I say fat, don't you say fat ; but do you say fat your own way.' "

" Eugene is caricaturing," said Ellen, " Phil. Sullivan was scarcely so bad as he represents ; although I must confess his mode of instruction was at times rather ludicrous. Yet it was perhaps better suited to the poor children he had to teach, than that of a more refined instructor ; and for all his blundering at the English, there was not one in the county a match for him at Latin or Irish."

" That is certainly true," said Eugene ; " it was from him I learned the rudiments of Latin, and he has taught it to half the cowboys in the parish, to keep them, as he said himself, out o' longin'. This may account in some measure for the acquaintance with Heathen Mythology, which some of our most ignorant poetasters possess, and which is so profusely and sometimes ridiculously made use of in our songs. I do not mean those blundering songs misnamed Irish, that are written by blockheads as utterly ignorant of the idiom of our language, as they appear to be of common sense ; but in songs which, though little known out of Ireland, must be familiar to all who have been any time in the country, — such as the following : — A young man meets a pretty girl in a morning, and falling head and ears in love with her at first sight, he breaks out with this rhapsody, —

> Are you Aurora or the goddess Flora ?
> Or are you Venus or the morning sun ? &c.

" Poor Phil. Sullivan is now no more, and those who once composed his school are dispersed to the four quarters of the globe — a new parish schoolhouse is built, but few attend it, in consequence of some attempt made to interfere with the belief of the children."

When we left the school-house, we were met by a sedate-looking old gentleman, who saluted us as he passed. " That," said Eugene, " is Father ———, our parish priest, a good and upright man ; but eccentric in his manners, and more so in his preaching — that the latter is affected for the purpose of accommodating himself to the comprehension of his hearers, I believe, for he is a man of learning, and shines in conversation, when in company with people who understand him ; but if you heard him from the pulpit, I doubt much whether you would be able to refrain from laughing.

" When the congregation are all composed, with their eyes fixed on him, he begins : ' There you are all of ye, looking demure and mim-mouthed, like as many saints, as if butter wouldn't melt in your mouths. Who would think, now, that half-an-hour ago you were busy scandalizing one another, making your remarks on this one's dress, and that one's face, while more of ye were bargaining about your pratas and corn ; and this is all done when you come here on the pretence of hearing the word of God on the Lord's day ; — but what do you do on the week days? — why you curse, and swear, and tell lies, and drink, and fight ; and worse than all that, you go scheming about at night, doing mischief to every one that doesn't please you ; and after doing all this, you'll come to me, hanging a lip like a motherless foal, and a whine in your face, to make your confession, and get absolution for your sins. But how can I give you absolution ? people that never think of God, only when the devil's at their elbow — And when I refuse ye, ye fall to blubbering, and say, O Father ——— dear ! hear me ; what will I do, if you don't hear me ? And what answer can I make ye, only that you'll go to hell and be damned — and indeed it's as true as I say it, if you don't mend your manners, that will be the end of ye. So I would advise you to mind what you're about, and don't forget that there's One above ye, that's taking note of all your misdeeds. I am sure you know yourselves there's no pleasure in the world in doing what's wrong, and you all know how contented you feel when you do what's right. Then take my advice, and " make your souls" without any delay, for the Lord knows which of you may be alive to see next Sunday.'

" That is but a very imperfect specimen of his powers ; for, in this rude style, he is a most merciless dissector of the human heart, and his hearers often wonder how he attains a knowledge of their most secret failings, even when they are not regular in their duty. Rude, however, as his oratory is, at times it is very impressive, and I have often seen his audience in tears. He possesses a strong influence over his flock, and I have frequently seen him plunge into the midst of an hundred fellows who were fighting with sticks, and with his horse-whip disperse the whole of them.

" There is a very unjust prejudice raised against our clergymen, from the supposition that they encourage or abet the disturbances that agitate this country. Nothing can be more unjust : they not only denounce and excommunicate all concerned in them, from the pulpit, but I have known them risk their lives in the endeavour to prevent outrages. I am sure, take them as a body,that there is not a more useful or exemplary set of men in the world, than the parish priests of Ireland. There are no doubt exceptions ; but what would become of the character of the clergyman of the Established Church, were individual instances brought forward to criminate the whole body ? For my part, although I am a Catholic, and of course must condemn the upholding an expensive church establishment at the charge of people who are not members of it, yet there are many clergymen of that church whom I esteem and respect. With the one belonging to our parish we are on the most friendly terms ; his family and ours are almost constantly together, and I

am sure love each other sincerely. It would be well
for you to bear in mind, that in this country *Protestant* and *Catholic* is not so much the distinguishing
name of a religious sect, as it is the *shibboleth* of a
political faction. There is, indeed, very little religion among the zealots on either side,—their own
aggrandisement, and the possession of power or po-
pularity, being their ruling motive. Poor Ireland
has been torn to pieces between these conflicting
parties, and has alternately been the dupe or the
victim of the one or the other. Among well informed
and really religious people, these distinctions are
little thought of."

"Nor should they be," replied I; "but, in my opinion, the influence of your clergymen over the mind
and conscience of their flock extends too far, when
used among ignorant and debased people. To restrain
them from what is wrong, it may be beneficial, but it
can also be turned to a bad purpose; and few intelligent people would like to have their conscience so
much in the keeping of men frail and erring in their
nature."

"Their influence is not so great as you imagine,"
replied Eugene; "we exercise a freedom of opinion
on many points; for instance, there are many Catholics who cannot believe that all other sects will be
eternally lost, and the enlightened of our clergy do
not insist upon the point."

"It is an article of belief," said I, "that in my
opinion is replete with mischief, and is the strongest
weapon in the hands of your adversaries against
emancipation. What can we expect, say they, from
people who believe we are running the broad road to
destruction? Even their pity can only extend so far
as to drag us from its brink forcibly, as we would
restrain a man from committing suicide. Would
there not be an end of our political and religious
freedom, the moment they got the ascendency?"

"It is certainly the most feasible argument they use," replied Eugene; "but at most we could not treat you worse than we have been treated, and if knowledge, by enlarging the mind, creates a more liberal feeling, its effects will extend to the poor Catholics as well as others. It is, after all, but a puerile argument; we find Protestants tolerated in France, and other Catholic countries. The evil you dread springs from ignorance, which produces bigotry, intolerance, and persecution, among Protestants as well as Catholics.—But I am sure you must be teazed with our incessantly talking about our country?"

"Far from it," said I, "the subject to me is very interesting."

"For once," said Ellen, "I am tired of it; let us shift the subject, if you please, to something else."

"Then I hope you will conduct us to the fairy haunts in the neighbourhood, and give us some of the traditions about them."

"With all my heart," said she; "but we do not need to travel far — this green mount on our left is said to be a favourite resort of the ' good people,' and as its summit commands a view of all the places of note in the neighbourhood, we may seat ourselves there." So saying, she led the way.*

As we were returning home, — " I see you are like the rest of your countrymen," said she, " a good listener; but you take care that we shall not know much of your adventures. You, that have been ranging the world over, amid scenes of every kind, must surely

* Here I had introduced some fairy traditions, which she recited with all the arch and witty accompaniments of voice and manner, which render even a common story interesting ; but having accidentally met with a very enter-taining book lately published, entitled, " Fairy Legends and Traditions of the South of Ireland," where I find similar stories, related in a style so much superior to mine, that it would have been presumption in me to follow the same track ; I have thought it proper to cancel that part of my MS. and must now refer the reader to the above work for the gratification of his curiosity.

have much more interesting subjects in store, than those who have been always at home."

"The life of a soldier is not so varied," said I, "as you may imagine; there is a sameness in his duty, and so little liberty of his own in all that he does, that he cannot see or feel objects through the same medium as those who travel on pleasure or business. In general, he is secluded in a barrack or a camp from the rest of the world, and therefore there can be little variation in his life at home or abroad. In war, he is placed in circumstances which often strongly excite his mind, but the repetition of even these, soon renders it incapable of the impression. When we had been some time abroad, we went into action with nearly as much indifference as we did any minor point of duty."

"Then we are led to believe, from what you say, that soldiers are thus rendered incapable of the finer feelings of humanity."

"Under particular circumstances it may have that effect," said I. "But, after all, there is no class of men so susceptible of feeling, if the proper chord is touched. I know many instances of their disinterested and generous conduct in assisting the distressed; and the story which I am going to relate may exemplify the manner in which their sensibilities may be wrought upon, even in the tumult and excitation of an assault, where, in general, the kindly feelings of nature are entirely excluded.

"The adventure is not one of my own, but it was related to me by my friend H——, whom you have heard me mention, and whose veracity I cannot question."

CHAPTER XIII.

AN AFFECTING SCENE.

" On the night of the storming of Roderigo," said he, " I was one, among others, who pressed forward on the French, up to the market-place, after they had abandoned the defence of the walls. They had ceased to make resistance, and the town was completely in our possession, when I was induced, along with three more of the regiment, to turn down one of the streets for the purpose of searching the houses for articles of value. Having entered two or three which were already filled by our soldiers, we ran farther on from the noise and riot, and stopped at a house which seemed to be superior to those around it. The first place we entered was the kitchen, where a few embers were glowing on the hearth, and emitting a faint light on the surrounding walls. An awful silence reigned through the house, which was only interrupted by the distant huzzas and riot of our troops. On throwing some wood on the fire, we were enabled by its light to find a lamp, with which we proceeded to search the other apartments of the house — Every thing was in order — no sign of confusion more than if the family had gone to bed in perfect security. This and the stillness that reigned around, altered the complexion of our minds, and tinged them with a feeling of solemnity which we could not account for. Had there been noise or disorder, or the appearance of any one having been there on the same errand as ourselves, we would have begun plundering without a thought ; as it was, we had gone through several apartments filled with articles of value, without touching any thing. On reaching the upper flat of the house, we were startled by hearing some one sobbing ; and proceeding towards the apartment from whence it issued, we discovered the door ajar, and a light in the room. We hesitated a moment, doubting whether it might not be some of the French soldiers who had fled from the ramparts ; and preparing ourselves for defence, should such be the case, we pushed up the door, and entered together. But the scene which presented itself arrested our steps at the entrance. Stretched on a couch lay a young female apparently dying. Her mother — for such we understood her to be—sat supporting her head upon her breast ; while the father, kneeling by her side, held a crucifix before her, — a female domestic kneeling at her feet, bathed in tears, completed the group, and all were busily employed in prayer. No notice was taken of our entrance, except a slight start when we first appeared ; their feelings were too intensely bent on the one object to attend to any thing else. Life seemed to be ebbing imperceptibly ; her eye was fixed and glazed ; but ere her soul fled its earthly tenement for ever, a strong convulsion seized her : this appearance of acute suffering wrought up the minds of her parents to the highest pitch of agony. We were so powerfully affected by the scene, that we forgot every thing else — forgot the exultation and excitement of victory—forgot the errand which we had come on. Nature claimed an undivided sway, and, wrapped in solemn and softened feeling, we stood rooted to the spot, gazing, with the tear of pity glistening in our eyes, on the lovely being who was expiring before us. The struggle was short, and the fearfully suspended groan which burst from the agonized father, proclaimed that all was over — the mother sat gazing on the dead, lovely even in death, with a vacant stupor in her eye, that told the unutterable nature of her grief.

" We were making a motion to depart, when the

father, for the first time, seemed to observe our presence, and going over to a box, he took from it a purse filled with money and offered it to us ; but we refused — for worlds we would not have touched any thing in the house. We shook hands in silence with the inmates, retraced our steps slowly down the stairs, and were soon involved in riot and confusion ; but we were not now in the mood for mixing in such scenes, and we regained our column on the rampart, with our minds filled with the solemn and affecting scene we had witnessed."

We had now reached the cottage, and as I intended to return to my detachment that night, I was pre-paring to depart, but they pressed me so warmly to pass another evening with them that I could not refuse, and a happier evening I never spent. After much varied conversation, kept up with great spirit by the family, we insensibly returned to our old topic, the state of Ireland, and canvassing the mo-tives and lawless proceedings of the people in the neighbourhood.

"Poor wretches !" said Eugene, " they know not what they are doing ; they feel themselves oppressed and miserable, and, like the inferior animals, they kick in the direction the pain is inflicted, but political aim they have none. In fact the poor creatures who are associated with these parties by choice or com-pulsion, are invariably the most ignorant part of the community, and I believe have not sufficient ability among them to carry any organized measure into execution. I have had opportunities of knowing them more accurately than many, for I have been once or twice at their meetings ; and whatever in-terested or designing men may advance to the con-trary, I assure you they are only actuated by one feeling—revenge on their oppressors ; and such a thing as an attempt to overturn the government was

never agitated amongst them. That sufficient misery
exists among the Irish to spur them on to desperation, I believe few people who know any thing of
the country will deny. Much of this misery is too
deeply seated to yield to any of the nostrums pre-
scribed for its cure; it is, like some of the diseases
of the body, which are best cured by supporting the
system, withdrawing all cause of irritation, and
leaving the rest to nature. But the most prominent
and apparent cause of it is, that there is no adequate
employment for the inhabitants, no extensive manu-
factures among them: the people, therefore, are
obliged to revert to the land for support, which,
from being let at a rack-rent, to supply the extravagance of the proprietors in another country, barely
yields a subsistence; and the poor cottar, even when
he submits to live on potatoes three times a-day,
exists in continual dread of being turned out, or
having his effects distrained for the rent, which, with
all his efforts, he is unable to raise. Living thus in
continual dread of utter starvation, is it to be wondered at that they should feel irritable; and that,
when they see their hard-earned gains rapaciously
forced from them, under colour of law, to support
clergymen of a different persuasion, or the non-
resident landlord, who, 'like the barren sand, imbibes
the shower,' but yields no return — is it to be wondered at that the poor peasant, thus goaded on to
destruction, should turn upon his drivers, and, over-
looking the primary agents in his miseries, vent his
blind fury on those who, from their subordinate
situation, come in closer contact with him? Thus
the tithe-proctor, the middle-man, or the stranger
who is introduced to occupy the land from which he
has been ejected, and has now no refuge left him
from famine, are the common objects of his resent-
ment. All these evils which I have described, are
acknowledged and lamented, and lectured upon at

great length by many *lazy* good people, who do not
put forth a finger to ease the burden, if we except the
exertions of certain Societies, who, with the best
motives, I have no doubt, distribute Bibles and
Tracts among our starving countrymen; but some
security against actual want is necessary before a man
can cultivate his mind, or make any great improvement in morality; and a religious tract, however
useful it may be in its proper place, is but an indifferent substitute for bread.

" There exists a strong desire to convert the
Catholics from the error of their ways; but what
benefit could accrue from unsettling their faith, without improving their conduct, I am at a loss to know.
Judging from that of the lower class of Protestants in
Ireland, I do not think they would benefit much by
the exchange. Whatever may be the difference between the two sects, the morality they teach is the
same : therefore I think the better plan would be, to
endeavour, by proper instruction, and humane usage,
to make them good Catholics."

" I perfectly agree with you on that point," said I ;
" for if some miraculous change does not take place
in human nature, there must ever be a difference of
opinion in religious matters ; and that which has most
influence on the conduct of its members must be the
best. A man's belief ought to be left to his own
conscience. The mind in process of improvement,
where it is left free and unbiassed, gradually opens
on the truth, and spurns its former error ; but force
or undue influence creates prejudice, and raises an
insurmountable barrier to its farther progress. All
that seems wanting to your countrymen is relief from
present misery, and instruction — then, if Protes-
tantism is a better religion than their own, they will
soon find it out. The energies of the Irish are at
present dormant — they are enveloped, as it were, in

the haze of morning ; but when the sun does burst
forth, theirs will be a glorious day."

"Yes," said Ellen, "they have in them the elements of a great people, and I am sure, were they
used as they ought to be, they would be submissive
and loyal to a fault.

> There never were hearts, if our rulers would let them,
> More form'd to be grateful and blest than ours !

"It gives me the highest pleasure, — it does my
heart good, to hear any one speak in liberal or kindly
terms of my poor country." Struggling with the
feelings which filled her bosom, unsolicited and spontaneously she burst forth into the melody of,

> Remember thee ! yes, while there's life in this heart,
> It shall never forget thee, all lorn as thou art :
> More dear in thy sorrow, thy gloom and thy showers,
> Than the rest of the world in their sunniest hours.
>
> Wert thou all that I wish thee — great, glorious, and free,
> First flower of the earth, and first gem of the sea,
> I might hail thee with prouder, with happier brow,
> But, oh ! could I love thee more deeply than now ?
>
> No ! thy chains as they torture, thy blood as it runs,
> But make thee more painfully dear to thy sons —
> Whose hearts, like the young of the desert-bird's nest,
> Drink love in each life-drop that flows from thy breast.

There was something peculiarly thrilling in her
voice — its low tones breathed the sigh of a broken
heart—the higher notes, wild and energetic enthusiasm.
She appeared to have sung the first two stanzas un-
consciously ; for as she finished them, observing us
listening, she blushed and stopped short. Through our
persuasion she was induced to continue ; but the glow
of feeling which had before animated her was gone,
the spell was broken, and although she still sung in a
superior manner, her voice had lost much of its former heart-searching effect.

With feelings of sorrow that I cannot express, I
took leave of this happy family, whose existence, as it
were by enchantment, in the midst of misery and
crime, put me in mind of those green and fertile spots
which we sometimes found embosomed among the
wild and rugged Pyrenees.

CHAPTER XIV.

ELLEN.

I HAD not proceeded far on my journey, when I
was overtaken by Eugene — " I have some little business in town," said he, " and I may as well accompany
you." In the course of our conversation, I took occasion to revert to his sister Ellen, whose character had
made a strong impression on my mind, — " She has
too much feeling," said he, " for her own happiness ;
she lives in a constant state of excitement of one kind
or another, which her scanty knowledge of the world
has not been sufficient to subdue. Time and experience, however, may rectify that fault. She will soon
be where she can have opportunities of observing the
world more accurately, for she is betrothed to a young
man, a distant relation on my mother's side, who
holds a situation in one of the public offices in Dublin.
Their marriage is fixed for the beginning of next
month, after which she accompanies him home. I
wish he may be sensible of the treasure he receives
in her hand, for she will not be content with a
divided allegiance — She will love him more devot-
edly than most women could do ; but she will expect
the same from him, and her mind is so sensitive, and
her heart so proud, that the slightest indication of
carelessness on his part will render her unhappy "

"Good-morrow to you, Master Eugene," said a countryman who was working in a field by the road side.

"Good-morrow, Rooney," said Eugene. "Have you got every thing put to rights again?"

"Indeed I have, sir; but it's yourself I have to thank for it. May my blessing and the blessing of God attend you and yours wherever you go."

"I will call in and see you as I come back."

"Arrah do, master — don't forget."

"That poor fellow," said Eugene, as we passed on, "had his house burned some time since, by a band of those deluded wretches who infest the country. I have several times introduced myself at their meetings, for the purpose of reasoning with them on the wickedness and folly of their proceedings; and some of the most rational of them have been induced, through my persuasion, to live peaceably; but others have threatened to attack my own house, for daring to interfere with them. I might, by giving information to the magistrate, have had the ringleaders apprehended; but besides having the national horror of an informer, I am well aware that it would be productive of no good in the country.

"On several occasions, by receiving timely information, I have been able to prevent the execution of their revenge; but in poor Rooney's case I was too late.

"Some time ago, a number of people in the neighbourhood lost possession of their small farms, through means of a pettifogging scoundrel of an attorney, who, by paying a large fine to the agent, took the land on lease, over their heads; the consequence was, that their little farms (previously too high) were raised in rent to double the sum. In this extremity they came to the resolution of resisting the advance of rent; the consequence was that they were forcibly ejected, and tenants brought from a distance to replace them, many of whom being intimidated by anonymous threatenings posted on their doors, or conveyed by letters, abandoned the houses ; but others, and among the rest Rooney, the individual whom we have just now passed, determined to keep possession and defend themselves against all who might dare to molest them. Rooney's obstinacy induced the Shanavests to resolve on forcing him out, and with that purpose they paid him a midnight visit ; but he and his son were ready for them, and in answer to their summons to open the door, he gave them the contents of a blunderbuss. This exasperated them to the highest pitch, and they used their utmost efforts to burst the door open ; but here he was also prepared, having barricaded the passage with the heavy parts of his furniture. I was informed of the intended attack by Billy M'Daniel, who had heard some hints of it from those concerned, and I hastened to the house to endeavour to save the poor people from their fury. When I arrived, they had succeeded in forcing the door, but were still impeded in their entrance by the things which Rooney had piled in the passage. I beseeched, I entreated them to desist ; but my voice was drowned in the vociferations and noise of the wretches, whose evil passions were now roused to extremity. One rascal (I know him well) had ran to a neighbouring cottage for a light, and now attempted to hold a bundle of flaming straw to the inside of the roof, for the purpose of setting it on fire ; regardless of the danger to which I was exposing myself, I knocked him down with my stick, but a blow on my head from some one behind laid me senseless on the spot. When I recovered, the burning roof of the cottage was falling about me ; fear lent me strength, and I sprung to my feet, when my ear was struck with the cries of a child. I plunged forward through the smoke to the place from whence the sound proceeded, and in a settle bed, surrounded by burning thatch and rafters, I found the poor innocent nearly suffocated. It was the work of a moment to snatch it up and bear it to the door, where I met the despairing mother, and threw it into her arms.

" ' God bless you and save you,' said she, ' whoever you are.'

" Feeling the hazardous situation I was in, and knowing that my motives might be misconstrued, and my actions represented in the worst light, I hurried homewards without speaking a word.

" I had not been many minutes at home, when I was startled by some one knocking at the door. Although I was conscious of having committed no fault, I felt alarmed, and my heart beat violently. On opening the window and looking out, I found it was Mr ——, the magistrate, with a party of soldiers. This at first confirmed my fears, but they were soon dispelled, for in answer to my inquiry, ' what he wanted ?"

" ' I would be obliged to you,' said he, ' if you would get up and come along with me, for some rascals have set Rooney's house on fire, and I am afraid have murdered some of its inmates.'

" Having muffled myself in a cloak, I came down and accompanied him to the house, which I had left half an hour before. It was now one burning mass, shooting up showers of sparks into the air. Rooney's son was with us, and in giving his relation to the magistrate, told what I have already related.

" ' They couldn't get in upon us,' said he, ' for we had thrown all the furniture into the passage, and had given them two or three shots, when one fellow pushed in with a lighted wisp in his hand, to set fire to the house; some of his own party knocked him down; but that did not save us, for they lighted the thatch of the house before they left the door. We then became desperate, and removing the things from the entry, pushed out, determined to live or die. The villains had escaped, but the whole roof was now in a blaze. There was no time to lose, and gathering our trembling half-naked family together, we rushed into the field before the house. On looking round the children, my mother gave a scream. ' Oh, my little Jane !' she cried, and sprang forward to the burning cabin. A little girl of four years of age had in the confusion been left in bed, where she was lying asleep, unconscious of the work of destruction going on. I instinctively followed my mother, and as she approached the door, I perceived a man burst from the burning house with the child—throw it into my mother's arms, and immediately disappear. I was so struck with surprise, that I could not follow him, it seemed like the work of some supernatural being.'

" We had now reached the house, where we found many of the neighbours assembled, and among them some, like myself, who had been there before. I was horror-struck at the dismal scene, and had there been any prospect of the least good being done by it, I would have had them all apprehended.

" In going round the premises with the magistrate, we met the poor woman, who was strolling about, mourning the desolation of her dwelling. The light of the burning house fell full upon my face as we met—she stared at me for a moment, and exclaimed, ' Aren't you the good gentleman who saved my child ? O! God Almighty bless you, for it is yourself—I know you by the blood on your face.'—I was confounded,—the magistrate looked doubtfully at me.

" ' There is really blood on your face, Mr M'Carthy

" ' There may be,' said I, endeavouring to recover my self-possession, ' for I feel my nose bleeding but you surely know me better than to suspect that I had any hand in this business.'

" ' Oh ! not at all,' said he. But I could see that

suspicion was raised in his mind. Had he been a man whom I could have trusted, I would have told him the whole story ; but I was too well aware of his disposition to say any thing about it ; and as I knew he would be questioning the woman concerning the circumstance when my back was turned, I sought out Rooney and told him every particular of the affair, and charged him to say nothing about it. It was lucky I did, for Mr —— had them examined very minutely on the subject next day, and endeavoured to draw something from them in confirmation of my being implicated in the affair ; but Rooney kept his promise faithfully, and the woman told him that she was sure now I was not the person she had seen. What she said about the blood on my face was perfectly correct, for my nose must have bled profusely when I was knocked down, as I found it crusted on my clothes next morning.

"'I have since assisted Rooney, and you see how grateful the poor fellow is.

" This affair has induced me to be more cautious, for the magistracy are so perfectly absolute, that I might have been sent off to New South Wales (if I got off with that) for my exertions on that night. Law is so summary here, and so little evidence required against a man whom they wish to ruin, that it reminds me of some place in your country, where it is said they were in the habit of hanging people first, and then trying them."

When we parted, Eugene made me promise to pay them an early visit ; but being unexpectedly relieved from the duty on that station, I never had the pleasure of seeing them again. Shortly after, I received several letters from him, wherein he detailed his sister's marriage and happiness with her husband, and when I last heard from him, she was the happy mother of three children.

CHAPTER XV.

A DRUNKEN FROLIC.

WHILE here, two of our sergeants, in a drunken frolic, took it into their head to go and see their sweethearts in Wexford. When they came thoroughly to their senses, they were far on the journey, and thinking their crime would be the same, they entered the town. Their absence being discovered, a party was sent after them, and they had not been many hours in the place, when they were found, and marched back prisoners to their regiment.

We expected they would have got off, by being reduced from their rank ; but the commanding officer seemed to consider their crime of too heinous a nature, to let them escape with an ordinary punishment. They were tried by a General Regimental Court Martial, and sentenced to be reduced to the rank and pay of private, to receive five hundred lashes, to be branded on the side with the letter D, and afterwards to be sent to (what is usually termed) a banished regiment. One of them was an intelligent man, who had been respectably brought up — the other a young man, scarcely twenty years of age: the former did not live to go abroad — he died in Dublin, I believe, of a broken heart; the other went abroad, but I never heard what became of him.

The impression throughout the regiment at the time was, that the sentence was most unreasonably severe, particularly that part of it that awarded the corporal punishment. Will that disgrace to the country never be done away with? I am perfectly convinced it could be done without, and those who advocate it, must be men who are either wofully ignorant of human nature, or whose passions obscure their reason, and induce them to act contrary to their better judgment; the latter is the most common of the two. I have known commanding officers, who have acted in this respect rationally and wisely, while their personal feelings were not strongly excited; but who, when they were so, committed the most flagrant injustice.

Why should there not be a definite code of military laws for the army? for that abstruse, vague, and indefinable thing called " the mutiny act," surely does not deserve the name. I defy any two persons separately, to make the same commentary on it. In it so much is left to the private opinion of Courts Martial, that the sentences passed by them are often preposterously unequal: for instance, I have known a man tried by one court martial, and sentenced to three hundred lashes, and another for the same crime, without any palliating circumstance in his favour, sentenced to fourteen days' solitary confinement. What are we to make of this inconsistency?—It is evident it proceeded from the temper of the individuals composing the court.

If these things appear hard or unjust, why not rectify them, by attaching a definite punishment to every crime, at least as far as circumstances admitted? The business of Courts Martial would then be clear and easy; nor would officers feel themselves in the unpleasant predicament in which they are often placed. Corporal punishment ought to be abolished altogether; I am perfectly convinced it could be done without. In many regiments we have strong proofs of the allegation; and the fact, that where punishment is most frequent, the men are the worst behaved, and *vice versa*, cannot be denied.

It cannot fail to humble a regiment to have one of their number flogged, and it ruins the individual. No man who has prided himself on his character, can look up after it: he bears a humiliating sense of disgrace about him for ever after, — "a worm that will not sleep, and never dies." My character, he will say, is gone, I can never hold up my head among my comrades ; all prospect of promotion is lost to me, for should my officers at any future period offer it, how could I, who have been tied up, and my back lacerated before the gaze of the whole regiment, ever feel confidence to command those who have witnessed my disgrace, and to whom I have been an object of pity or scorn, either of which is alike humiliating to a mind not entirely callous.

Many may wonder at my warmth on this subject ; but if they had, like me, seen the dreadful extremity to which it was at one time carried, they would cease to be surprised. Who that has ever seen a man stripped before the gaze of a regiment, his limbs bound to the halberts, and the knotted scourge lacerating his flesh, while the surgeon stood by to measure by the pulse the amount of human agony which the poor wretch could suffer, would ever wish to see it again ?

The first man I saw flogged, received eight hundred lashes, for desertion — it would have been more merciful to have shot him. But men have been known to receive a thousand lashes before they were taken down from the halberts ; and on occasions where nature could not bear the punishment awarded at once, they have been brought out again, and again, to have their half-healed backs torn open afresh ! They have been known to faint under their punishment, and again be flogged into life ! On other occasions their agony was lengthened out by giving the lash by tap of drum, allowing half a minute to elapse between each tap, and when the mangled back was cut through the skin, and the bare muscle quivered under the scourge, the only mercy extended was to inflict the rest of the punishment on some other part of the body ! And yet all this was done under the eyes of people professing Christianity and civilization — who were yearly inundating Parliament with petitions against flogging negroes with a cart-whip — yes, while the blood of their countrymen was sprinkling a barrack square, and their cries were ringing in their ears! They saw it not — heard it not — their feelings were too fine for aught but distant misery. The groans of their tortured countrymen were given to the wind — no voice was heard in their behalf — no arm was raised to save.   Yes, there were a few who vindicated the cause of insulted humanity, and they live in the grateful remembrance of the soldier ; but their efforts were rendered ineffectual through the opposition of men whom I dare not trust myself to speak about.

How individuals can be found to stand up in the senate of a free and enlightened country, and vindicate this brutal and inhuman mode of punishment, is an anomaly not easy to be accounted for.

Thank God! the times I have described are gone past — men cannot now be treated in that manner without investigation; but still enough remains to make us wish its abolition.   Though flogging is now seldom resorted to at home, I am afraid it is still too prevalent in our colonies abroad, and may in a great degree cause that debasement of mind, and habits of inebriation, which we observe in the generality of those soldiers who have been stationed long in the East or West Indies.

If any crime committed by a soldier in the army deserved corporal punishment, the individual should no longer be a member of it : after such punishment, he ought to be discharged, as unworthy to be a soldier. It may be argued that many would then commit crime, when engaged in an unpleasant service, to get their freedom ; but those who would say so, know little of human nature.   Most men who have any character to uphold, consider disgrace worse than death ; and if they had witnessed, as I have done, the reluctance with which soldiers, in general, left their regiment, when sick, even on the eve of battle, and what anxiety they evinced to join, when restored to health, they would think differently. Many schemers there are in a regiment, certainly; but under any circumstances they would be useless characters — there are drones in every hive. To inspire and cherish the manly honourable spirit I have described, it is only necessary to treat men as if they possessed it. Soldiers have their failings, and their prominent vices, it is true; but they generally lie on the surface, and their neighbours in civil life have this advantage of them, that they " have the better art of hiding;" but in point of disinterested feeling, and generosity of character, I question much whether the soldier would lose by the comparison.

The besetting sin of the British soldier is drunkenness, (the parent of many others,) produced, in a great measure, by the leisure time which he has in general hanging on his hands. I am sorry the only effectual cure for this has not been pushed to the necessary length, — I mean urging the men to improve their minds, and affording them the means, which would not only make them more useful soldiers, but enable them to fill up their spare time with advantage to themselves.

As an instance of this, there were a few of us in the habit, instead of spending our idle time in the public-house, of walking down by the river side, carrying our books with us, and alternately reading and conversing. Some of our comrades who had been addicted to drink, sometimes joined us for the sake of the walk; and from the pleasure they derived from the conversation, and the new ideas awakened in their minds, they voluntarily gave up their old habits, and became converts to our system. We procured books on the various subjects to which our attention was excited, and although not quite masters of the subject, it would have surprised many people to have heard our disquisitions on Natural Philosophy, History, &c. Music was a favourite amusement also, and by forming small parties, we were never at a loss to pass the time, and when on guard, (the most irksome time to others,) we found it the most pleasant. Our number was not great, certainly, but a little encouragement and countenance from our officers might have done much. The detached situation of the regiment often broke up our party, but still we cherished the germ of intellectual improvement; and if I have in any way gained the start of my comrades in this respect, it has been by my application while in the army, for when I first entered it, my education was entirely confined to the elements of reading, writing, and arithmetic.

I know there are men who look upon the increasing intelligence of the lower classes of society with a fearful eye, considering it as the precursor of revolution and anarchy. The man who thinks so, must have a " worthless neivefu' of a soul." Education, by improving the understanding and ripening the judgment, leads men to see clearly their own interest and follow it steadily, and of course will always render them tractable to the existing government, where that government is not tyrannical and unjust. None have any reason to fear the spread of knowledge, but those whose actions loathe the light.

CHAPTER XVI.

THE DESERTER.

I was one day on the main guard in Kilkenny, when a deserter, passing through under escort to Dublin, was delivered to our charge. The poor fellow was accompanied by his mother and two sisters. Such unusual company with a man in his situation excited my curiosity, and inquiring into the particulars of his case, he told me that his father had died about two years before, leaving his family, consisting of his wife and six children, the lease of a small farm of twenty acres, at a moderate rent; he was the elder child, and only son of the family, and the charge and cultivation of the land principally devolved on him.

For two years things went on prosperously; but at the end of that time the lease expired through the failure of the last life on which it depended. This was a sudden and unlooked for event; but as they had been regular tenants, they had never doubted for a moment that they would get their lease renewed. In this, however, the poor creatures were mistaken, for when Frank called on the agent, he found that unless he could raise twenty pounds in cash, to give by way of fine, the farm would be given to some person who would give it. Sorrowful enough he returned home, and communicated this intelligence to his mother and sisters, who were thunderstruck; for raising twenty pounds in cash was out of the question. Many plans were thought of, but none fully answered the purpose, for when all their efforts were exerted, they were only able to raise twelve pounds out of the twenty. The day on which Frank was to give in his answer was fast approaching, and as a last resource, it was determined that he should apply for the loan of the required sum to a gentleman, a friend of his father's, who lived in an adjacent village: unluckily for poor Frank, when he went there, the gentleman was in Dublin, and was not expected home for a month.

Depressed and melancholy, he was returning home, not knowing what to do, when he met a recruiting party beating up through the town. The thought

struck him instantly that he might raise the necessary
sum by enlisting, and acting from the impulse of the
moment, without nicely weighing the consequences,
he took the king's money; and after he got his
bounty, went and took up the lease. He had never
mentioned the affair to his mother, and she believed
that the money was received from his father's friend.
The truth, however, could not be long concealed, for
the sergeant came out to inform him that he had
orders to send his recruits to head-quarters, and it
would be necessary for him to be in readiness to leave
home in three days. He was, therefore, obliged to
disclose what he had done to his mother. It was
dreadful news to the poor woman, for, independent
of her great affection for him, he was her principal
dependence in cultivating the farm. " What use can
the lease be to us," said she, " when we have nobody
to mind it ?" Frank felt the truth of what she said ;
but he endeavoured to console her by saying, that as
Tim Brachnie, their neighbour, was on the point of
marrying his elder sister Sally, they would not miss
him, for Tim was well able to manage the land. As
for himself, he was happy at having it in his power
to secure a living to the friends he loved so much,
and he was sure that he would agree better with the
life of a soldier than labouring at home; he might
soon rise to be a sergeant, perhaps make his fortune
in the East Indies, and come home and make them
all happy.

However Frank might please himself with these
speculations, they afforded little consolation to his
mother. But there was no helping the matter : he
was obliged to bid his friends adieu, and march to
join the depot in Chatham, the regiment being in the
East Indies.

Shortly after his arrival, a draft was selected for
embarkation to join the regiment. Frank was among
the number, and he wrote home, taking a farewell of

his friends. The time of his embarkation was fast approaching, but he had received no answer to the letter he had sent home; he felt grieved at this. " Could I but see them for one half hour," thought he, " or at least get a letter from them before I go, I would feel satisfied;" but the day previous to the intended embarkation arrived without any letter. As he was sitting melancholy in the barrack-room pondering over this unaccountable neglect, one of his comrades told him that some one wanted him outside the barrack gate. Frank's heart leaped to his mouth, he made haste to obey the summons, and entering a room of the public-house to which he was directed, he was struck mute with astonishment on perceiving his mother and two of his sisters, who flew into his arms, clung round him, and cried and laughed by turns. " When do you go, my child?" said his mother. " To-morrow," replied Frank. " For God's sake, is that true. O Frank! what will I do? You are going where I will never see you again; you'll never live to get there, and what will become of your poor mother, when she hears of your death?—but she'll never live to hear of it, if you go." Poor Frank was sadly perplexed. " I have walked a hundred miles in Ireland, and two hundred and fifty in England," said his mother, " besides crossing the salt ocean, and your poor sisters walking foot for foot with me—and God knows we hadn't much to live on — our money wasn't very plenty, and the people in this country are not so ready stretching out their hands as the poor Irish. Now, Frank, you're going to leave us for ever, and if you do, your poor mother will never see Ireland again, for she'll die on the road, in a strange country, and what will become of your poor sisters?" This was touching Frank on a tender point—a vague resolution flitted through his mind—he had found the life of a soldier not so much to his liking as he at first expected. " I wouldn't wish to advise you to desert,"

said one of the sisters, who saw Frank wavering;
" but how can you leave us and your poor mother
forlorn here." " Och, the king, God bless him !" said
his mother, " will never miss you out of so many,
and the Lord knows your poor mother would miss
you all the days of her life."

Frank had summoned his honour and fair fame to
his side ; but what do they know of these things in
the bogs of Ireland ? thought he — His oath — ay, that
was a tickler ; but isn't it like a custom-house oath—
And then his poor mother. Frank yielded to their
solicitations. The next point was to make his escape ;
but that was soon arranged,—he was dressed in a suit
of his elder sister's clothes, and under the cloud of
night they set off on their return home.

They had a weary journey travelling to Bristol,
where they embarked on board the packet for Water-
ford, and were safely landed on Erin's green isle once
more. They had travelled a long day's stage on their
way home, and thinking themselves safe, were sitting
in their lodging-house refreshing themselves with a
cup of tea, when the sergeant who had enlisted Frank
came into the house, and presented a billet to the
landlady. He had been ordered to remove to another
station, and was so far on the way with his party
He knew Frank's mother the moment he came in,
and coming over inquired for her family, and when
she heard from her son. The poor woman was so
confused, that she did not know what she was saying,
and stammered out some nonsense, which, along with
the petrified appearance of the daughters, raised a
suspicion in his mind. Frank, in his female dress, sat
holding down his head, — " Is this your daughter
Peggy that 's looking so bashful ?" said the sergeant,
putting his hand out to raise up Frank's chin, when
he saw enough of the face to understand who it was.
Frank saw he was detected, and dropping any attempt
to disguise himself farther, lifted the stool on which

he was sitting, to knock the sergeant down, as the only means of effecting his escape ; but the sergeant had beckoned in his party, who were standing at the door, and he saw that resistance would be madness, and therefore submitted to his fate with the best grace he could. He was sworn in a deserter and committed to jail, having previously resumed his own dress, and was thus far on his way to Dublin, accom panied by his mother and sisters, who were determined, as they said themselves, to follow him to the *end of the world.*

What became of poor Frank afterwards I never heard, but happening to be in Chatham about two years after, I inquired at one of the sergeants of the depot, and found his story perfectly correct. I had even the curiosity to go to the house where they had effected his disguise, the landlady of which corroborated the story so far as his mother and sisters being in the house, and the soldiers coming there after him when he was gone.

I have little left worthy of relating that occurred while stationed in Kilkenny, but I cannot dismiss the subject without paying a tribute of respect and admiration to the character of the clergyman who acted as chaplain to the troops in that place—the Rev. Mr Rowe, rector of St Mary's. Joined to an indefatigable discharge of his duty, the purest benevolence, and a liberal mind, he possessed an eloquence that caught the attention of the most illiterate and careless. Our men were never very remarkable for their church-going propensities, but we had not been long in Kilkenny when the greater part of the regiment voluntarily attended his Sunday evening sermons. Without stooping to coarseness of expression, he rendered himself plain and intelligible to all ; and by his earnest and affectionate manner, endeared himself to his hearers. His preaching had a very visible

effect on the conduct of many of our men, and I am
sure they all remember him with feelings of esteem
and veneration. He was no time-server, " with doc-
trines fashioned to the varying hour," but rigidly
followed the example of his Master in being " no
respecter of persons." It would be well for the people
of Ireland were all the clergymen of the established
church like Mr Rowe.

As a specimen of the familiar manner in which he
drew the men's attention, I was once on the jail guard
when he came to visit the prisoners. Those of the
guard not posted as sentinels were always called in
on such occasions, and when we were assembled he
read some passages of Scripture ; but while he was
reading the men's attention wandered. Perceiving
this, he shut the book, and looking round his audience,
" I will tell you a story," said he ; every eye was
fixed on him ready to hear the promised tale :—

" There was once a gentleman possessed of great
riches, and he lived up to his income, enjoying all that
this world could afford. He was on the point of
setting out on a pleasure tour, when he took suddenly
ill and soon after died. Some time after, a gentleman,
who had been on very intimate terms with the
deceased, but ignorant of his death, called at the
door, and asked the servant if his master was at
home ; the servant replied, in melancholy accents,
' Alas, sir ! my master has gone to his long home —
he is dead.' ' Dead !' said the gentleman, horror-
struck with the news, but recovering himself, —
' Well,' said he, ' it is the road we must all go sooner
or later — but I hope he has gone to heaven ?' The
servant, who knew his master's wild manner of living,
shook his head. ' What !' said the gentleman, ' do
you doubt it ?' ' I don't know,' said the servant,
' but when my master was on the eve of going a
journey, he was always talking about it, and making

great preparations some days before he set out; but during his illness I never once heard him mention *heaven.*'

" Are you, my friends, making preparation for that long journey that we must all soon take ?"

He then took advantage of their attention being awakened to impress upon them the necessity of that preparation.

CHAPTER XVII.

LIKENESSES.

ABOUT the period of which I am now writing, the service of a number of our men expired. Where they were good characters they were strongly pressed to re-inlist ; but many of them seemed to be satiated with their seven years' apprenticeship, —among the others, some of my comrade sergeants, who were induced to leave the service in disgust at the conduct of some of their officers, one in particular, whose situation brought him in closer contact with them. He had risen from the ranks to the situation which he then held, by dint of a species of *noisy activity*, which was at that time in great request. It was not enough to bid a man do a thing, but the command must be accompanied with a few oaths, in a stentorian voice, that roused every echo within a mile ; and it would have been diverting and ludicrous in the extreme, to a person unaccustomed to the business, to hear an order given by the commanding officer when in the field, ringing along through the chain of underlings, increasing in strength and vociferation, until it reached the quarter for which it was intended. I am not sure whether I have conveyed to the reader a clear idea of what I wish to

describe ; but if he has ever been along-side a dog
kennel, and watched the progress of their sweet
voices, from the first note sounded by the master of
the band, until the whole pack, tagrag and bobtail,
joined in the melodious concert, he will have some
notion of what I mean. The officer in question considered this quality so essentially necessary to the
character of a non-commissioned officer, that those
who did not abuse or blackguard the men under their
command, were considered unfit for the situation.
So particular was he in this respect, that if he heard
of a sergeant being praised by his company, that
individual was set down in his mind as a candidate
for the first private's coat that might be vacant.
" You are one of the good fellows, I believe," he
would say, addressing the offending non-commissioned
officer, " Damme, I'll good fellow ye."

He had a system of favouritism which he pursued
in the corps, to the almost total exclusion of any, but
those *he* recommended to the situation of a non-commissioned officer. The power he possessed to do
this was partly acquired by his own presumption, and
partly by the indolence or apathy of the officer commanding. The result, however, was, that men were
promoted to the situation who could not write their
own name ; being consequently dependent on their
inferiors for doing their duty, they could scarcely be
very fit persons to hold the situation, and as they
could not help being conscious of their inability, it
must have been irksome and unpleasant to themselves.
In this, however, they were the more like himself,
for without any great stretch of imagination, his
writing might have been mistaken for Arabic ; as to
the other parts of a gentleman's education, he knows
best whether he possessed them or not.

But I am digressing — I was talking of the sergeants leaving the corps when their period of service

expired. Several of them were sent for, and promised great things if they would re-inlist; but from the reason I have already mentioned, they declined doing so. The consequence was, that during the short time they remained in the regiment, they were treated by him in the harshest manner; this was low illiberal conduct, and certainly did no good to the service.

In the absence of senior officers, we were some time under the command of a young man, who was newly promoted to the rank of major. He had the elements of a good commanding officer in him, and in his discipline endeavoured to copy Colonel Lloyd; but the nervous manly spirit was wanting—the perfect self-confidence in his own powers and judgment, which the original possessed. Vacillating and infirm of purpose, he was alternately led by some officer or another; and although he disliked the one whose portrait I have given in the preceding page, yet he had not resolution enough to oppose the measures which he carried by dint of impudence. Thus his efforts to imitate Colonel Lloyd were often rendered farcical. For instance, in endeavouring to establish the cleanliness and regularity of messing, which the corps was so remarkable for, while under the command of Colonel Lloyd, the men were encouraged to provide extra dishes, on the anniversaries of any of our battles, which, in addition to the whisky purchased for the occasion, took away a good deal of their pay, as these red-letter days occurred very frequently. The consequence was, that the men were getting so much the epicure, in a small way, that they would willingly have held anniversaries on every day of the year, had it not been that as the lining inside increased, the covering of the outside was getting thinner. This, however, soon wrought its own cure. But after all, Major C—— was a warm-hearted feeling gentleman; all he wanted, was experience, and a little more knowledge of human nature

I have no doubt but by this time he is an excellent officer.

He was succeeded by one whom I need not name, we all knew him well enough. The first time I remember him in command of the regiment, he was superintending a punishment, which he ordered to be given by tap of drum. As he paced up and down the square, listening to the cries of the poor wretch, with a countenance, in which the green and yellow were striving for predominance, with tne dark tinge which it had naturally—" he grinned horribly a ghastly smile," which I think I see before me at this ,nstant, in all its native deformity ; but we were not much troubled with his company during the fighting days. I have ransacked my memory, endeavouring to find some good action he had done while in the corps, to throw into the scale against the rest of his conduct : but I am obliged to give up the task in despair.

It may be asked, was there no bright reverse to oppose to this picture ? Yes there was,—Captain G——, witty, intelligent, and good humoured, with his face reflecting all the good qualities of his heart ; Captain D—— C——, the kind and benevolent, who still cherishes his kindly feeling to the old corps, and has done more for the individuals who belonged to it than any man in the regiment ; Captain K——, a gentleman of refined manners and education ; Captains C——, B——, and A—— ; and last, though not least, a man who ought to have been a major a dozen years ago—he had been in India with the corps, and commanded the light company through the Peninsula ; but he is still a captain, although many must have passed over his head in the course of two-and-twenty years. Though rather unpolished in his manners, he was a good officer—not very eloquent ; however, the speech he made to his company, previous to their being engaged for the first time in Portugal, will long be remembered : —

" The French are before you, my lads—let us fight manfully: if we live we'll be an honour to our country, and if we die," (lowering his voice,) " it's no great consequence."

Some may be inclined to think, from my warmth on the subject of flogging, and the freedom with which I have treated the character of officers, that I may myself have smarted under the lash; or at least that I feel envious and disappointed at not being promoted in the service. When I first set out in my narrative, I resolved to keep myself in the back ground; and I might have closed my story without telling the public farther than what they now know, were it not that my statements might suffer from surmises similar to that I have mentioned; but for the sake of truth, and in justice to myself and the service, I think it necessary to state, that I did not long remain a private. I entered the service at fourteen years of age, was corporal before I was sixteen, and by the time I attained my eighteenth year, I had risen to that rank which few men who inlist as private soldiers can ever hope to pass in the British army. During my service, I have held situations that required something more than ordinary ability and steadiness, and I possess testimonials of character from my various commanding officers that I have every reason to be proud of.

If I have spoken freely of the abuse of power in the army, I have done it through a natural hatred to oppression and tyranny, which every thinking man must feel; and as a subject of a free and enlightened country, I claim a right to speak my sentiments. I have no prejudice against the aristocracy of the army—far from it—there are many of them whom I esteem and respect—many of them intelligent and liberal minded men, who would do honour to any profession; but there are also others of a different stamp, supercilious, overbearing tyrants, who think

their fellow-men created to be their slaves, and ignorant swaggering coxcombs, whose puppyism must
disgust all under their command. I have spoken of
them as they merited,—let each claim his meed of
praise or censure as he may think himself deserving
it.

I believe few people set out in life with higher
notions of rank or greatness than I did. The reading
I indulged tended to increase it,—even the favourite
tragedy* which we were in the habit of reciting on
Saturday in school, taught me that there was something in noble blood that shone in the countenance,
and inflamed the heart, though the possessor were
born in a shed, and bred among beggars—some
impress that marked the refined gold of creation.
This was imposing in theory, and finely calculated
for the ideal world I then lived in ; but when I
entered upon the stage of the great world, and had
an opportunity of seeing those favoured individuals,
I felt as much disappointment as the poor woman,
who ran half-a-dozen miles to see the king, and after
all discovered that he was only a man. The result
was, that I learned to look on gold lace and epaulettes
without being dazzled, and in forming my opinion of
the individual to go a little deeper than his splendid
outside. The haughty contempt or insolence of a
superior, and the cringing sycophancy of under-
strappers, many of whom were ready to hunt down
on the slightest hint any poor devil who had the
misfortune to incur the displeasure of his officer,
gave me the keenest mortification ; but it threw me
on my own energies, and taught me to exist within
myself, independent of the smiles or frowns of those
around me : although my body was constrained, my
soul was free — and I could detest a tyrant, and
despise a blockhead, whatever his rank might be.

---

* " Douglas," which I admire for its composition and dramatic effect ; but
detest for the venal sentiments which it is calculated to convey.

Let it not be thought, however, that I dislike men, because they stand above me in the scale of society — far from it. Where they are good men, I respect and esteem them the more, that they are so in spite of the power and temptation they have to be the contrary. I have invariably found, that the real gentleman is mild and unassuming in his manners, and possesses more feeling for his fellow-creatures, than those who start into rank or wealth.

CHAPTER XVIII.

STORY OF RESTON.

From Kilkenny the regiment removed to Dublin, where, being quartered in a barrack outside the town, the dull sameness of our duty was broken in upon by little worthy of relation. One incident, however, I may relate, that will not only support opinions advanced in this work, but also give me an opportunity of doing justice to an individual, which inadvertence only caused me to delay so long.

While in Kilkenny we got a musician from a militia regiment to teach our band. He was a first rate performer; but in saying so, I sum up all his good qualities, for a more ignorant mulish blockhead I never met with. Our officers, listening only to the sweet sounds which he elicited from the various instruments, thought he could not fail to make our band as good musicians as himself, and proud of his acquirements, they granted him every indulgence; but he had no more art in communicating his knowledge of the science to others, than the clarionet on which he played; and his morose overbearing temper actually kept the regiment in a constant broil. Not a day passed, nay, scarcely an hour, without a complaint from him, against some one or another; and as those complaints were sometimes listened to, and the individuals complained of punished in some shape to please him, the life of a musician in the regiment was no enviable one.   Among them was a young lad of the name of Reston, whose growing talent, in spite of every obstacle, threatened to outdo his master — this roused his jealousy, and he prohibited him, on various pretences, from the use of both music and instruments, by which he might have improved himself; but, not content with this, he tormented him by all the nameless methods which a superior in the army can, I am sorry to say, too often do with impunity. Poor Reston was known to the officers and his comrades as a boy of remarkably precocious talent, not in music alone, but in every thing ; and naturally of a proud spirit, he could ill brook the insult and oppression which was heaped upon him, and seeing that his enemy was supported in every thing that he did, his mind was wrought up to desperation, and he deserted — taking his passage in a vessel from Dublin to Glasgow, where his parents resided.

On his arrival there, instead of endeavouring to palliate his offence, they represented it to him in the most heinous light, urged him, as the only way to amend his fault, to return to his regiment immediately ; and lest any thing might deter him, his mother accompanied him to Dublin, and gave him up to the commanding officer.   Reston was pardoned, and recommenced his duty ; but the spirit of his oppressor was in no way altered — he took every opportunity of provoking him.   Reston's feelings were keen in the extreme ; but he suffered patiently for a length of time, until one morning, when the regiment was going out to drill, provoked beyond measure by taunts and insults, he replied in terms that were construed into something resembling mutiny — this was immediately reported by the

fellow who had aggravated him — the consequence
was, that he was tried by a court martial on the field,
and punished. He did not receive more than twenty-
five lashes, when he fainted and was taken down —
his back was little hurt, but the scourge had entered
his soul — he never recovered it. He begged his
friends strongly to purchase his discharge, and they
made the necessary application at head-quarters, but
it was resisted at the regiment. Seeing this, his
mother travelled to London herself, and petitioned
His Royal Highness for her son's discharge, representing her own services to urge its being granted ;
but the usual official routine being gone through, the
required permission was again combated at the regiment, and declined at head-quarters. The consequence was, that poor Reston was driven to despair,
and seeing no hope of being relieved by any other
means from the oppression under which he groaned,
he again deserted, and has never since been heard of.

Thus, a young man of genius, and abilities of no
common kind, was ruined, to keep in countenance
one of the veriest blockheads that ever appeared in
human shape, who at length sunk into well merited
disgrace, but not before many good men were
punished, and otherwise unjustly used for his sake.

I have alluded to his mother representing her
services to the Commander-in-Chief — I shall now
give her character, and then leave the reader to judge
whether she had not some claim upon the indulgence
of those in office at head-quarters.

She was the individual who distinguished herself
so nobly at Matagorda near Cadiz, while the French
were besieging the latter place in 1810. Her husband was then a sergeant in the ninety-fourth regiment, and one of the detachment that occupied that
fort, when the French bombarded it with thirty piece
of cannon. It may be easily conceived what havock
would be created by so much artillery playing upon

a place not more than an hundred yards square, and it may also be imagined that few women could have maintained ordinary courage or self-possession in such a place: but from the commencement of the action she behaved in a manner which it is scarcely in my power to do justice to. The bomb-proofs being too small to contain the whole garrison, some of the men had huts formed on the battery, and among the rest was that of Mrs Reston. When the French opened upon us, she was wakened out of her sleep by a twenty-four pound shot striking the facine where her head lay; but nothing daunted, she got up, and removing her child, a boy of four years old, down to the bomb-proof, she assisted the surgeon in dressing the wounded men, who were fast increasing on his hands, for which purpose she tore up her own linen and that of her husband. Water being needed, one of the drum-boys was desired to go and draw some from the well in the centre of the battery; but he did not seem much inclined to the task, and was lingering at the door with the bucket dangling in his hand, — "Why don't you go for the water?" said the surgeon. — "The poor thing's frightened," said Mrs Reston, "and no wonder at it: give it to me, and I'll go for it." So saying, she relieved the drummer from the perilous duty, and amid the dreadful discharge of artillery playing on the battery, she let down the vessel to fill it with water — she had scarcely done so, when the rope was cut by a shot; but she determined to get her message with her, and begging the assistance of a sailor, she recovered the bucket, and brought it filled with water down to the bomb-proof, where her attention to the wounded soldiers was beyond all praise. In the intervals, she carried sand bags for the repair of the battery, handed along ammunition, and supplied the men at the guns with wine and water; and when the other two women (who had been in hysterics in one of the bomb-proofs, from the time the action had commenced,) were leaving the battery, she refused to go. Next morning, our ammunition being expended, we ceased firing, and the French, seeing the dilapidated state of the fort, sent down a strong force to take possession of the place; and our men were mustered for their reception, when Mrs Reston was at her post with the others, determined to share in the danger. It was a critical moment, for had they got under the range of our guns, our efforts would have been unavailing. Through the ruinous state of the fort, three guns, all that we could bring to bear upon them, were crammed with loose powder, grape, ball cartridge, &c. to the muzzle, ready for a farewell shot, and when they came within two or three hundred yards of the fort, we poured their contents into the very heart of the column, and laid the half of them prostrate on the earth. Those who survived took to flight — their batteries again opened, and a fresh supply of ammunition having arrived for us, we returned their salute; but the place being found untenable, the surviving part of the garrison were withdrawn by the boats of our fleet.

Mrs Reston still exhibited the same undaunted spirit. She made three different journeys across the battery for her husband's necessaries and her own. The last was for her child, who was lying in the bomb-proof. I think I see her yet, while the shot and shell were flying thick around her, bending her body over it to shield it from danger by the exposure of her own person. Luckily she escaped unhurt, and still lives, and is at present residing in Glasgow. But will it be believed that she never received the smallest token of approbation for her intrepid conduct, and the service which she rendered on that occasion?

After her husband was some time discharged, she

was induced, at the instigation of officers who were
well acquainted with her heroic conduct, to make
a representation to the Commander-in-Chief, who
warmly recommended her case to the Secretary at
War; but the cold reply was, that he had no funds
at his disposal for such a purpose. Generous, noble
nation! surely the advocates for economy had little
to find fault with here.

Mrs Reston is now advanced in years,* and
although her husband enjoys the regulated pension
for his services, he is unable to work for his subsistence, and surely one shilling and ten-pence a-day
to support two individuals, is no great excuse, as it
has been made, for not making any exertion in her
favour.

The only instance of the kind, exclusive of that
now related, that I witnessed in the course of my
service, was in the person of a woman who lived as
the wife of a captain of one of the light companies of
our brigade. She accompanied him through the
campaign, exposed to all the dangers and privations
attending on such a life, with a devotedness that no
legally married woman could have surpassed. At
the battle of Vittoria, when the army was engaged,
she was left with the baggage; but hearing from some
of the disabled men that the captain was wounded,
she mounted her horse, and galloped down into the
scene of action, regardless of the danger, to seek out
and relieve him wherever he might be. She found
him when he had breathed his last, and stopped by
him until he was buried. This was an appalling
blow for her: she was left friendless in a strange
country; but those who paid her any little attention
in the captain's lifetime, now felt no compassion for
her. Her gold watch, her favourite pony, and all

* Since the publication of this work, her husband is dead, and she is
now living in the poor-house of Glasgow.

that she formerly held through her protector, were taken from her, and a short time after, I saw her struggling through the mud on the line of march, with the shoes torn off her feet. She soon after disappeared, but what became of her I do not know.

CHAPTER XIX.

A LETTER.

I HAD letters from home that my father had been in bad health for some time, and I now received one, saying, that no hope was entertained of his recovery, and if a furlough could be procured, to come home without delay, as he had expressed an anxious wish to see me. I lost no time in making the necessary application, and being successful, I went in search of a vessel. I found one that had put in to Dublin through contrary winds, and was now ready to sail the moment it was fair. I was impatient to get forward; but as there was some prospect of the wind coming round in our favour, I took lodging in a house on the quay. I had been acquainted with the people who kept it, as they had lived in Wexford previous to their coming to Dublin. Having mentioned the vessel that I intended to take my passage by, Mrs L—— asked her husband if that was the vessel Eliza was going in. On his replying in the affirmative, " I am glad of it," said she, " our friend may be able to pay her some attention on board, and perhaps be of some service to her when she lands at Glasgow. I know I can trust you with her story," said she to me; " and when you hear it, I am sure you will feel as much interest in the fate of the poor creature as I do." Without following Mrs L——

through all the various digressions and windings of her story, I have taken the liberty to relate it, according to the knowledge I afterwards had an opportunity of acquiring : —

Eliza R—— was the daughter of a respectable farmer in the county of ——. She was the eldest of the family, and considered the beauty of the small village she lived in. There was a soft loveliness about her features, and a benignity beaming in her mild blue eyes, expressive of purity and peace within. Her modesty and goodness of heart had made her a favourite with all her neighbours ; and she was so retired and correct in her conduct, and unremitting in her religious duties, that she was looked upon as a superior being. Eighteen years of Eliza's life had passed away without any event occurring to disturb its even current. Many of the young men of the village would willingly have proposed for her hand ; but they were restrained by an awe which her beauty and conduct had inspired.

It was about this time that a gentleman belonging to the revenue department, whose business led him to the coast, came down from Dublin ; and there being no house of public entertainment, he begged a lodging for the short time he had to stop from Michael R——. It was instantly granted ; and he had scarcely become an inmate of the house when he cast his eyes on Eliza, and his heart was inflamed with a passion which he determined, if possible, to gratify. Her modest retiring disposition left him little room to make familiarity with her ; but observing that she was a rigid attendant on mass, he feigned a devotion which he did not feel, and by this pretence had an opportunity of escorting her to chapel. His person and manners were prepossessing, and his language fluent. But it is unnecessary to enter into a detail of the measures he took to accomplish his purpose ;

suffice it to say, that he won the heart of the too confiding Eliza,—he had sworn to make her his wife, and she believed him, — all was arranged between them,—he was to go to Dublin, and settle his affairs, provide a house for her reception, and return to marry her and conduct her home. The unsuspecting parents saw his partiality for her, and felt proud of it ; they little knew the serpent they were fostering in their bosom. Poor Eliza parted from him in the faith of a speedy return, and dreamed of years of happiness, which, alas ! she was never to enjoy.

The time of his promised return elapsed, and day after day rolled on without him making his appearance. She now began to feel dreadful anxiety, — she had received no direction how to write, and had no means of learning any thing concerning him. He must be sick, thought she, or some accident has befallen him, or he would be here ; and she grieved that she knew not where to seek him, that she might tend and watch over him. She was soon doomed to be unde-ceived — a neighbour, who had been at Dublin, called upon her father with some articles which he had employed him to purchase. " When you were in Dublin," said Michael, " did you see any thing of the gentleman who lodged with us before you went away ?"

" That I did," replied the visiter, " I took a parcel for him from Mr W——'s."

" He told us he was to be back here again in a week ; but something unlooked for has kept him, for we haven't seen a sight of him since."

" I don't think he'll be able to come at present," said Billy, " for when I was in Dublin his wife was very ill."

" His wife !" exclaimed Eliza, who had been an attentive listener to the conversation.

" Ay, his wife," said Billy ; " he was married about two years ago to a lady belonging to B——."

Eliza heard no more; she had summoned up all her energy to meet the confirmation of the dreadful news; but the struggle was too much — nature gave way, and she sunk lifeless from her chair. They ran to her assistance, and having raised her, succeeded by slow degrees in bringing her back to life On recovering, she felt that she was ruined for ever; but the necessity of keeping her own secret, acted as a counterpoise to despair, and induced her to smother her feelings. Her parents were not surprised at her fainting, for they were aware of his attentions, and they could feel for her situation; but they had no knowledge of the extent of her misery. She was partially recovering from the effects of her grief, when she found herself in a way which she could not long hope to conceal. Her agony of mind now became excessive; she could not endure that her disgrace should be known in the neighbourhood, and she determined on leaving her home, and travelling to some distant part of the country. Packing up her clothes, and taking some money with her, she travelled to the nearest port, where she embarked for Dublin, and having found Mrs L——, to whom she was related, she confided to her the story which I now give to the reader. But not being able to procure any means of subsistence, and hearing that employment was more likely to be had in Glasgow than any other place, she resolved on going there, where, far from any one who knew her, she might drag out a miserable existence: and for this purpose she had taken her passage in the vessel I intended to go with. I was introduced to her by Mrs L——; but she shrunk from observation, and seemed to feel uneasy at being observed. Seeing this, I did not obtrude myself on her notice; but I could not see her " pale wasted cheek, and brimfu' e'e, or hear her heart-bursting sighs," without lamenting over this wreck of human happiness.

The wind remaining contrary for two or three days, I felt so uneasy that I determined on proceeding by coach ; but previous to doing so, I recommended Eliza to the care of my friend B——, who was waiting his passage by the same vessel, his term of service having expired. The sequel, which I may as well relate here, was communicated to me in a letter from him a few days after my arrival at home : —

" Two days after you left us, we sailed from Dublin harbour, in company with two other vessels bound for Glasgow. The wind being fair, we had ran down the coast a good way before dark ; but as the night came on, the weather got hazy, and the wind veered more to westward, blowing very fresh, and continued increasing : by ten o'clock it was a perfect storm. All hands had been on deck from the time it grew dark, and as we had been rather pinched for room, the passengers turned into the vacant births ; but I had never any liking to being below in bad weather, and remained on deck. The night looked frightful — the mist was such, that we could not see the vessel's length a-head — and the wind blowing fearfully in upon the shore. The captain had never been on the coast before, and seemed to have no confidence in his knowledge of it, and in his confusion lost sight of every precaution. I was well aware of our danger, and mentioned it to the captain. ' I can't help it,' was his answer, ' I can see no light—to lie-to, I would inevitably drift — and to tack with this wind would be impossible ; all I can do is to keep the vessel close to the wind—perhaps it may clear up.' I saw there was little hope, and my mind turned to the poor creatures in the cabin, who were lying sick in the births ; if there was any chance for them, it must be on deck, and going below for the purpose of getting them up, I found Eliza in dreadful agony,—the pains of premature labour had seized her through excessive sickness. I endeavoured to persuade her to come up, but she could not stir. I overheard one of the sailors on deck sing out that he saw a light. 'Thank God!' said I, 'we may be saved yet.' 'Is there danger?' said Eliza. I could not conceal it. 'You had better try to get up on deck, I will assist you; if you have any chance of being saved it will be there.' 'O, no!' said she; 'let me remain, I do not wish to be saved; God will have mercy on me, and the waves will cover my shame!' Hearing a great bustle, I ran up the ladder, — 'Lord have mercy on us,' said one of the sailors, 'we are all lost.' 'How? how?' said I. 'Don't you see the breakers a-head.' I did see them too plainly: we were close upon them. I ran down to the cabin, and partly by force, partly by entreaty, got Eliza out of her birth; and getting her in my arms, I got to the foot of the companion ladder. I was half-way up the ladder, when a crash that would have roused the dead pealed in my ear, mingled with the despairing shriek of the crew. The shock threw me back on the cabin floor, and my head coming in contact with the iron ring of the hatch, I was rendered for a few moments insensible. The stern of the vessel had been torn asunder, and it now yawned beneath me; the water rushed in — I remember no more. I was saved, miraculously saved; but Eliza escaped from the censure of an unfeeling world."

Poor Eliza had indeed escaped from the censure of the world; but her seducer still lives: if he is not lost to every feeling, his remorse must be great. Poor B—— had a narrow escape with his life: when the vessel went to pieces, he had clung to a piece of the wreck, and was washed ashore on it; but he and one of the crew were all that were saved.

CHAPTER XX.

MY FATHER'S LAST HOURS.

It was late at night when I reached Glasgow, and I travelled on to my father's house, my mind filled with a fearful anxiety that he was not in life, and I knocked at the door with a palpitating heart — a light beamed across the hall window — I heard a low moan —another —then my mother's voice inquiring, " Who is there ?"

" It is me," replied I.

The door opened—" Thank God," said she, " that you have arrived, for your poor father has been anxiously expecting you, and was beginning to despair of seeing you before his eyes were closed for ever."

" Is he so ill ? Oh ! let me see him."

A hectic flush tinged her pale cheek, while she motioned me to be silent, and leading me into another room — " My child," said she, " you may prepare yourself for the worst, for little hope remains of his recovery. He has been confined to bed—no, not to bed, for the nature of his malady will not allow him to lie ; but he has sat in his arm-chair, with his head resting on a pillow before him, for three weary months — no interval of rest — no cessation of pain ; but he is calm and resigned, no murmur passes his lips, and his only wish is, that he may be permitted to see his child and die. He is now so weak that I think it would be imprudent for you to see him, without preparing him for the meeting." But her precautions were unavailing—he had heard my voice when I entered, and he now called upon her. The

next minute I was at his side, bedewing his hand
with my tears — he attempted to speak, but his voice
was choked in the utterance. I looked up in his
face, the hue of death was upon it — he gasped for
breath, and fell back in his chair. The agony I felt
at that moment was indescribable, for I thought he
was dead. My mother having used the necessary
means for his recovery, a long low moan succeeded
her endeavours ; he slowly unclosed his eyes, and she
motioned me to leave the room. When I next saw
him, he was prepared for the meeting ; a flush of joy
animated his wasted features while he said, " My
dear boy, I begged that I might see you once more
before I closed my eyes in death. That prayer has
been granted : I can now say, ' Lord, now lettest thou
thy servant depart in peace.' "

" And can you forgive all my folly and ingratitude
— forget all the distress I have occasioned you ?"

" Forgive you ? oh, yes ! you little know a parent's
feelings. But there is One whom you have offended,
whose pardon I hope you desire and ask — One who
delights to forgive — ah ! cling to Him, my child, He
will never forsake you. I will soon have crossed
' that bourne from whence no traveller returns.' In
a short time you will have no father ; but it would
smooth my passage to the tomb, to think that you
felt inclined to throw yourself into the hands of the
living God, and beg his assistance to curb that un-
stable spirit, which has caused you and us so much
misery ; and that we shall yet meet, no wanderer lost,
a family in heaven — there is joy in the thought."

I felt my heart softened more than it had been in
all my misery : surely adversity is no tamer of the
human heart — at least, I never felt it so. I am of
opinion that it is calculated rather to draw forth the
darker passions of our nature, and shut up all the
holy avenues of the soul. I wished to sit up with

my father that night, but my mother urged me to
retire to rest. I did so, but I could not sleep ; I lay
ruminating on my past life, and on my father's situation, my mind stung with remorse. I had learned
that his distress of mind, when I first went abroad,
had been great, and that insensibly his health had
sunk, and that his disorder (which proved eventually
to be a cancer of the stomach) had been lingering on
him for some years — I therefore could not but consider that I had contributed to the state he was now
in.

He grew rapidly worse ; he was never satisfied
when I was out of his presence, and I generally sat
up with him at night. His malady caused him the
most excruciating pain, but he bore it with the
greatest patience and fortitude. He had always been
remarkable for his piety, but it was that unostentatious
kind of it which shews itself more in actions than
words : the world was receding from his view, but he
did not feel or feign those ecstasies which we often
have described in the obituary of religious people ;
his was an humble confidence, alike removed from
despondency and presumption. It was remarkable
that this gave offence to some of his more enthusiastic
brethren. One, in particular, having called upon
him, seemed to feel disappointed that he was relating
no heavenly raptures or beatific visions, and very
anxiously endeavoured to draw him into some confession of this kind.

" My friend," said my father, " you seem disappointed that I do not speak in certain and rapturous
terms of my future state ; but if we consider that when
we have done our utmost, we are but unprofitable
servants, we ought to beware of presumption, and not
give the reins to a wild imagination, on the verge of
a solemn eternity, and on the point of entering the
presence of the Judge of all the earth. I feel a

confidence in my Almighty Creator — I know he is a God of truth, and I rely on his promise — I know he is a God of love and mercy, and I have given up my all into his hands ; more than this I dare not say."

The stranger felt reproved, and urged the subject no farther.

All his affairs had been previously settled — he arranged every particular concerning his funeral, and counselled me on my conduct after his decease, with the utmost calmness ; but I could not listen to it, although I was persuaded that he would not recover : there was something so heart-rending, and to me so premature, in the contemplation of his death, that I could not bring myself to reply to any of his suggestions.

He was now near his end ; but the more his body wasted, his intellect grew clearer — his soul seemed to wax strong in the anticipation of its freedom, and rejoice in the prospect of shuffling off its mortal coil.

It was nearly three weeks since I had returned home ; my mother and I were sitting beside him, when he expressed a wish to lie down in his bed. This he had attempted before I came home, but from the excessive pain it produced, he was obliged to abandon the idea. He now, however, felt assured that he could lie, and we carried him to the bed, but it was in vain ; the horizontal posture caused him such agony that we were obliged to raise him, when he fainted in our arms. I thought he was dead — we placed him on a sofa — he recovered — one bright flash of intellect pervaded his features — for a few minutes he seemed as if perfectly well ; and observing us weeping, he was surprised, and asked the reason. He appeared neither to feel pain, nor to remember that he had felt any ; a gleam of hope shot across our minds that he might yet recover. — Ah no ! his soul was on the threshold, pluming her wing for an eternal flight ! — She fled — the celestial fire that animated his features, gave place to the cold damp of death — his lip quivered — one convulsive gasp, and he was no more !

The day arrived on which I was to follow my father's remains to the tomb. A torpid feeling had pervaded my mind since his death, nor did I feel any of those emotions which people in such circumstances are said to feel — he was even consigned to the grave, and the last sod smoothed over it, and yet I waked not to sensibility. When I returned home, our relations and friends were assembled, and although there was much commonplace expression of grief, and just encomiums passed on his character as a man and a Christian, still my heart was like a fountain sealed up. The last friend had departed, and I sat on the sofa on which my father had breathed his last, absorbed in the same melancholy stupor. The day had been stormy, and the pattering rain dashed against the windows, while the wind, sweeping along in sullen gusts, whistled through the casement, now wild and irregular — now low and mournful ! There was something in this that struck a kindred chord within my bosom, and melted my whole soul. Oh ! there are answering tones in nature, responsive to every feeling of humanity, from the light note of gladness, to the dying accents of despair !

I awakened, as it were, from a dream, to all that desolateness of heart, which those only who have felt can understand, and looking round the room, became conscious that I was alone in every sense of the word — bereft of my best friend — he who had centred all his care and solicitude in me — he whom I had repaid with ingratitude — he who, had he lived, would have been my director and friend, was gone for ever, and I was left alone in the world, " a wretch unfitted with an aim."

It was my father's wish that I should procure my discharge, and settle at home in some business, to which I was by no means averse : I therefore lost no time in taking the necessary step for that purpose, and procured my freedom. Previous to my being emancipated, I had looked forward to the event as the consummation of all my wishes. I thought that when I could once breathe freely, all other good things would follow, and I indulged in many Utopian dreams ; but when the much desired object was accomplished, I found myself surrounded by difficulties. I had gone into the army a mere boy, my service had been principally abroad. The life of a soldier is not one where people learn worldly wisdom, and I now felt myself as much a child in that respect, as when I first left my native home to seek for reputation in the wars.

I was acquainted with no business to which I could turn my attention, and I endeavoured to procure a situation of some kind ; but here my boyish sins and military life were visited upon me. The cool calculating people of my native city felt no inclination to employ one who had manifested so much unsteadiness in his early days ; and besides this, they considered an individual who had been in the army the very worst person they could employ — they were all lazy good-for-nothing fellows ; in short, there exists an insurmountable objection to such men — the moral character of the individual is nothing — he has been guilty of being in the army, and that is sufficient. My father's arrangements in my favour, that might have secured me against these evils, were set aside, for want of some formality of law, and my bark was thrown on the ocean of life, to be driven along by the current, without compass or

chart to guide its course — He who would have been
my pilot,

—— had reach'd the shore,
Where tempests never beat, nor billows roar.

My own efforts were of little avail to combat the
difficulties that I had to encounter. My father's
friends and acquaintances, remembering all my childish follies, and the greater number of them being dull
thorough-paced men of business, whose blood had
glided through its icy channel in the same even
current from the time they came into the world,
could not believe that a warm imagination might lead
a boy astray from the path of prudence, without his
heart being depraved. They saw nothing in me but
the blackguard boy, who had ran away from his
parents; and they rung eternal cautions in my ears,
accompanied by wise shakes of the head, and doubts
lavishly expressed of my steadiness. They could ill
dissemble the thorough contempt they had for my
capacity for business: no wonder, they had all out-
stripped me in the necessary qualifications of chica-
nery and selfishness — I acted from natural impulse,
and often wrong ; but it was myself that suffered —
they acted systematically, their eyes fixed steadily
on their own interest, ready to take advantage of the
follies of those around them. I speak from experience. I have found individuals who hypocritically
deplored my want of wisdom, while in the act of
taking advantage of my folly : while others, on the
pretence of caring for my soul's salvation, wished to
imbue my mind with their religious prejudices, and
cramp my conscience within the narrow bounds
marked out by their particular sect; and when I
claimed a right to think for myself on these matters,
they shunned me as a reprobate, or decried me as
an infidel. I have found many things to disgust me
in my passage through life ; but never any thing

equal to the hypocritical cant of many professing sectarians.

Thus, as it were, cut off from society, and my place filled up in it, I did not possess the necessary courage to force through these difficulties, and I remained in an undecided state for some time. My manners had not been framed in the world's school, and I felt all that *mauvaise honte* that people of a sensitive mind generally feel in such a situation, which, along with a proud feeling that caught fire at the slightest look, or word indicative of contempt, rendered my progress in the world almost a thing impossible.

This feeling induced me to decline the assistance of those who wished to afford me an opportunity of mixing with it, and I retired within myself, unknowing and unknown, affecting to feel contempt for those whom I was afraid to mix with. I was in danger of sinking into a complete misanthrope, and I confined myself so much to the house and my books, that my health began to be impaired. My mother, seeing the apathy and torpid state into which I was fast sinking endeavoured to arouse me to some exertion, and her arguments had so much effect, that it made me resolve to try some business; but nothing could induce me to do so in Glasgow. I accordingly set about removing to a different part of the country—embarked in a business that I knew nothing about — neglected all the necessary caution which a more intimate knowledge of the world would have taught me — became the dupe of those who chose to take the trouble to deceive me — looked forward to results without calculating the intermediate steps, and in a short time had the pleasure of being as poor as ever. But here let me pay a tribute of gratitude to individuals, who, in a strange place, came generously forward with their advice and purse to assist me, when I needed assistance—who, though truly religious people, did not ask me, before they offered it, what church I sat in, or what my early life had been — The effects of my ignorance of business could not then be rectified ; but I shall ever retain a grateful remembrance of their disinterested goodness.

It is useless to go through all the circumstances that induced me to resume the uniform of a soldier : suffice it to say, that it was the result. My only consolation now is, that in spite of my folly, and the untoward circumstances which have occasionally thwarted my passage through life, I can look back on my errors with a conviction that they were more of the head than the heart.

THE END.

Also published in facsimile in *The Spellmount Library of Military History* and available from all good bookshops. In case of difficulty, please contact Spellmount Publishers (01580 893730).

HAMILTON'S CAMPAIGN WITH MOORE AND WELLINGTON DURING THE PENINSULAR WAR by Sergeant Anthony Hamilton
Introduction by James Colquhoun

Anthony Hamilton served as a Sergeant in the 43rd Regiment of Foot, later the Oxford and Buckinghamshire Light Infantry. He fought at Vimiero and took part in the retreat to Corunna, vividly describing the appalling conditions and the breakdown of the morale of the British Army. He subsequently fought at Talavera, Busaco, the Coa, Sabugal, Fuentes de Oñoro, Salamanca and Vittoria. He also volunteered to take part in the storming parties of the sieges of Ciudad Rodrigo and Badajoz. During these actions, he was wounded three times.

Published privately in New York in 1847, this rare and fascinating account has never before been published in the United Kingdom.

RANDOM SHOTS FROM A RIFLEMAN by Captain John Kincaid
Introduction by Ian Fletcher

Originally published in 1835, this was the author's follow-up to *Adventures in the Rifle Brigade* – and is a collection of highly amusing, entertaining and informative anecdotes set against the background of the Peninsular War and Waterloo campaign.

RECOLLECTIONS OF THE PENINSULA by Moyle Sherer
Introduction by Philip Haythornthwaite

Reissued more than 170 years after its first publication, this is one of the acknowledged classic accounts of the Peninsular War. Moyle Sherer, described by a comrade as 'a gentleman, a scholar, an author and a most zealous soldier', had a keen eye for observation and an ability to describe both the battles – Busaco, Albuera, Arroyo dos Molinos, Vittoria and the Pyrenees – and the emotions he felt at the time with uncommon clarity.

ROUGH NOTES OF SEVEN CAMPAIGNS: in Portugal, Spain, France and America during the Years 1809–1815 by John Spencer Cooper
Introduction by Ian Fletcher

Originally published in 1869, this is one of the most sought-after volumes of Peninsular War reminiscences. A vivid account of the greatest battles and sieges of the war including Talavera, Busaco, Albuera, Ciudad Rodrigo, Badajoz, Vittoria, the Pyrenees, Orthes and Toulouse and the New Orleans campaign of 1815.

ADVENTURES IN THE RIFLE BRIGADE IN THE PENINSULA, FRANCE, AND THE NETHERLANDS FROM 1809–1815 by Captain John Kincaid

Introduction by Ian Fletcher

This is probably the most well-known and most popular of the many memoirs written by the men who served under Wellington in the Peninsular and Waterloo campaigns. The author, Captain John Kincaid, served in the 95th Rifles, the most famous of Wellington's regiments, a regiment which 'was first in the field and last out'. Kincaid fought in most of the great campaigns in the Peninsula between 1809 and 1814 and at Waterloo, in 1815, where he served as adjutant to the 1st Battalion of the Regiment.

THE MILITARY ADVENTURES OF CHARLES O'NEIL by Charles O'Neil

Introduction by Bernard Cornwell

First published in 1851, these are the memoirs of an Irish soldier who served with Wellington's Army during the Peninsular War and the continental campaigns from 1811 to 1815. Almost unknown in the UK, as the author emigrated to America straight after, it includes his eye-witness accounts of the bloody battle of Barossa, the memorable siege of Badajoz – and a graphic description of the battle of Waterloo where he was badly wounded.

MEMOIRS OF THE LATE MAJOR-GENERAL LE MARCHANT by Denis Le Marchant

Introduction by Nicholas Leadbetter   Foreword by Dr David Chandler

Only 93 copies of the memoirs of the founder of what is now the RMA Sandhurst were published by his son Denis in 1812. His death at Salamanca in 1841 meant that Britain was robbed of its most forward-thinking officer. This facsimile edition is enhanced with additional watercolour pictures by Le Marchant himself.

THE JOURNAL OF AN ARMY SURGEON DURING THE PENINSULAR WAR by Charles Boutflower

Introduction by Dr Christopher Ticehurst

A facsimile edition of a rare journal written by an army surgeon who joined the 40th Regiment in Malta in 1801 and subsequently served with it in the West Indies, South America and the Peninsular War. Described by his family 'as a man of great activity and a general favourite with all his acquaintances', he saw action from 1810 to 1813 including Busaco, Ciudad Rodrigo, Badajoz and Salamanca – gaining a well-deserved promotion to Surgeon to the staff of Sir Rowland Hill's Brigade in 1812.

THE DIARY OF A CAVALRY OFFICER 1809-1815 by Lieut-Col William Tomkinson

Introduction by the Marquess of Anglesey

The importance of *The Diary of a Cavalry Officer* for students of the Peninsular War of 1808-14 and of the Waterloo campaign of 1815, as well as its capacity to interest and inform the nonspecialist, is attested to by its scarcity in secondhand bookshops. It is eagerly sought after by both types of reader. There is hardly a serious account of the Peninsular 'running sore' (to use Napoleon's own words), which was a chief reason for his downfall, or of Waterloo, that does not rely in some degree on Tomlinson.

In Spain and Portugal he served with distinction for nearly five gruelling years in the 16th Light Dragoons, later 16th Lancers, one of the best cavalry regiments in the Peninsula.

Some of the important and patently accurate details of many actions in which he took part appear in no other accounts.

But it is chiefly for the penetrating comments on both esoteric and homely, mainly non-military, situations that the general reader will welcome this reprint.

As a temporary staff officer Tomkinson was at times close to Wellington and his detailed account of the Iron Duke's working day when not actually in the field is unique.

For a free catalogue, telephone

Spellmount Publishers on

01580 893730

or write to

The Old Rectory

Staplehurst

Kent TN12 0AZ

United Kingdom

(Facsimile 01580 893731)

(e-mail enquiries@spellmount.com)

(Website www.spellmount.com)